For Better, For Worse

This interdisciplinary volume explores the fictional portrayal of marriage by women novelists between 1800 and 1900. It investigates the ways in which these novelists used the cultural form of the novel to engage with and contribute to the wider debates of the period around the fundamental cultural and social building block of marriage. The collection provides an important contribution to the emerging scholarly interest in nineteenth-century marriage, gender studies and domesticity, opening up new possibilities for uncovering submerged, marginalized and alternative stories in Victorian literature. An initial chapter outlines the public discourses around marriage in the nineteenth century, the legal reforms that were achieved as a result of public pressure and the ways in which these laws and economic concerns impacted on the marital relationship. It beds the collection down in current critical thinking and draws on life writing, journalism and conduct books to widen our understanding of how women responded to the ideological and cultural construct of marriage. Further chapters examine a range of texts by lesser-known writers as well as canonical authors structured around a timeline of the major legal reforms that impacted on marriage. This structure provides a clear framework for the collection, locating it firmly within contemporary debate and foregrounding female voices. An afterword reflects back on the topic of marriage in the nineteenth century and considers how the activism of the period influenced and shaped reform post-1900. This volume will make an important contribution to scholarship on Victorian Literature, Gender Studies, Cultural Studies and the Nineteenth Century.

Carolyn Lambert is an independent scholar and a Visiting Lecturer at the University of Brighton, United Kingdom.

Marion Shaw is Emeritus Professor of English at Loughborough University, United Kingdom.

Routledge Studies in Nineteenth-Century Literature

For a full list of titles in this series, please visit www.routledge.com.

For Better, For Worse

Marriage in Victorian Novels
by Women

**Edited by Carolyn Lambert
and Marion Shaw**

Routledge
Taylor & Francis Group

LONDON AND NEW YORK

First published 2018 by Routledge

2 Park Square, Milton Park, Abingdon, Oxfordshire OX14 4RN
52 Vanderbilt Avenue, New York, NY 10017

*Routledge is an imprint of the Taylor & Francis Group, an informa
business*

First issued in paperback 2019

Library of Congress Cataloging-in-Publication Data
Names: Lambert, Carolyn (College teacher) editor. |
Shaw, Marion editor.
Title: For better, for worse: marriage in Victorian novels by
women / edited by Carolyn Lambert and Marion Shaw.
Description: New York: Routledge, 2017. | Series: Routledge
studies in nineteenth-century literature | Includes
bibliographical references and index.
Identifiers: LCCN 2017021949
Subjects: LCSH: Marriage in literature. | English fiction—
19th century—History and criticism. | English fiction—Women
authors—History and criticism.
Classification: LCC PR878.M36 F68 2017 |
DDC 823/.8093543082—dc23
LC record available at https://lccn.loc.gov/2017021949

ISBN: 978-1-138-28564-4 (hbk)
ISBN: 978-0-367-88604-2 (pbk)

Typeset in Sabon
by codeMantra

Contents

Acknowledgements

The editors would like to thank our contributors who have worked so hard to make this volume, we believe, a significant addition to nineteenth-century literary scholarship. We wanted to ensure that the women's voices that were raised, often courageously, in the fierce debate around marriage in the nineteenth century and beyond, were responded to by women academics in our own time. This volume represents a wide selection of their views and uncovers some surprising interpretations of canonical authors as well as bringing into the light some lesser-known writers who deserve more scholarly attention.

1 Introduction

The Lottery of Marriage

Carolyn Lambert

Nineteenth-century marriage was a socially constructed gamble in which the odds were weighted heavily in favour of existing social, cultural and legal power structures. The spiritual authority of the church, the legal authority of the judiciary and social and cultural expectations all combined to assert the pre-eminence of marriage, home and family life as the foundation of society. Marriage was also, as Elsie Michie discusses, an essential part of the economic fabric, a form of exchange and accumulation, a secure foundation on which financial and social stability could be built in an increasingly unstable world (Michie, 5–12).[1] Yet between 1800 and 1900, marriage evolved from 'an economic institution to a private relationship' (Hammerton, 2). Tensions began to be articulated between the material purpose of marriage – to provide a stable home and financial future – and the higher emotional expectations of a companionate marriage. This idea of marital friendship, advanced by John Stuart Mill in *The Subjection of Women* (1869) and by later feminist writers, was 'inconsistent with legal and economic inequality' and demanded behavioural changes from both men and women as well as legal reforms (Hammerton, 156). Writers as diverse as Sarah Stickney-Ellis, Florence Nightingale and Harriet Beecher-Stowe questioned the nature of the choice of a life partner based on little or no knowledge:

> A man and woman come together from some affinity, some partial accord of their nature which has inspired mutual affection. There is generally very little careful consideration of who and what they are,-no thought of the reciprocal influence of mutual traits,-no previous chording and testing of the instruments which are to make life-long harmony or discord,-and after a short period of engagement, in which all their mutual relations are made as opposite as possible to those which must follow marriage, these two furnish their house and begin life together.
>
> (Beecher Stowe, 12–13)

The effects of this inability to make an informed choice of marriage partner were compounded after the wedding ceremony when the romantic expectations of young women were confronted by the reality of mundane domesticity. Above all, the doctrine of coverture – at marriage husbands assumed possession and total control of their wives' property and their children – was the cause of wide-ranging campaigns for the reform of statutory regulation. These controversies presaged a century of legal and social challenges and a debate about the nature and purpose of marriage, much of which found its way into contemporary fiction.

The Nature of the Debate

Many of the activists campaigning for reform struggled with the conflict between the need for judicial change and the cultural hegemony of daily life. The ebb and flow of the debate and the partial success or failure of attempts to amend the legislative framework that disabled women within marriage are illustrative of the magnitude of the undertaking. Calls for reform were also calls for a fundamental re-appraisal of nineteenth-century cultural and domestic mores including mounting a challenge to a patriarchally structured society that sought to control every aspect of life. Reformers, whether overtly or implicitly, demanded a realignment of the division between public and private life which confined women to a restrictive domestic environment and a role predicated solely on the family. As Mary Lyndon Shanley notes, campaigners 'forcefully challenged what they regarded as society's sentimentalization of family life' (Shanley, 7). However, the activists did not challenge women's roles within the home: rather, they demanded opportunities for women to participate in public life, including calling for employment opportunities.[2] What Kelly Hager has described as 'the crisis of marriage' during the nineteenth century therefore means that the nature of the debate is 'confused, constantly under revision, and divided in [its] aims', and this is reflected in the texts discussed in this collection.[3]

The diverse nature of the debate around marriage is reflected in the life experiences of the women authors whose works are discussed in this book. Only two of them, Charlotte Yonge and Rhoda Broughton, were unmarried. The remainder were variously widowed, separated, happily and unhappily married, mothers or childless.[4] Their life histories illustrate the gap between the ideal of life in the domestic citadel and the reality of the economic struggle for survival. Frances (Fanny) Trollope, Eliza Lynn Linton, Florence Marryat, Margaret Oliphant and Mrs Henry Wood all wrote to earn money to support themselves and their families. Death, madness, domestic violence and incompatibility intervened to undermine the apparently secure refuge that marriage offered to these women. While activists were campaigning for the right for women to work outside the home and to keep their own earnings, the reality for many women was a choice between finding some sort of income or starving. Indeed, Trollope only avoided starvation in America through the generosity of her travelling companion, Auguste Hervieu (Neville-Sington, 133). Class also affected the opportunities available to women. Women authors were, by definition, middle class and educated, as were the reformers. Working-class women had fewer and riskier options, although the Langham Place group, with the help of another early feminist, Jessie Boucherett, opened a business school for girls which still operates as the charity, Futures for Women.[5]

The History of Reform

At the beginning of the nineteenth century, divorce petitions were exceedingly rare. In 1801, as Hager notes, Jane Addison was granted a divorce 'by private Act of Parliament [...] on the grounds of her husband's incestuous adultery with her sister' (Hager, 33). From 1801 until 1857 when the Divorce Act was passed, only three other women succeeded in divorcing their husbands. This was partly on the grounds of cost: only the wealthy had the means and the requisite connections to petition for a private Act of Parliament. However, Joan Perkin notes that almost half of the seventy-four petitioners for divorce from 1803 to 1827 were in fact middle class, a pattern that continued into the 1850s (Perkin, 23). Stuart Anderson similarly argues that the cost of divorce was probably considerably lower than the figures presented by the Campbell Commission, just as the class of applicants was more varied (Anderson, 436). This was partly due to the attitudes of the various Lord Chancellors in power during this period, their stance towards divorce and their manner of conducting legal proceedings. In addition, the estimated costs of divorce quoted by the 1853 Royal Commission on Divorce and Matrimonial Causes (from £700 to several thousand pounds if there was protracted litigation) were greatly exaggerated, although the £475 that about half the petitioners paid in the first half of the nineteenth century was certainly far beyond the reach of most people (Perkin, 23).[6]

The 1836 Act for Marriages in England enabled ministers of churches other than the Church of England to conduct marriages. As Unitarians, for example, William and Elizabeth Gaskell had to be married in St John's Parish Church in Knutsford in 1832 rather than in a Unitarian chapel. The act also made it possible for non-religious civil marriages to be held in register offices that were set up in towns and cities. The act was followed four years later by the most prominent and public statement of marriage: that of Queen Victoria and Prince Albert. However, despite her position as a national symbol of marital bliss and maternal fulfilment, as Hager notes, Victoria had long-standing reservations about the lottery of marriage which she continued to express privately in her letters and journals more than twenty years later (Hager, 1).

In 1839, the year before the marriage of Victoria and Albert, the reality of domestic life behind the closed doors of what Wilkie Collins described as 'the secret theatre of home', was brutally exposed (Collins, 64). The marriage of Caroline and George Norton graphically illustrated the way in which women were often trapped in a privately conducted power struggle to preserve their sanity, their health, the care and welfare of their children and their own economic survival. Caroline's story and her quest for justice are outlined succinctly and clearly by Shanley (Shanley, 22–29). She and her husband were profoundly mismatched and in 1836, the fragile truce in the Norton household was finally shattered. George's case for 'criminal conversation' between Caroline and Lord Melbourne was dismissed without the jury ever leaving the jury box. However, the irrevocable damage to her reputation, and more specifically, George's refusal to allow her access to her children, infuriated Caroline and motivated her to campaign for a change in the law. She persuaded Thomas Talfourd MP to introduce a bill giving mothers the right to appeal for custody of children under seven. She then embarked on her own public campaign producing a series of leaflets outlined in the timeline at Appendix A of this book, arguing for legislative change. The pamphlets highlight a variety of injustices to women, insisting that wives needed the protection of the law in cases where their husbands, their natural protectors, failed them.

The outcome of Caroline Norton's activism was the Custody of Infants Act (1839). The Act enabled women with sufficient means to petition the equity courts for custody of children up to the age of seven and for periodic access to children aged over seven. However, '[a] mother could not avail herself of even these limited rights if she had been found guilty of adultery' (Shanley, 137). It was a further eighteen years before a clause in the Divorce and Matrimonial Causes Act (1857) allowed judges discretion to award custody orders as they deemed appropriate. Nevertheless, Caroline Norton's was the first significant female voice to be raised in public protest against marital injustice. Like many of the women authors considered in this collection, she wrote poetry and novels and became the editor of two magazines to support her family. In her writings on custody, as Elisabeth Gruner notes, 'she shapes her trials into a story, indeed, almost a novel' (Gruner, 306). Her rhetoric however, as Gruner argues, 'consistently associates women with the private, the family, the sphere of domesticity' (Gruner, 306). In this sense, Norton aptly illustrates the tension that continued throughout most of the nineteenth century between the public and the private, the gendered division of labour and the struggle women faced to make their voices heard.

Their own private networks formed an important source of support for women. In the 1850s, a more formal network was established that became known as the Langham Place circle.[7] The Langham Place circle, led by Barbara Leigh Smith, began a systematic campaign for legal reform that was highly organized and sophisticated in its approach. Leigh

Smith took the masculinized language and gendered constructs of the law and used them as a weapon to attack embedded legal and hegemonic injustices suffered by women. In her publication *A Brief Summary in Plain Language of the Most Important Laws of England concerning Women* (1854) she sets out, with devastating clarity, the full extent of women's disabilities. Her approach was radically different from that of Caroline Norton's impassioned personal appeal, but so were her circumstances. She was unmarried at the time, one of five illegitimate, but openly acknowledged, children of the radical MP Benjamin Leigh Smith, who gave each child a legacy of £300 a year for life, providing his daughter therefore with an independent income and financial security. The Langham Place group followed the widespread success of Leigh Smith's pamphlet (a second edition was issued in 1856 and a third in 1869) with a petition to Parliament for the reform of married women's legal rights to property. Again, their views differed markedly from those of Caroline Norton who accepted the cultural convention that husbands provided for and protected their wives. By contrast, the Married Women's Property Committee insisted that married women were entitled to their own property and to any income they themselves earned. As Shanley argues, whereas Norton appealed to the differences between men and women to justify her appeal, they 'insisted that the state recognize the fundamental and equal rights of men and women to possess property, regardless of marital status' (Shanley, 33).

This petition, signed by a number of women novelists including Elizabeth Gaskell, attracted attention partly because of a parallel campaign for reform launched by the Law Amendment Society. Both the Langham Place petition and the Law Amendment Society's resolution condemning the common law rules of property respecting married women were placed before Parliament. However, at the same time, the House of Lords was debating a bill to create a civil Divorce Court. As Shanley explains, '[up] to this point the two measures had been conceived of and dealt with [...] independently, but from the spring of 1856 through 1857 the issues of married women's property and divorce law reforms were inseparably linked' (Shanley, 35). The Divorce and Matrimonial Causes Act of 1857 allowed divorce through the law courts, instead of the slow and expensive business of a Private Act of Parliament. However, under the terms of the act, the husband had only to prove his wife's adultery, but the wife had to prove her husband had committed not just adultery but also incest, bigamy, cruelty or desertion – in other words, the grounds for divorce were not changed nor was the sexual double standard abolished. As Hager notes, this codification of divorce meant that 'private life became increasingly more policed and standardized; all legal stories of marriage and divorce would now be told using the same language and the same narrative cues' (Hager, 39).

It was a further thirteen years before the Married Women's Property Act was passed in 1870, establishing for the first time, the principle of a married woman's right to keep any income earned through work in addition to any land she inherited and any money up to £200. The Married Women's Property Act of 1882 further allowed women to keep what they owned at the time of marriage. The discourse around both the 1857 Divorce Act and the Married Women's Property Act of 1870 was however complicated by consideration of what was meant by coverture. As Rachel Ablow notes, different accounts of coverture 'were mobilized to very different political ends' (Ablow, 11). Feminists, as Shanley argues, consistently demanded the legal equality of men and women and just as consistently, 'Parliament would respond by protecting the most vulnerable women from exploitation and abuse' but refused to give women the resources to protect themselves (Shanley, 77). During the 1870s, feminists repeatedly 'attacked a wide range of laws that reflected [...] Parliament's assumption that women should be defined, at least in part, by their domestic and reproductive functions' (Shanley, 78).

One of the areas of concern for feminists remained a woman's right to custody of her children which they argued was an integral part of their marital subjection. The Infant Custody Bill of 1873 was opposed by feminists as being weak and inadequate, ignoring the fundamental principle for which they were fighting – that of the equal legal rights of both parents to custody. The passing of the Married Women's Property Act of 1882 gave encouragement to campaigners that the principle of equal rights within marriage had been established and that this would filter through into other legislation. Parliament however rejected calls for equal parental rights and the Infant Custody Act of 1886, while it made the welfare of children the determining factor in deciding questions of custody, nonetheless made the father the sole legal guardian during his lifetime.

The Matrimonial Causes Act of 1878 in effect amended the Divorce Act of 1857 by making divorce less costly to obtain. It also allowed women victims of a violent marriage to obtain a separation order. However, as Shanley notes, evidence concerning the practical outcomes of this increased protection is ambiguous. While the act did enable women to leave their violent husbands, they were not allowed to divorce and re-marry and some magistrates used their discretionary authority regarding their assessment of a woman's future safety to send wives back to their abusive husbands. 'A husband's repeated abuse of his wife, no matter how severe, was not considered as serious an offense against marriage as a single instance of a wife's infidelity' (Shanley, 170). The Summary Jurisdiction (Married Women) Act of 1895 closed a century of campaigning by allowing a wife who left her husband on the grounds of his wilful neglect or persistent cruelty to petition for maintenance for herself and her children and for custody of her children.

Critical History

There is an emerging scholarly interest in literary representations of marriage. A number of earlier texts deal mostly with the historical reforms that emerged during the period 1800–1900. Shanley's *Feminism, Marriage, and the Law in Victorian England, 1850–1895* (1989) provides a clear and comprehensive account of the activities and impact of the feminist campaigners and continues to be widely referred to. Although Perkin's *Women and Marriage in Nineteenth-Century England* (1989) has a lucid and well-structured first chapter on women and the law, Perkin often loses focus and seems to be overwhelmed by her material, failing to give a clear account of her argument. The book is also inadequately referenced.

Literary criticism of women and marriage in the nineteenth century is first addressed by Jenni Calder in *Women and Marriage in Victorian Fiction* (1976). Calder writes eloquently but with insufficient depth, and like Perkin, her book is inadequately referenced. In *Victorian Women's Fiction: Marriage, Freedom and the Individual* (1985), Shirley Foster examines the domination of the theme of love and marriage in Victorian fiction and explores the ways in which women writers in the mid-nineteenth century confronted the conflict between the expectations of marriage and the alternatives presented by a single life. Foster gives a competent account of her chosen theme but her study is limited to five authors and she draws no overall conclusions from her analysis. In addition, the sub-titles to her chapters (for example, 'Elizabeth Gaskell: The Wife's View') suggest a pre-determined approach to the exploration of her chosen theme which could close down consideration of other ways in which women writers resisted the cultural hegemony of domestic life. Valerie Pedlar focuses on the imaginative representations of male madness in *The Most Dreadful Visitation: Male Madness in Victorian Fiction* (2006). Although her focus is on men, she includes a chapter on madness and marriage. In this chapter, Pedlar situates her examination of three sensation novels by Charles Reade, Anthony Trollope, Eliza Lynn Linton and Mary Braddon securely in their historical and literary context and makes an important contribution to an under-represented theme.

Ablow's *The Marriage of Minds: Reading Sympathy in the Victorian Marriage Plot* (2007) is a creative and nuanced approach to the topic. Ablow builds on the 'ethical turn' that literary criticism has recently taken, arguing that the Victorian novel was akin to the concept of a good wife. She focuses her account on the relationship between reader and text and on that between husband and wife taking coverture as an organising principle and offering refreshing new readings of some canonical texts. Her book is well matched by Hager's *Dickens and the Rise of Divorce: The Failed Marriage Plot and the Novel Tradition* (2010) which argues compellingly that the crisis in nineteenth-century marriage is not adequately accounted for in our theories about the rise of the novel. Hager argues that eighteenth- and nineteenth-century texts were rich in failed marriage plots that pre-figure legal reform. She offers a revisionist reading of Dickens's novels against the context of the rise of feminism in the period, interpolating her analysis with factual accounts of marital failure and public debates about marriage and divorce. A James Hammerton's comprehensive examination of divorce and family breakdown in Victorian and Edwardian marriages, *Cruelty and Companionship: Conflict in Nineteenth-Century Married Life* (1992), is firmly grounded in historical evidence. Hammerton draws on records of the Divorce Court which came into being after the passing of the Matrimonial Causes Act of 1857 and on press reports of the magistrates' courts which tried suits of separation and maintenance under the Matrimonial Causes Act of 1878 to shed light on the intimate effects of conflict between husbands and wives. This enables him to discuss a range of social issues, including identifying 'a clear pattern of women's resistance against husband's power', and to provide a nuanced and subtle account of the tension between the patriarchal and companionate models of marriage (Hammerton, 6).

Tim Dolin claims that '[t]he reform of the property laws affecting married women was the most fundamental of all feminist legal and social reforms in the nineteenth century' (Dolin, 4). His creative exploration of the impact of property reform on narrative makes an important contribution to debates about identity and gender, setting out the ways in which economic considerations linked to marriage rippled out into the personal and domestic sphere. Dolin however focuses on the female owner of land. In *Women and Personal Property in the Victorian Novel* (2010), Deborah Wynne explores Victorian women's fascination with commodities, the acquisition of portable property that was apparently of little financial value. She argues convincingly that the issue of property ownership is much more complex and nuanced than modern commentators have acknowledged, linking the ownership of 'things' to the possession of social power and the creation of a self-identity and associating this in turn to the debates around the Married Women's Property Acts. Elsie Michie develops the theme of the 'vulgar question of money' in her investigation of the increasing tension between the economic basis of marriage and the growth of the moral imperative: *The Vulgar Question of Money: Heiresses, Materialism and the Novel of Manners from Jane Austen to Henry James* (2011). She focuses primarily on courtship and the way in which 'the choice between two women becomes a means of articulating nineteenth-century social tensions between the desire for wealth and advancement and the need to regulate one's own behavior by another set of values' (Michie, 6).

Ginger Frost's book, *Living in Sin* (2008), draws on a wide range of sources from the long nineteenth century to provide a nuanced account of marital non-conformity among couples of all social classes.

Although these couples, despite high-profile partnerships like those between George Eliot and George Henry Lewis and Harriet Taylor and John Stuart Mill and radical movements such as the Owenites, remained in the minority throughout the Victorian period, Frost argues that these couples 'threw into disarray the traditional definition of marriage' and helped to drive forward the reform agenda (Frost, 2).

The most recent contribution to the debate is Talia Schaffer's magisterial monograph *Romance's Rival: Familiar Marriage in Victorian Fiction* (2016). In her wide-ranging analysis, Schaffer argues that what she defines as a 'familiar' model of marriage where a woman makes a safe, rational, non-erotic choice of a known suitor as opposed to marriage to a dashing romantic rival, continued to permeate Victorian fiction alongside the new romantic ideal and that this two-suitor plot helped Victorians to work through fears about marriage. Schaffer's nuanced reading of the historical context emphasizes the disenfranchisement and disempowerment of women and acts as an appropriate corrective to our 'excessive focus on desire' in our reading of these texts which 'has obscured the extent to which female characters were able to make strategic decisions about their lives through the agency of marriage' (Schaffer 13).

While the books by Calder and Foster put down important critical markers, it is some time since their publication and therefore an appropriate moment for a re-examination of this theme by a new generation of academics. Foster's study is important because she uses a range of letters and non-fiction to contextualise her argument, but her book is limited to five novelists. Foster's claim that many nineteenth-century female novelists have been undeservedly neglected and that the major ones are further illuminated by being considered alongside their less familiar contemporaries, is developed further by the studies in *For Better, For Worse: Marriage in Victorian Novels by Women*. The scope of Pedlar's book, by choice, is limited to a consideration of male madness. Although she analyses texts by women writers in her chapter on marriage, her principal focus is on the sensation novel. Ablow's book focuses on canonical texts by five authors and is an extended presentation of her metaphorical links between the concept of marital and readerly sympathy. It is a series of encounters rather than a sustained consideration of fictional marriages and the novelist's contribution to contemporary debate. Hager's book aligns most closely with *For Better, For Worse: Marriage in Victorian Novels by Women,* but her focus is solely on the work of Dickens. Schaffer's wide-ranging study extends consideration of marriage into a range of non-sexual and same-sex partnerships highlighting the extent to which cultural and social expectations were destabilized during this period and the complexity and ubiquity of the discourse that surrounded marriage. *For Better, For Worse: Marriage in Victorian Novels by Women* builds on this work by focusing closely on the work of women novelists and on their presentations of the intimacy of marriage and its impact on the lives of both men and women.

The Female View

Women's discourse during the long struggle for marriage reform was conducted in a variety of forums: formal and informal, public and private. Several of the novelists whose texts are considered in this book contributed to the debate in other ways, such as through journalism and reviews, and all of them were part of a female network through which they continued private conversations about the public debate and sought to find their own solutions to a relationship that was simultaneously intimate yet at the core of public life. Letters, for example, were a ubiquitous part of nineteenth-century life, freely entering and leaving the home, effortlessly breaching the boundaries and conventions that protected domestic space. A reliable, regular, and comprehensive postal service meant that letters could be conveyed efficiently and economically without fear of interception. Letters however had an ambiguous status, since as well as being personal correspondence between two people, they were also public property in that they were read and shared between a circle of friends and acquaintances, and were therefore liminal objects, as Rosemarie Bodenheimer notes 'on the boundary of public and private discourse' (Bodenheimer, 8).[8] Nevertheless, they were an important way in which women could discuss ideas, develop their thoughts and become part of interlocking circles of friends and activists.[9]

Journalism offered women a public space in which to openly debate their concerns. Barbara Onslow notes that '[i]t provided an arena to debate directly those social and political issues from which women were excluded at all levels of government, a vehicle to promote political and religious beliefs, a channel to educate or influence other women' (Onslow, 16). Valerie Sanders notes the ubiquity of articles on marriage in contemporary periodicals and Mona Caird's essay on marriage in the *Westminster Review* precipitated an avalanche of some 27,000 letters to the *Daily Telegraph* (Sanders, 25).

Advice books, or what Hammerton describes perhaps more accurately as 'prescriptive literature' (Hammerton, 73), were another way in which women's role in marriage was debated in public. Leonore Davidoff and Catherine Hall discuss the ways in which Sarah Stickney Ellis, one of the most popular of the advice writers, sought to promulgate the idea of marriage as a safe and stable institution, a bulwark against the political and social unrest of the external public world (Davidoff and Hall, 180–84). Yet her writing reveals the underlying tensions between the concept of the submissive wife whose proper role was to be confined to domestic tasks and the ways in which she could exercise moral power and influence over her husband. It was a tactic of avoidance rather than mitigation which argued for the suppression of women and the supremacy of patriarchal control.[10]

Novel writing was, for many women, their chosen way of interrogating the cultural concept of marriage, of engaging with the wider public debate that raged across the century. Novels enabled the reader to pass beyond the boundaries of the courtship plot and its resoundingly reassuring conclusion – 'Reader, I married him' – and to follow the consequences of choices made (Brontë, 479). As Sharon Marcus notes, '[t]he nineteenth-century novel was one of the most important cultural sites for representing and shaping desire, affect, and ideas about gender and the family' (Marcus, 8). Whereas courtship novels looked forward to an idealized future, marriage novels looked back on an idealized past from a disrupted and chaotic present. Novels could explore the deep structure of the institution of marriage in a nuanced way that could help to shape thought, to pose questions and to proffer answers. Marriage, at the end of a courtship novel, is presented as a form of stasis. The texts discussed in this book show women writers challenging this textual closure as not representative of their lived lives, but instead, seeking to move the narrative forward just as contemporary discourse sought to challenge the social, cultural and legal hegemonies that preserved married women in stasis.

For Better, For Worse: Marriage in Victorian Novels by Women

This collection is arranged as far as possible in chronological order. The timeline at Appendix A shows some of the key events and texts connected with marriage and its reform between 1800 and 1900. The novels discussed in this collection are inserted into this timeline which shows the longevity and vigour of the debate that centered around marriage reform and the strength of the resistance to change. Marriage, as Hager notes, is 'not a stable entity': it is 'multiplicitous and shifting' (Hager, 33). The institution of marriage was at the heart of social, cultural and economic life in the nineteenth century: hence the urgency of the discourse and its appearance in such a wide range of texts: fiction, journalism, parliamentary bills and reports, private letters all deal with aspects of marriage. The timeline also illustrates the re-iteration of legislative reform as the boundaries that separated women from the goal of individual rights and equality before the law for both married and single women were gradually eroded. No single Act of Parliament achieved what activists demanded although they became increasingly more sophisticated in their arguments and in their use of the political system to achieve change.

The collection opens with a discussion of three interlinked novels by Frances (Fanny) Trollope dealing with the picaresque marriage of the eponymous Widow Barnaby. The novels track the marital career of the Widow Barnaby and her third husband, Major Allen as they make their swashbuckling way across England, Australia and America. The success or failure of their attempts to secure a fortune and social status for themselves through deceit and cunning depends on the strength of the relationship between them, and the novels record the development of their marriage from suspicion and concealment to open admiration and dependence. It is an ironic and joyous inversion of the nineteenth-century model marriage in which gender and roles are continuously subverted.

Emily Morris discusses two novels by Charlotte Yonge: *Heartsease* (1854) and *The Clever Woman of the Family* (1865). Morris's chapter adds to recent critical debate that calls for a more nuanced approach to apparently overtly conservative and anti-feminist writers such as Yonge. She argues that Yonge presents a more complicated and ambiguous treatment of marriage in these novels than has previously been recognized suggesting that it is perhaps not the best choice for every woman. Morris points out the links between the two novels, exploring the ways in which Yonge re-considers ideas about personal happiness for women in the interval between the publication of the two texts. As Morris notes, Yonge is a writer with a didactic purpose and the alternatives to the harsh realities of marriage that she offers in these novels are located in spiritual and non-patriarchal relationships.

Marion Shaw provides a sensitive account of Elizabeth Gaskell's *Sylvia's Lovers* (1863). Written entirely in dialect it is in some ways the least accessible and certainly the most unremittingly tragic of Gaskell's novels. Shaw situates her analysis of the text securely in its historical context, focusing her discussion on the psychological drama that is enacted between the three protagonists: Sylvia, her husband Philip and Charley Kinraid, the man she loves. Shaw considers the way in which the various kinds of obsession presented in the novel, warp individual and collective psychologies and lead to damaged and restricted lives. Sylvia and Philip's marriage is founded on a secret, a lie told by Philip which makes Sylvia believe that she has no other choice than to marry him and the resulting despair and disillusion of both of them fuelled by Philip's obsession for Sylvia, are what drive the narrative to its bleak conclusion.

Frances Twinn offers an account of a crowded marriage in her consideration of *East Lynne* (1861) arguing that while Mrs Henry (Ellen) Wood overtly portrays a conventional view of marital behaviour within a Christian marriage, the sub-text of the novel reveals her underlying sympathy with the tensions and pressures that drive Isabel Vane's transgressive behaviour.

Carolyn W. de la L. Oulton considers Rhoda Broughton's sensation novel *Cometh up as a Flower* (1867) arguing persuasively that Broughton used the tropes of sensation fiction less to create a disruptive, thrilling experience for her readers and more to portray her heroine Nell Lestrange's short and sad life after she is tricked into a conventional marriage with a wealthy man she does not love. Nell openly describes her sexual attraction to her lover but in an ironic inversion of the expected seduction narrative, is compromised, less by her sexuality, than by her own naivety.

Instead of being either seduced or experiencing a happy ending with her lover with all misunderstandings resolved, Oulton's analysis shows how Broughton uses Nell's narrative to reveal a darker domestic realism that is ultimately far more destructive and dramatic than the conventions of sensation fiction.

Meredith Miller provides a wide-ranging and considered analysis of marriage in George Eliot's *Daniel Deronda* (1876) in the context of both domestic-national and imperial power. Miller's sophisticated argument addresses criticism that *Daniel Deronda* is a novel of two halves by showing how Eliot blends fictional modes to create a nuanced portrayal of the ways in which individual psychologies and questions of national identity and power intersect. She considers the array of marriages in the novel and the ways in which these are enmeshed within the overall narrative structure to provide a critique of nation, empire, culture and gender. In doing so, Miller provides a fresh reading of what has been considered a fractured text, enabling it to be viewed as a single, subtle, inter-related narrative.

Joanne Shattock adds an important dimension to the collection in her discussion of two of Margaret Oliphant's little known novels, *The Ladies Lindores* (1883) and its sequel, the novella *Lady Car* (1889). Shattock locates her discussion of these texts in the context of Oliphant's journalism and non-fiction writing: a reminder of the diverse ways in which many of the novelists represented in this collection not only engaged with the debate around marriage but also earned a living. Shattock points out that Oliphant was sceptical that legal reform could in itself alleviate the marital disability suffered by women and was adamantly opposed to divorce because of the effect on children. Shattock traces the subtle ways in which Oliphant's views became more nuanced over the course of her long writing career and analyses how these views are embedded in the two novels.

Tamara S. Wagner discusses Mrs Henry (Ellen) Wood's late novel *Court Netherleigh* (1881) and examines the ways in which Wood disrupts the anticipated ending of the courtship plot by emphasizing the need for marriage to be based on pragmatic economics and financial security rather than on romantic expectations. Wagner considers *Court Netherleigh* as an inverted example of 'prescriptive literature': a fictional manual that sets out the ways in which women can destroy their marriages. She links her analysis to Wood's own inter-textual re-working of her earlier sensation novel *East Lynne* (1861) showing how the reduction in sensational elements in the later text enables Wood to focus on the intimacies of the marital relationship and its destruction as a result of the banalities of everyday reality rather than by adultery.

Laura Allen discusses the neglected novel by Mary Eliza Haweis – *A Flame of Fire* (1897). Like Margaret Oliphant, Haweis was also a journalist, who used her non-fiction writing to argue for legal reforms that would abolish women's disability in marriage. Allen outlines the ways in which Haweis' personal experiences underpin this text and provide a politically charged account of a marriage.

Catherine Pope contributes a disturbing portrait of both real-life and fictional marriages in her challenging chapter on Florence Marryat, focusing on marital violence. Pope grounds her argument securely in the various contemporary discourses around the ideology of marriage. She examines critical reactions to Marryat's novels, making a compelling case for Marryat as a uniquely radical voice raised in protest against widespread domestic violence. Pope emphasizes Marryat's courage in not only unflinchingly exposing the appalling reality of wife-beating in her fiction but in persisting in demanding equality in marriage, despite the sustained criticism she endured from the critics and the press. Marryat used her own experiences to devastating effect in her fiction, refusing to be silenced and encouraging other women to resist male oppression.

Rebecca Styler provides a fascinating account of some little-known feminist Utopian fiction that appeared on the cusp of the nineteenth and twentieth centuries. She considers Jane Hume Clapperton's *Margaret Dunmore: or, A Socialist Home* (1888), Elizabeth Burgoyne Corbett's *New Amazonia: A Foretaste of the Future* (1889), Amelia Mears' *Mercia, The Astronomer Royal: A Romance* (1895), Florence Ethel Mills Young's *The War of the Sexes* (1905) and Irene Clyde's *Beatrice the Sixteenth* (1909), analysing the ways in which these texts radically re-constructed gender relations, addressing issues of women's oppression and presenting visions of alternative matriarchal societies. Although the texts vary in their particulars and are confined to representations of middle-class living, all the authors argue that women's economic emancipation is the primary marriage reform that is required.

Victoria Margree addresses a wide range of short fiction in her stimulating chapter arguing that the short story allowed women to address controversial subjects in a form that was less exposed to criticism than the novel and that also benefited from the expansion in the periodical market during the nineteenth century that required short pieces of fiction to satisfy public demand. Margree provides an informed overview of the short story between 1800 and 1900, starting with Maria Edgeworth's 'The Limerick Gloves' (1804) and Laetitia E. Landon's 'Sefton Church' (1834) and moving on to supernatural, gothic and uncanny tales such as Rosa Mulholland's 'Not to Be Taken at Bed-Time' (1865), Edith Nesbit's 'Man-Size in Marble' (1893), Rhoda Broughton's 'The Man with the Nose' (1872) and Netta Syrett's 'A Correspondence', published in the notorious *Yellow Book* in 1895. She concludes her chapter with Margaret Oliphant's 'A Story of a Wedding Tour' (1894).

Marlene Tromp's chapter rounds off the collection in fine style, drawing together historical and critical threads to weave a feminist account of marriage, and analysing *Middlemarch* (1872) as an expression of female power within marriage, pointing out neglected aspects of violence by women towards their husbands.

This collection resonates with women's voices: nineteenth-century women writers are linked to twenty-first-century women academics in a conversation that still continues. In the period under discussion, women refused to allow their voices to be silenced, finding creative ways to subvert the cultural hegemony and to directly and indirectly attack the injustices they faced within marriage. This collection represents a tiny sample of their work.

Notes

1 See also Leonore Davidoff and Catherine Hall. *Family Fortunes: Men and Women of the English Middle Class, 1789–1859*. London: Hutchinson, 1987, p 322. Charlotte Brontë commented acidly on the financial impetus behind marriage in her novella 'Henry Hastings' (1839) in which her narrator advertises for a wife, saying that he is not too particular about 'an eye too few or a row of teeth minus […] provided only satisfactory testimonials be given of the possession of that one great and paramount virtue, that eminent and irresistible charm, C-A-S-H!' ('Henry Hastings' in *Tales of Angria*, Heather Glen ed, Harmondsworth: Penguin, 2006).

2 See for example the writing of Marion Kirkland in Susan Groag Bell and Karen M Offen eds. *Women, the Family, and Freedom: The Debate in Documents, Volume One, 1750–1880*. Stanford, CA: Stanford University Press, 1983, pp 192–99, the work of the Langham Place circle who established the Society for the Promotion of the Employment of Women and the writing of Florence Nightingale in Florence Nightingale, Mary Poovey ed. *Cassandra and Other Selections from Suggestions for Thought*. London: Pickering and Chatto, 1991.

3 Kelly Hager. *Dickens and the Rise of Divorce: The Failed-Marriage Plot and the Novel Tradition*. Farnham: Ashgate, 2010, pp 3–4 and p 10 n1. See also Shirley Foster. *Victorian Women's Fiction: Marriage, Freedom and the Individual*. Beckenham: Croom Helm Ltd, 1985, pp 6–16 for a more detailed discussion of the dualism of the calls for reform which both advocated change yet still regarded marriage and motherhood as the female idea.

4 See Elaine Showalter. *A Literature of Their Own: British Women Novelists from Bronte to Lessing*. London: Virago Press, 1978, p 47. 'My research shows that of women writers born between 1800 and 1900, a fairly constant proportion – about half – were unmarried. In a number of cases, women married late in life, after they had established a professional reputation and were able to earn a good market price for their books. Married women writers…were frequently motivated to publish by their husband's financial failure, illness, or death, and thus took on double burdens of support. The effect of such financial needs can easily be traced in the too-rapid production of competent, not-quite-realized fiction.'

5 The age of female consent had been twelve from the sixteenth century. In the nineteenth century, intercourse with a girl under ten became a felony, and intercourse with a girl between the ages of ten and twelve was a misdemeanour. However, the age of consent was raised to thirteen in 1875, and to sixteen in 1885. There was no compulsory education for girls until 1870.

6 Anderson argues from his examination of court records that 'whereas between 1801 and 1840, 50% of the petitioners were spending less than £165…

between 1841 and 1857, 75% were paying less than £250, as the increasing cost of the action was partly offset by the decreasing proportion of petitioners who had to sue. By the end of the period nearly a third spent nothing on the action (Anderson, 438).

7 Kathryn Gleadle discusses an earlier group of radical Unitarian activists who campaigned during the 1830s and 1840s who developed 'a powerful social, political and cultural critique of modern society, and women's role within it' (Gleadle, 6).This group, she argues, formed the basis of the women's rights movement of the 1850s. Kathryn Gleadle. *The Early Feminists: Radical Unitarians and the Emergence of the Women's Rights Movement, 1831–1851*. Basingstoke: Macmillan Press, 1995. See also Carolyn Lambert. *The Meanings of Home in Elizabeth Gaskell's Fiction*. Brighton: Victorian Secrets, 2013, 80–83.

8 For a more detailed discussion of letter as discourse, see, for example, Joanne Shattock, 'Elizabeth Gaskell: Journalism and Letters', in Laurel Brake and Marysa Demour eds, *The Lure of Illustration in the Nineteenth Century: Picture and Press*. Basingstoke: Palgrave Macmillan, 2009 and David Barton and Nigel Hall, eds, *Letter Writing as a Social Practice*. Amsterdam/Philadelphia, PA: John Benjamins Publishing Company, 2000.

9 Elizabeth Gaskell's letter to Eliza Fox of c 1 January 1856, is an example of the ambivalence many women felt about Barbara Bodichon's petition to amend the law on married women's property: J A V Chapple and Arthur Pollard eds. *The Letters of Mrs Gaskell*. Manchester: Manchester University Press, 1997, p 379.

10 See also Hammerton, pp 73–82 for a further analysis of the work of writers of prescriptive literature.

Works cited

Ablow, Rachel. *The Marriage of Minds: Reading Sympathy in the Victorian Marriage Plot*. Stanford, CA: Stanford University Press, 2007.

Anderson, Stuart. 'Legislative Divorce – Law for the Aristocracy?' in Gerry R Rubin and David Sugarman eds. *Law, Economy and Society, 1750–1914. Essays in the History of English Law*, pp 412–44. Abingdon: Professional Books Limited, 1984.

Beecher Stowe, Harriet. *Little Foxes; or, the Insignificant Little Habits Which Mar Domestic Happiness*. London: Bell and Daldy, 1866.

Bodenheimer, Rosemarie. *The Real Life of Mary Ann Evans: George Eliot, Her Letters and Fiction*. Ithaca, NY and London: Cornell University Press, 1994.

Brontë, Charlotte. *Jane Eyre*. London: Smith, Elder, & Co, 1877.

Calder, Jenni. *Women and Marriage in Victorian Fiction*. London: Thames and Hudson, 1976.

Collins, Wilkie. *Basil*, Goldman, Dorothy ed. Oxford: Oxford University Press, 2000.

Davidoff, Leonore and Hall, Catherine. *Family Fortunes: Men and Women of the English Middle Class, 1789–1859*. London: Hutchinson, 1987, p 322.

Dolin, Tim. *Mistress of the House: Women of Property in the Victorian Novel*. Aldershot: Ashgate, 1997.

Foster, Shirley. *Victorian Women's Fiction: Marriage, Freedom and the Individual*. Beckenham: Croom Helm Ltd, 1985.

Frost, Ginger S. *Living in Sin: Cohabiting as Husband and Wife in Nineteenth-Century England*. Manchester: Manchester University Press, 2008.

Gruner, Elisabeth Rose. 'Plotting the Mother: Caroline Norton, Helen Huntingdon, and Isabel Vane'. *Tulsa Studies in Women's Literature*, Vol 16, No 2 (Autumn, 1997), pp 303–25.

Hager, Kelly. *Dickens and the Rise of Divorce: The Failed-Marriage Plot and the Novel Tradition*. Farnham: Ashgate, 2010.

Hammerton, A James. *Cruelty and Companionship: Conflict in Nineteenth-Century Married Life*. London and New York: Routledge, 1992.

Marcus, Sharon. *Between Women: Friendship, Desire and Marriage in Victorian England*. Princeton, NJ: Princeton University Press, 2007.

Michie, Elsie B. *The Vulgar Question of Money: Heiresses, Materialism and the Novel of Manners from Jane Austen to Henry James*. Baltimore, MD: The John Hopkins University Press, 2011.

Neville-Sington, Pamela. *Fanny Trollope: The Life and Adventures of a Clever Woman*. London: Penguin Books, 1998.

Onslow, Barbara. *Women of the Press in Nineteenth-Century Britain*. Basingstoke: Macmillan Press, 2000.

Pedlar, Valerie. *The Most Dreadful Visitation: Male Madness in Victorian Fiction*. Liverpool: Liverpool University Press, 2006.

Perkin, Joan. *Women and Marriage in Nineteenth-Century England*. London: Routledge, 1989.

Sanders, Valerie. 'Marriage and the Antifeminist Woman Novelist' in Nicola Diane Thompson ed. *Victorian Women Writers and the Woman Question*, pp 24–41. Cambridge: Cambridge University Press, 1999.

Schaffer, Talia. *Romance's Rival: Familiar Marriage in Victorian Fiction*. Oxford: Oxford University Press, 2016.

Shanley, Mary Lyndon. *Feminism, Marriage, and the Law in Victorian England, 1850–1895*. Princeton, NJ: Princeton University Press, 1989.

Wynne, Deborah. *Women and Personal Property in the Victorian Novel*. Farnham: Ashgate, 2010.

2 Frances Trollope and the Picaresque Marriage

Carolyn Lambert

In an age when marriage was preceded by a period of ritualized court-ship that ostensibly celebrated the idea of romantic love but was actually based on economic necessity, hard bargaining and fiscal power, disil-lusion at the disjunction between expectation and reality was perhaps inevitable. Sarah Stickney-Ellis takes a pragmatic view of the problem in *The Wives of England* (1843) when she explains the reason for the title of her first chapter: 'Thoughts Before Marriage':

> [I] would venture to recommend a few inquiries to those who have not yet passed the rubicon, and with whom, therefore, it may not be too late to retract, if they should find they have not correctly calcu-lated the consequences of the step they are about to take; or, what is still more probable, if they have not coolly and impartially estimated their own capability for rendering it one of prudence and safety both to themselves and others.
>
> (Stickney-Ellis, 11–12)

Stickney-Ellis's measured tone is in sharp contrast to the plethora of newspaper and journal articles, police reports, cartoons and even polit-ical debates that depicted horrific tales of domestic violence, but she is both clear and robust in her advice. Young women too often see marriage as a 'petulant rebellion' against the restraints of home and parental au-thority and are seduced by the attentions of 'a polite and flattering lover' (Stickney-Ellis, 14). Yet while she urges caution and taking sufficient time to properly assess the would-be husband's character, she also admits that the cultural restraints imposed on young women make this impossible:

> It is one of the greatest misfortunes to which women are liable, that they cannot, consistently with female delicacy, cultivate, before an engage-ment is made, an acquaintance sufficiently intimate to lead to the dis-covery of certain facts which would at once decide the point, whether it was prudent to proceed further towards taking that step, which is universally acknowledged to be the most important in a woman's life.
>
> (Stickney-Ellis, 22)

Stickney-Ellis moves on to discuss a range of character traits that would make a man unsuitable as a husband, among which, she lists symptoms of insanity, including 'a highly excited and disordered state of the nervous system' (Stickney-Ellis, 24). This was Frances (Fanny) Trollope's own experience of marriage.

Fanny met her husband, Thomas Anthony Trollope in 1808, and after a relatively brief courtship, they married on 23 May 1809. Thomas Anthony's proposal of marriage was made formally in writing and in his letter he set out his financial position (Neville-Sington, 32). Fanny replied with an equally candid outline of her own pecuniary situation although this apparently carefully calculated, level-headed approach to their union was underpinned by expressions of great affection on both sides. But on 4 May 1809, three weeks before their wedding, Thomas Anthony wrote a letter that Frances Eleanor Trollope, Fanny's daughter-in-law calls 'a most curious piece of self revelation' (Frances Eleanor Trollope, 35). In this letter, Thomas Anthony explains that he distrusts over-emphatic expressions of feeling and that he feels 'afraid of raising doubts to the prejudice of my own sincerity by professing too much, or declaring myself in too vehement a manner' (Frances Eleanor Trollope, 36). Frances Eleanor Trollope provides an acute analysis of the way in which this reluctance became an entrenched emotional withdrawal that antagonized his family and alienated both his children and his clients and colleagues:

> In latter years ill-health, and the extraordinarily incautious use of powerful drugs, no doubt increased his nervous irritability until he lost power to control it. But here in his own avowed theory of life, we see the germ of the deepest mischief.
>
> (Frances Eleanor Trollope, 37)

Thomas Anthony's addiction to calomel, the opiate referred to by his daughter-in-law, seriously impaired his judgement and irretrievably damaged his relationships. His practice as a lawyer failed, and the inheritance on which the family were relying to solve their financial difficulties also vanished when Thomas Anthony's uncle re-married and produced a large family. Fanny Trollope, like other novelists discussed in this collection, turned to writing to support herself and her family. As Anthony Trollope reports in his *Autobiography* (1883), Fanny applied herself with energy and determination to the enforced change in her circumstances, rising at 4 a.m. every morning to produce book after book (Trollope, Anthony, 21). Her industry was well rewarded and her books continued to be reprinted until the early 1880s when, as Pamela Neville-Sington notes, they suddenly ceased to appear (Neville-Sington, 366). Her son Anthony, whose debts she paid and for whose first novel she found a publisher, disassociated himself from her after her death, dismissing her as 'neither clear-sighted nor accurate; and [...] unable to avoid the pitfalls of exaggeration' (Trollope, Anthony, 27).

Trollope explores the theme of marriage in several of her novels.[1] In *One Fault* (1840) for example, which references the Reform Act of 1832, she writes about a marital tragedy in which the partners are irreconcilably divided by the husband's domineering and tyrannical behaviour towards his wife.[2] The trio of novels dealing with the Widow Barnaby published between 1839 and 1843 superficially could not be more different, yet these texts trace the career of the eponymous Widow Barnaby as she struggles to survive, like her creator, against the vicissitudes of fortune. Whereas *One Fault* is an account of a failed marriage very like Trollope's own, the texts that deal with the Widow Barnaby's marital adventures offer a satirical view of this most intimate of relationships, taking the romantic ideals of the courtship plot and subverting them. The Widow is far removed from Stickney-Ellis's sheltered, virginal and inexperienced girls who will be offered as commodities in the marriage market. Instead, Trollope gives an unwaveringly ironic account of her heroine as a figure of fun, but one who is undeniably powerful as she manipulates, lies and cheats to achieve her goal of marriage to a man of appropriate wealth and status. She charts her destructive path through life with total disregard for anyone who cannot or will not assist her in fulfilling this aim. Yet as an analysis of the novels will show, the Widow's third and final marriage to Major Allen does ironically fit the pattern propounded by writers of advice literature like Stickney-Ellis. It does so by inverting the gendered power relationship of nineteenth-century marriage, showing the Widow as determined to act in her own financial and social interests without being constrained by legal and cultural expectations. As Ann-Barbara Graff points out, the novels explore 'the possibilities of the domestic imploding some of the popular misconceptions about domesticity, women's sphere, and the role of women in society' (Graff, 69)

The Widow Barnaby was commissioned by Richard Bentley & Son together with a planned sequel. This suggests therefore that Bentley recognised that there was a ready market for a set of comic novels about a widow searching for a new husband. Contextually, as this collection of essays illustrates, Trollope's novels appeared at a time when courtship, love and marriage was an endemic concern in both fiction and non-fiction writing. It is suggestive therefore that Bentley was confident about both potential sales and the satirical treatment of the subject matter which exposed and critiqued what happened within the domestic sanctuary of home, brilliantly expanding Harriet Beecher Stowe's comment that

> [h]ome is a place not only of strong affections, but of entire unreserve; it is life's undress rehearsal, its back-room, its dressing-room,

from which we go forth to more careful and guarded intercourse, leaving behind us much *débris* of cast-off and every-day clothing.

(Beecher Stowe, 10)

In this chapter, I explore the marital journey of the Widow Barnaby and Major Allen as they make their picaresque way through England, Australia and America. I focus on three major themes: the power struggle between them, the performances they enact for each other as well as for the outside world and the plots and subterfuge they initiate for their survival.

Power

The Major and the Widow engage in a power struggle from the moment of their first meeting. This takes the form of a series of verbal duels based on the need for knowledge about each other's social and financial position. The presentation of the Widow at this stage is largely comic and the Major's lies become increasingly flamboyant. At the end of *The Widow Barnaby* (1839), the Widow undertakes a pragmatic assessment of her circumstances, re-invents herself with chameleon-like facility, and marries the Reverend Patrick O'Donaghue. After his sudden death, she finally becomes the wife of the Major, having first ensured that 'all she had should be firmly settled upon herself' (Trollope, 1839, Vol 1, 392). There is a clear separation in their marriage between business and emotion. Theirs is a calculated relationship, transacted in terms of gains and losses even when these are not necessarily expressed as monetary values.[3]

Their marriage, at least initially, is one of mutual, concealed antagonism with each vying to gain power and control. At the start of *The Widow Married: A Sequel to The Widow Barnaby* (1840), the balance of power in the relationship, socially, domestically and fiscally, appears to lie with the Widow who flaunts her family connections and her 'tightly-settled, and regularly-remitted income' that supplies all their expenses (Trollope, 1840, Vol 2, 22). The Widow's control of the family finances is extremely unconventional[4]:

> [H]is notions of a well-regulated family economy might have led him to prefer taking his lady's income under his own immediate and separate control; but here, after a somewhat spirited trial on occasion of the two first quarterly payments, he gave in.
>
> (Trollope, 1840, Vol 2, 23)

The Major retaliates by concealing the extent of his gambling winnings from his wife and by refusing to share these with her on the grounds that to do so, would deprive their newly born daughter of her inheritance. The passage of dialogue in which husband and wife each seek to achieve control is masterly in tone and content. Terms of endearment are used as weapons to deflect unwelcome demands and questions. Facts and emotions are hidden behind a façade of urbane domesticity. Trollope concludes:

> There was occasionally a vast deal of fondness displayed on both sides, yet a sharp observer might sometimes have fancied that there was some latent feeling of suspicion and reserve at their hearts.
>
> (Trollope, 1840, Vol 2, 25)

Underlying and unspoken tensions in the marriage are expressed physically through mutual pinching and when the Widow's garrulity threatens the Major's new identity and their life in London society, the power struggle becomes more overt with the Major seizing his wife's wrist to silence her and the Widow tugging sharply to disengage herself.[5] By the time the O'Donaghue family (as they are now known) arrive back in London, the Major is firmly in control of both his wife and his daughter Patty, and culturally appropriate gendered roles have been re-established. His threats are overt: if they do not obey him or if they question him, he will leave. His assertion not only brings his family firmly under his control, it makes clear their mutual need for survival and reliance on each other for success.

The Widow and her daughter reflect on their situation in Chapter XIX mid-way through the novel at a hinge point in the narrative. Geographic locations are used as staging posts in preparation for the family's assault on London society. Roles, identities and behaviour are tested and modified as the family moves up the social scale and the stakes become ever higher. The 'judicious exhortation' referred to in the chapter heading alludes both to the Major's instructions to his wife and daughter and to the Widow's attempts to manage Patty. He is determined that they should remain secluded for their first two months in London and ruthlessly imposes his will on his wife and daughter. From this point on, the Widow actively supports the Major in his machinations and she and Patty become assets in his campaign to exploit their social connections and make their fortune. Their relationship becomes more of an equal partnership. The narrative arc of their marriage reaches equipoise in *The Barnabys in America; or, Adventures of the Widow Wedded* (1843).

The names they adopt at various stages of their relationship reflect the history of the power play in their marriage.[6] When they are first married and reliant on the Widow's income and social connections for status, the Major adopts the name of her previous husband, the Reverend O'Donaghue. After their narrow escape from prosecution in London, he arrives in America as Major Allen Barnaby – his own real name coupled with that of his wife's first husband. The narrative continues to reflect the fluctuations of their power struggle and acts as a satirical commentary on cultural expectations of marriage. It is the Widow who brazenly adopts a public (and erroneous) persona as a novelist writing about America – an ironic inter-textual reference as Tamara S. Wagner notes to Trollope's *Domestic Manners of the Americans* (1832) (Trollope, 1843, Vol 3, ix) – and the Major who continues to lead a hidden life of illicit gambling and fraud, a secret watcher waiting in the shadows to take advantage of an opponent's weakness.

Their power struggle is conducted along gendered lines revealed clearly in the Widow's bizarre dream that provides a complex and layered account of the relationship between husband and wife, the role of women novelists and social ambition. Trollope describes the Widow falling asleep as having forgotten herself 'when a power nobler than memory took its place' (Trollope, 1843, Vol 3, 162). She has not in fact 'forgotten herself' at all but instead enters in her dream into a heightened state of self-awareness in which 'she became in sleep the subject of her own high imaginings' (Trollope, 1843, Vol 3, 162). She envisages herself as a famous novelist – the persona she has created in order to enter American society. She addresses her husband familiarly as 'Donny' telling him 'It is not *you* who have written all these books; and if, as you all justly enough say, a title must and will be given [...], it cannot be given to *you*. [...] It must and will be given to ME' (Trollope, 1843, Vol 3, 163). The Widow claims public acclamation and recognition as a novelist for herself as a woman with emphatic capitals. She is asserting herself as the more powerful partner, the one who will be acknowledged with a higher social status, the diametric opposite of the supportive Victorian wife who stays in her husband's shadow. She has no intention, as Trollope makes clear, of submitting 'to the degrading position of a merely ornamental appendage to her more highly gifted husband's establishment' (Trollope, 1843, Vol 3, 255). She is also resistant to his peripatetic lifestyle occasioned by his illegal activities. The constant destabilization of their home disrupts her attempts to achieve social recognition but equally, she is capable of doing battle on her husband's behalf and is consistently the one who comes up with creative schemes to save them both.

Discussions between husband and wife in this final novel of the series reveal a continuing exchange of information about their different plans and expressions of mutual respect. A deeper degree of affection enters their marriage as the Major increasingly comes to respect his wife's adept performances. The narrative focus moves to the Widow with the Major playing a supporting role as they work together equitably and harmoniously. Gendered roles are disrupted: the Widow '(not manfully but) womanfully called upon her genius to help her' (Trollope, 1843, Vol 3, 213). The Major acknowledges her as his 'best trump' and kisses her hand rather than seizing her wrist (Trollope, 1843, Vol 3, 232). The Widow becomes a figure of considerable power both within her marriage and in the external world. The Major turns to her for help when they are both in imminent danger of exposure. This time, his silence is that of respect rather than the desire to conceal his true feelings and motivation as was the case at the start of their marriage. Superfluous characters are shed so that the novel focuses exclusively on the relationship between the Widow and the Major.

Performance

Both the Widow and the Major are moral chameleons and this is reflected in their changing physical appearance. In *Sartor Resartus* (1834), Carlyle uses the work of the fictional German philosopher Teufelsdröckh to meditate on the way in which clothes are symbols that make manifest inner meaning and thereby the state of a culture and society (Carlyle, 205).[7] The Widow unleashes her inner character after her marriage to her first husband, the apothecary Mr Barnaby, when she becomes larger than life in every sense, tall in stature and outlandish in appearance, rouged and ringleted, embellished and garnished with her satin-stitch embroidery. Mariana Valverde discusses the way in which female dress in the nineteenth century signified moral status as well as social position. Flamboyant clothing and a love of 'finery' were associated with prostitution. While Trollope ostensibly uses the Widow's love of fashionable clothing to comic effect as a means of criticizing her ostentatious nature, there is a clear link between her expanding girth and her sexuality, her power over weaker individuals and over the narrative itself which she increasingly dominates. Her appetites are insatiable and she will stop at nothing to satisfy them. Her love of sensuous fabrics is a public statement of her wealth as well as a reflection of her own desires, and she displays her extensive wardrobe to the well-connected Mrs Beauchamp in order to infiltrate American society. Display and the veneer of social position replace letters of introduction and verifiable social connections. The Widow's new American character is given birth as each sumptuous piece of velvet, satin and lace is produced from the large hampers she has imported from England.

Ann-Barbara Graff, in her discussion of the role of the widow in literature, notes that 'the widow is routinely identified as a subversive threat to gender roles and the locus of comic instability, misadventures and entanglement' (Trollope, 1839, Vol 1, xxvii). The Widow Barnaby's gendering is unstable: she is tall, has large hands and her behaviour is masculine. The Widow's quasi-hermaphrodite appearance and behaviour emphasize her originality as a female picara. As Helen Heineman notes, by placing a female adventurer at the heart of the narrative, Trollope 'added a new dimension to the treatment of women in fiction' (Heineman, 157). Wily, utterly selfish, constantly seeking stimulation and new environments in which to exercise her dominant personality the Widow is the antithesis of the conventional submissive Victorian heroine. She pursues potential husbands relentlessly, her sexual voracity indicated by her flamboyant clothing with its excess of frills and furbelows, but she is equally ruthless in discarding companions whom she can no longer exploit. She has sufficient means to lead a quiet domestic life like her aunt, Betsy Crompton, who is in complete control of her 'time, energy and finances' but chooses instead to seek fame and fortune and a social status and recognition beyond her means (Trollope, 1839, Vol 1, xi).

She is the embodiment of Teufelsdröckh's theory of clothes as architecture: they are 'the site and materials whereon and whereby his beautified edifice, of a Person, is to be built' (Carlyle, 28) and she constructs a variety of personas to suit her current circumstances. Her satin stitch embroidery is the physical manifestation of her modus operandi – she 'embroiders' the truth to suit her own ends. '[T]here is NOTHING', she asserts, 'which makes so prodigious a difference in a lady's dress, as her wearing a great profusion of good work!' (Trollope, 1839, Vol 1, 92). Satin stitch is a flat stitch used to completely cover a section of the background fabric. The implication is that the Widow covers up the things she wishes to hide from society, principally her social and financial status, by obscuring these under layers of visually distracting decoration. Yet there is a disjunction between the delicacy of her work and her physical and social crassness. Satin stitch 'must be worked very evenly to give a good effect; silk thread is the most suitable to use' (Anon, 192). The Widow is not without skill, and her abilities, and the way in which she uses them for her own ends, become more apparent over the narrative arc of the three novels.

The Major, equally, changes his mode of dress to align with the role he has chosen to play. The most consistent manifestation of his character is that of a dandy as he attempts to gamble and cheat his way to a fortune. James Eli Adams discusses the development of middle-class masculinity asserting that '[t]he dandy shadows the Carlylean hero as the mark of the theatricality from which Carlyle anxiously sought to dissociate his heroes, but which seems inseparably bound up with their vocation' (Adams, 35) and this theatricality, discussed in more detail below, is certainly a key characteristic of the Major. Jessica Feldman points to the difficulty of pinning down the concept of the dandy, arguing that dandyism is 'always at the periphery of one's vision' and it is this very elusiveness that the Major relies upon for survival (Feldman, 1). Ellen Moers points out that 1830 was the year 'to renounce the Regency and vilify the dandy class' (Moers, 167). However, like *Sartor Resartus*, Trollope's novels straddle the divide in culture between Regency and Victorian England. They illustrate a movement 'from an outmoded Romantic vision towards a Victorian social actuality' (Carlyle, xxxiii). The Major, like the Widow, is an exaggerated version of a fashionable Victorian gentleman. His appearance 'including moustaches, favouris, collier grec, embroidered waistcoat, and all, was very nearly as remarkable as her own' (Trollope, Vol 1, 142).[8] The Major does not have the dandy's physical hyper-sensitivity, nor does he share the dandy's austere and dignified style, whose perfection lay in its simplicity (Moers, 31). He does however have no occupation or obvious source of support and as with the hero of Thomas Henry Lister's *Granby,*

> [t]here was a heartlessness in his character, a spirit of gay misanthropy; a cynical, depreciating view of society, an absence of highminded generous sentiment, a treacherous versatility, and deep powers of deceit.
>
> (quoted in Moers, 24)

Deception and fraud are linked to the theme of disguise. As Major Allen, he steals O'Donaghue's identity to pass himself off as a clergyman, shaving off his magnificent whiskers, a flamboyant symbol of his virility. The comedy darkens in the second and third novels in the series as the Widow helps the Major commit forgery, a capital crime, in order to re-enter society. The Major is a consummate performer, unlike his wife who cannot conceal her essential character. The Widow changes her costume and her script but the Major is altogether a darker, more protean character:

> With as much genuine coarseness, he had infinitely more tact than his vulgar wife, and was, in truth, so able an actor, that with an object of sufficient importance before him, he was capable to sustaining many characters extremely foreign to his own.
>
> (Trollope, 1840, Vol 2, 193)

The relationship between the Major and the Widow in the first two novels in the series is based on mutual, unspoken knowledge. Their most intimate moments are as much a performance as their public lives, the façade of the marriage they present to the outside world. It is an ironic inversion of the concept of separate spheres: for the Barnabys, there is no safe sanctuary, no division between the public and the private. Both home and society are equally fraught with the danger of exposure. Towards the end of *The Barnabys in America,* they perform as much for each other as for an audience, skilfully planning each public appearance and negotiating how best to manage the 'business' equitably, playing to their individual skills. The peak of their performance comes when the Major cross-dresses as his wife to escape their pursuers. This charade, although presented comically, encapsulates a number of important narrative themes that have been drawn throughout all three novels in the series. The power struggle between them reaches its culmination in this novel, and the Widow is acknowledged as a 'master spirit' (Trollope, 1843, Vol 3, 321). '[Y]ou must give my powers full scope' she tells her husband, 'I'll get you out of this scrape, as cleverly as I did from that of Big-Gang Bank' (Trollope, 1843, Vol 3, 313). In a neat reversal of their earlier relationship, the Widow controls the Major's speech, holding up her finger to stop him speaking, and threatening to abandon him to his fate, just as he threatened to abandon her in *The Widow Married*. Their acting has a serious purpose, and the Widow's disguise as a shabby countrywoman is as out of character as that of the Major cross-dressing as a woman.

To this end, she sets the stage carefully for their performance and issues precise stage directions to the performers. The Major promises that he 'shall neither mistake the order of the subsequent scenes nor forget my cue' (Trollope, 1843, Vol 3, 316). Trollope had a lifelong love of the theatre and amateur dramatics and indeed used this experience to embark on what she hoped would be a money-making scheme in Cincinnati. Like the Widow, Trollope arrived in America with no letters of introduction and struck the inhabitants of Cincinnati as being an unfashionable, inelegant and unrefined curiosity who did not conform to the social norms. She attempted to use her theatricals to both enter and enliven local society, and amateur dramatics feature in several other of her novels (Neville-Sington, 126–30).

Fanny's Cincinnati theatricals were based on an urgent need to earn some income. The Widow's production is founded on an equally urgent imperative to escape from their creditors and a possible capital charge. Her instructions include listing the costume her husband will wear – the Widow's 'large long cloak, petticoats, [...] Leghorn sun-bonnet and white lace veil' (Trollope, 1843, Vol 3, 314). The Widow herself will get ashore disguised as an old countrywoman. The Major will be allowed 'five minutes retreat' to transform himself into his wife, a pantomimic, hastily contrived means of escape for both of them (Trollope, 1843, Vol 3, 316). His cross-dressing is however, his wife instructs him, to be preceded by an exaggerated display of masculinity. He must tell their pursuers that his wife is horribly sick, then 'swagger a little about the horrid bore of travelling with women' (ibid). While this is an essential part of the Widow's plan, designed to maximise their chances of success, it is at this critical point in the narrative that the gendering of each of them is ironically clearly asserted. The Major's feminine masquerade amounts to little more than adopting some external signifying items of dress and a parodic interpretation of female behaviour. Indeed, he believes he will find it impossible to walk in a convincingly feminine way. Instead, his most important contribution to their escape will be the use made of his 'own *peculiar* talent' for acting (ibid, 315), and the Widow makes it clear that a good deal of the success of her plan will depend on this. It is the Major's masculinity therefore, his performance of patriarchal care as he balances the need to care for his sick wife with his commitments in the external public sphere, that will provide the context for the deception so deftly plotted by the Widow. Equally, the Widow's chosen disguise as an old countrywoman with 'a shabby old bonnet pulled low over her face, a very worn-out shawl, a common cotton-gown pulled up through the pocket-holes and [...] sleeves pushed up considerably above the elbow' (ibid, 319) re-locates her in the submissive feminine, a woman of no importance both in herself and in her gender.

The alignment of the 'costumes' of the Major and his wife symbolises the porous nature of their sexualities and the fluidity with which power and control within their marriage move from one to the other. The description of the Major's costume recalls the floating draperies with which the Widow attempted to disguise her increased embonpoint and indeed her social and sexual rapacity, before her reunion with her previous suitor, Lord Mucklebury. The Widow's large shawl effectively conceals 'the outline of his person' (Trollope, 1843, Vol 3, 318). Their similarity in height and build and the way in which the Major not only wears his wife's clothes but is able to take on aspects of her character through his physical performance, emphasises the protean nature of the sexuality and gendering of both of them.[9] They are indeed 'a perfect pattern couple' (Trollope, 1843, Vol 3, 322).

Hands, gestures and the gaze all play an important part in these performances and in narrative development and are an illustration of how deeply embedded Trollope is in the art of the theatrical. The Major's 'smiling mustache' symbolises his insincerity – the upward turn of his whiskers gives a false impression of good humour and social conviviality, disguising his far from benign intentions (Trollope, 1840, Vol 2, 40). His facial hair is also an indication that he is not what he seems. Susan Walton points out that 'until July 1854 most British soldiers were barred from sporting facial hair; moustaches were restricted to a few regiments and beards were banned except in unusual circumstances' (Walton, 233). The Major's absurd account of his personal defeat of Napoleon at the battle of Waterloo further undermines any plausible account he tries to give of his military experience (Trollope, 1839, Vol 1, 165). Mrs Stephenson gazes at the Widow in fascination through her glasses and is instrumental in exposing the Major's scheming with the clarity of her sharper focus. The Major's card cheating involves sleight of hand and the Widow's hands embroider her clothes as her tongue embroiders her social status and wealth. Domestic skills such as needlework are mocked by Trollope and used to suggest the Widow's lack of education, both literal and emotional. Agnes Willougby's travelling library has more value than her inability to do satin stitch. Yet Betsy Crompton's addiction to literature leads her to seriously misread character, and all three novels contain a narrative thread of parody of readers and reading as well as the aforementioned inter-textual references to *Domestic Manners of the Americans*.

Plots and Subterfuge

Plots and subterfuge bind the Widow and her husband together. Their marriage begins as a tactical one as they plan their campaign of social warfare. At first, their energies are taken up with delicate domestic ne-gotiations each seeking to outmanipulate the other, each with the unspo-ken knowledge of past secrets that are constantly weighed in the balance of their marital dance. Their fight for control over each other, for money and for the commodities and status both are determined to achieve, is a savage counterpoint to the idealised marriage of the Huberts and to the increasingly desperate manoeuvrings of Matilda Perkins to find a husband, no matter how unsuitable. This phase in their relationship is temporarily brought to an end when the Major tells his wife: 'This is silly work, my love, squabbling about which of us is capable of carrying on the war with the most skill' (Trollope, 1840, Vol 2, 45). From this point on, their not inconsiderable joint skills are mostly focused externally on manipulating social situations and relationships to their advantage. By the time they reach America, they respect each other's skills and abilities and understand how to use these to their mutual advantage.

The language used to describe their machinations is one of warfare: treasons, spoils and stratagems are their modus operandi. In *The Widow Married,* they arrive back in London to make an assault on the Widow's wealthy relatives. The Major's 'system of tactics dictated very strong regu-lations': his is an army discipline that he has no hesitation in imposing on his unruly wife and daughter (Trollope, 1840, Vol 2, 92). They are to 'carry on the war' by working together to ensure that appearances are kept up and their lack of money carefully concealed. A double deception is being practised here: the family are putting on a performance so that they 'appear like people of fashion' (Trollope, 1840, Vol 2, 93). The Major is planning to trick a gullible heir out of his fortune through gambling which was increas-ingly being viewed as 'an illegitimate form of financial risk'.[10] His caution and the immense care with which he balances an acceptable social façade with the risky illicit activity he is undertaking is made explicit in the head-ing to Chapter XVI which includes the phrase 'Military tactics' (Trollope, 1840, Vol 2, 161). Once again, the Major has to control his wife, telling her that she can have no other officers to their planned social re-union with the Huberts not because of the difference in rank between the officers and General Hubert but because the General is 'a sort of man that one never invites to meet – sporting gentlemen, who live by their wits' (Trol-lope, 1840, Vol 2, 169). The Major's calculations, both fiscal and social, are precise, and he will not 'spoil a great game by mixing it up with a little one' (Trollope, 1840, Vol 2, 169). The climax is reached at their grand party at which the Major plans to take Ronaldson's fortune by cheating at cards:

> It was not long before the business of the third drawing-room com-menced; not, indeed, that most important part of it for the bringing

on of which the whole costly entertainment was arranged, but such little skirmishing affairs as sometimes mark the coming on of a battle on which hangs much.

(Trollope, 1840, Vol 2, 358)

This use of language continues into the final volume in the series, *The Barnabys in America* where it is associated with the Widow who grasps her pen firmly, and replenishes it with ink 'as confidently as ever soldier drew his sword, or cocked his pistol' (Trollope, 1843, Vol 3, 141). The gendered associations, the phallic pen and sword, and the Widow's unquestioning confidence in her own abilities demonstrate that she is now in control of planning and carrying out their campaign. It also foreshadows the narrative climax of the novel, discussed earlier, when the Major and his wife literally swop roles and identities as he cross-dresses as the Widow to escape his pursuers. The Major conducts a parallel campaign in America to that of his wife's drive for social status and recognition with his secret life among the conmen of New York which he views as a battle, a trial of skill. He is content to let them make the first move:

He knew that it would not be made in the same style, or with the same weapons to which he had hitherto been the most accustomed; but [...] left [sic] them attack him in what manner they would, [...] he waited with no small degree of impatience for the opening of the campaign.

(Trollope, 1843, Vol 3, 290)

Trollope outlines in considerable detail the way in which the Major forges a bill of credit in order to obtain double the amount of cash. This both continues the ironic inter-textual references to *Domestic Manners of the Americans* highlighting the exploitative and ruthless nature of speculation in both the Old World and the New, and emphasizes the darkness of the Major's character. He is uncompromisingly predatory, both sexually and financially. His attempted assault on Agnes Willougby in which 'his huge hand grasped the elbow of Agnes, and he held her forcibly back' (Trollope, 1839, Vol 1, 154) is mirrored by his unhesitating use of forgery and identity theft.

Conclusion

Trollope's account of the Barnabys' marriage is always nuanced. The struggle for power and control within their relationship ebbs and flows and moments of equipoise are reached. Their mutual enjoyment of performance and the manipulation of social situations to their own advantage bind them together, and their relationship moves from one of financial and social convenience to one of genuine respect and regard.

Trollope uses the innovation of a series of novels based on the picaresque adventures of the Widow with consummate skill. In each novel, the narrative arc gradually tightens to focus on the relationship between the Major and the Widow and subsidiary characters are moved off-stage. Over the series of novels, we follow the development of the marriage as it deepens with each of their failed schemes when they become more aware of each other's skills and foibles and learn how to balance and use these to their common purpose.

The Barnabys' marriage is hardly the stereotypical one portrayed in most nineteenth-century novels, nor does it overtly follow the model propounded by writers of prescriptive literature such as Sarah Stickney-Ellis: the submissive wife managing the home and meeting the needs and wishes of her husband.[11] In many ways, it is a joyous romp as the two adventurers invent increasingly preposterous schemes to secure their financial and social status. The novels offer a rich seam of cultural and social commentary, ranging from the intimate to the national, the absurd to the profound, all of which Trollope explores with gusto and an unerringly satirical eye. Yet ironically, their marriage does curiously fit the ideal model propounded by Sarah Stickney-Ellis. Despite the Major's threats to abandon his wife and child, he stays with them. The pair learn to live with each other's faults and, as they sail away at the end of *The Barnabys in America*, the reader is secure in the knowledge that they will continue to work together in their own inimitable way. Trollope's own marriage of course did not follow this pattern and, despite its early promise, became instead unremittingly tragic. In the Widow Barnaby novels, she perhaps re-worked her own experiences and in doing so, produced one of literature's strongest female characters and the portrait of a marriage that is anything but conventional. The constant interchange of roles and appearance between the Widow and the Major reflects the shifting power in their relationship and the unsettled nature of their domestic and financial arrangements, a reflection to some extent of Trollope's own experiences as she travelled and worked unremittingly to try to support her own family.

Notes

1 See for example *Town and Country* (1848) and *The Life and Adventures of a Clever Woman* (1854).

2 See Elsie B Michie. 'Frances Trollope's One Fault and the Evolution of the Novel', *Women's Writing*, Vol 18, No 2 (2011), pp 167–81 for a discussion of the novel that positions it between Jane Austen's *Pride and Prejudice* (1813) and Anthony Trollope's *He Knew He Was Right* (1869). Helen Heineman, *Mrs Trollope: The Triumphant Feminine in the Nineteenth Century*, Athens: Ohio University Press, 1979, pp 188–92 also discusses Trollope's exploration of marriage in this novel.

3 See Elsie B Michie, *The Vulgar Question of Money: Heiresses, Materialism and the Novel of Manners from Jane Austen to Henry James*, Baltimore,

MD: The John Hopkins University Press, 2011, for a comprehensive account of the role of money and the wealthy woman in the nineteenth-century
courtship and marriage narrative.

4 As Abigail Burnham Bloom points out in her introduction to *The Widow
Married*, the Widow's inheritance from her first husband would legally be
managed by the Major (Trollope, Vol 2, xi).

5 Jessica Feldman's description of the dandy outlines many characteristics
which the Major shares and displays in his private and often misogynistic
relationship with his wife: 'Aloof, impassive, vain, the dandy has a defensive
air of superiority that shades into the aggression of impertinence and cruelty.
Military in bearing and discipline, the dandy is also as fragile and whimsical
as a butterfly' (Feldman, 3).

6 Tamara S. Wagner points out in her introduction to *The Barnabys in America*
that the 'obfuscation of identity or, literally, creation of a fake identity, is
extremely common in nineteenth-century fiction dealing with emigrating
fortune-seekers, absconding criminals or bankrupts, but Trollope's series
stands out in taking these successful imposters as her heroes and heroines'
(Trollope, Vol 3, xiii).

7 Sandra M Gilbert discusses the way in which the Industrial Revolution facilitated the development of fashion and the deployment of individual taste in
clothing, 'a heightened awareness of the theatrical nature of clothing itself'
(Gilbert, 392). She also notes the 'significant nineteenth-century tradition of
writing about androgyny, hermaphroditism, transvestism, and even trans-
sexualism' (Gilbert, 407, note 22 and 413 op cit).

8 Ann-Barbara Graff notes that a 'collier grec' was a wire cage moustache
(Trollope, Vol 1, 400, note 30).

9 See Vern L Bullough, Bonnie Bullough, Cross *Dressing, Sex, and Gender*,
Philadelphia: University of Pennsylvania Press, 1993, for a comprehensive
account of the way in which cross-dressing represents a symbolic incursion
into territory that crosses gender boundaries. Feldman also discusses the
ways in which dandies challenged the development in the nineteenth century of the two-sex system arguing that we need to 'understand the dandy
as neither wholly male nor wholly female, but as the figure who blurs these
distinctions, irrevocably' (Feldman, 11). This applies equally of course to
Trollope's presentation of the Widow.

10 For a more detailed discussion, see David C Itzkowitz, 'Fair Enterprise or
Extravagant Speculation: Investment, Speculation, and Gambling in Victorian
England', *Victorian Studies*, Vol 45, No 1, Victorian Investments (Autumn
2002), pp 121–47.

11 James A Hammerton points out that Stickney-Ellis's private views were at
odds with her public statements: 'On the eve of her own marriage, at thirty-
eight, to the missionary, William Ellis, she questioned his ability to cope
with her strong will and accustomed independence, and was quick to rebuke
him for the 'unreasonable' demands he made on her time' (Hammerton, 78).

Works cited

Adams, James Eli. *Dandies and Desert Saints: Styles of Victorian Masculinity*.
Ithaca, NY: Cornell University Press, 1995.

Anon, *Practical Needlework: An Illustrated Guide*. London: Book Club Associates, 1980.

Beecher Stowe, Harriet. *Little Foxes; or, The Insignificant Little Habits which
Mar Domestic Happiness*. London: Bell and Daldy, 1866.

Carlyle, Thomas. *Sartor Resartus*. Kerry McSweeney and Sabor Peter eds. Oxford: Oxford World's Classics, 1987.

Feldman, Jessica R. *Gender on the Divide: The Dandy in Modernist Literature*. Ithaca, NY and London: Cornell University Press, 1993.

Heineman, Helen. *Mrs Trollope: The Triumphant Feminine in the Nineteenth Century*. Athens: Ohio University Press, 1979.

Moers, Ellen. *The Dandy: Brummell to Beerbohm*. London: Secker & Warburg, 1960.

Neville-Sington, Pamela. *Fanny Trollope: The Life and Adventures of a Clever Woman*. London: Penguin Books, 1998.

Stickney-Ellis, Sarah. *The Wives of England*. London: Fisher, Son, & Co, 1843.

Trollope, Anthony. *An Autobiography*. David Skilton ed. London: Penguin Books, 1996.

Trollope, Frances. *The Widow Barnaby* (1839). Ann-Barbara Graff ed. Vol 1. London: Pickering and Chatto, 2011.

Trollope, Frances. *The Widow Married; A Sequel To The Widow Barnaby* (1840). Abigail Burnham Bloom ed. Vol 2. London: Pickering and Chatto, 2011.

Trollope, Frances. *The Barnabys in America; or, Adventures of the Widow Wedded* (1843). Tamara S. Wagner ed. Vol 3. London: Pickering and Chatto, 2011.

Trollope, Frances Eleanor. *Frances Trollope: Her Life and Literary Work from George III to Victoria*, Vol I. London: Richard Bentley and Son, 1895.

Valverde, Mariana. 'The Love of Finery: Fashion and the Fallen Woman in Nineteenth-Century Social Discourse'. *Victorian Studies*, Vol 32, Part 2 (1989), pp 169–88.

Walton, Susan. 'From Squalid Impropriety to Manly Respectability: The Revival of Beards, Moustaches and Martial Values in the 1850s in England.' *Nineteenth-Century Contexts: An Interdisciplinary Journal*, Vol 30, No 3 (2008), pp 229–45.

3 Imperfect and Alternative Marriages in Charlotte Yonge's *Heartsease* and *The Clever Woman of the Family*

Emily Morris

Novelist Charlotte Yonge (1823–1901) is often classified as an antifeminist Victorian woman writer, who, though very popular in her heyday, is too invested in conservative religious and gender values to be enjoyable, or even readable, to a modern audience. While these aspects of her works can be hard to stomach, the overt antifeminist views are invaluable in adding layers to our understanding of Victorian concepts of gender roles and their fulfilment, and indeed the popularity of her books suggests that what is frustrating now was, for many then, inspiring, entertaining and meaningful. Assertions such as 'I have no hesitation in declaring my full belief in the inferiority of woman, nor that she brought it upon herself' (Yonge, 1877, 1) and the slightly more generous 'A woman of the highest faculties is of course superior to a man of the lowest; but she never attains to anything like the powers of a man of the highest ability' (2), which open Yonge's collection of essays *Womankind* (1877) seem to leave little room for any proto-feminist ideas. However, as Tamara S. Wagner points out, 'Most of the novelists labelled – or branded – as typical antifeminists held ambiguous, even contending, views on various, not necessarily interrelated, agendas' (Wagner, "Narratives", 5).

This chapter focuses on the particular ambiguity of Yonge's depictions of marriage, which complicate her conservative reputation while seeming to participate in the celebration of traditional hierarchical gender roles. Her novels *Heartsease* (1854) and *The Clever Woman of the Family* (1865) explore the question of whether marriage is the best choice for every woman, as well as describing its imperfections. *Heartsease* is a novel specifically focused on describing a marriage, and the later *Clever Woman,* a more overtly controversial and antifeminist novel, develops both themes and character types from *Heartsease* in ways that suggest Yonge reconsidering notions of happiness. Though both novels end with their heroines ensconced in marriage and motherhood, these unions are not presented as the unquestioned happy resolution for women of many Victorian (and other) novels. As June Sturrock points out, Yonge's 'female characters have interesting alternatives to marriage, while in her

plots she carefully avoids treating marriage as the inevitable resolution'
(Sturrock, 50). Instead, questions and challenges are at the forefront of
both novels and the answers, fulfilment and resolution are to be located
in religious faith, relationships between women and alternative unions
that take place in spite of, and with more ease and joy than, traditional
patriarchal marriages.

Yonge's personal and religious backgrounds underlie her queries of
the traditional marriage plot. Yonge herself was never married and records of her life give no evidence that she ever contemplated marriage or
formed any romantic attachments to men. She was a devoted daughter,
and a devoted student and follower of Tractarian minister and family
friend John Keble.[1] She lived as a near-member of her brother's household in a cottage on his estate, first with her mother and then with the
sister of her brother's wife, Gertrude Walker (Hayter, vii–viii). Yonge's
greatest use of her time and energy was in her writing and her editorship
of the magazine *The Monthly Packet,* tasks that she saw as her particular calling in helping to spread Keble's message and in informing and
guiding young female readers in matters spiritual and practical. Wagner
argues that Yonge 'translated her belief system into compelling fictions
of everyday life' and that 'she did so in a self-conscious development,
even deliberate recuperation, of a growing mass readership. To capture
the voracious Victorian reader by remaking popular paradigms was part
of the project' (Wagner, "Introduction", 216). This remaking involves a
strong focus on religious and conservative values, but as Kristine Moruzi
proves, Yonge's authority as editor of the *Monthly Packet* is another
remaking. Moruzi suggests that in the context of the magazine, the
'seemingly paradoxical position of agency and submission is arguably a
consequence of Yonge's religious beliefs and her status as both a professional author and a single woman' (Moruzi, 64). Sturrock reads Yonge's
female characters' unmarried professional lifestyle as religious devotion,
but also a comfortable choice, suggesting that for women like them, who
took on religious work instead of the work of marriage,

> one advantage of God over man as a goal is that he is not likely to
> ask one to abandon one's serious pursuits to care for him, as after
> all one's serious pursuits can be conveniently interpreted as caring
> for him. And statistically he is far less likely to distract from one's
> serious pursuits by pregnancy.
>
> (Sturrock, 60)

The delivery and rearing of children are acknowledged to be a huge in-
convenience as well as a great danger in Yonge's novels. The convenience
that Sturrock sees here in the goals taken on is reflected in the undercur-
rents of dissatisfaction and trouble in the marriages in Yonge's fiction,
as well as in the alternative resolutions. The traditional expectations of

female fulfillment through self-sacrifice and devotion to husband and children that pervade Yonge's fiction and *The Monthly Packet* come from a woman who did not fulfill those expectations. Yonge's vocational authority and domestic situation reflect the same reluctance to recognize marriage and motherhood as uncomplicated, unmitigated and unvarying paths to happiness as do certain aspects of her novels.

The earlier of the two novels, *Heartsease, or the Brother's Wife*, develops the idea of marriage as a familial enterprise and centres on female influence within marriage. It also suggests that a woman should be prepared for heartache and difficulty stemming from the imbalance of power that a traditional marriage entails. The brother's wife of the novel's subtitle is Violet Martindale, married at the beginning of the story at fifteen years old to Arthur Martindale, who is both older and of higher social status than she. Violet is overwhelmingly attractive, both physically and in her sweet and submissive disposition, and the Martindale family, initially dismayed by Arthur's choice and her low connections, quickly grow to love her. The one member of the family with whom her relationship is most important and most fraught is Arthur's sister Theodora, a headstrong and proud, though essentially selfless and good young woman who is gradually influenced by Violet to embrace both feminine submissive wifehood and deep and life-changing religious faith. The gift of faith in trials does not begin with Violet though. She is greatly influenced by the eldest Martindale brother, John, a partial invalid who is grieving the death of his own beloved, Helen. Helen is the initial source of the faith and self-sacrifice that John in turn teaches Violet. The path of influence is, then, Helen to John, John to Violet and finally Violet to Theodora, whose tendencies toward feminist questioning and out-of-control behaviours make her the character who is shown to most need guidance, especially if she is one day to become a wife herself. Theodora proves this when her first engagement ends because, as she writes to her mother, 'Mr. Fotheringham tried to exercise a control over my actions to which I could not submit' (261). It is through and to Violet that she learns to submit: 'in all the tossings of her mind she had, as it were, anchored herself to her docile, gentle sister-in-law, treating her like a sort of embodiment of her better mind. Violet's serenity and lowliness seemed to breathe peace on a storm-tossed ocean; and her want of self-assertion to make Theodora proud of submitting to her slightest wish without a struggle' (284). Theodora can submit to one who does not demand it as her due, as a husband might, but rather leads by feminine example, and Theodora later does take what she has learned into her romantic relationship when she becomes Fotheringham's wife.

The case of Theodora insists on the valuable influence of close female relatives. Yonge also promotes this influence within marriage, suggesting that it is more than simply a two-way street. The influence that John exerts over Violet begins in an episode where they are described as though they are husband and wife, not brother and sister-in-law. In order to recover from the birth of her first child and the anxiety brought on by the economic responsibilities of wifehood, Violet and her baby are sent to the seaside with John, on what reads like a honeymoon. Violet's 'enjoyment was excessive,' she sees the scenery as 'a perfect vision of delight,' she 'crie[s] out joyously' (112) and is generally shown here, with John rather than Arthur, as at her happiest. John's father says of the pair, 'They are so comfortable together, it is a pleasure to see them' (137), and John claims Violet 'is a particularly agreeable person, and we do very well together' (137). He suggests that Theodora should join the party as 'a very good opportunity for them to grow intimate' (137) – that is, to develop the same kind of relationship that he and Violet now have. The sense is that Arthur's marriage should intimately involve the whole family, that it is not simply a relationship between two people. In many ways this influence is that of a sister, too, as John is simply a stand-in for his deceased fiancée Helen, whose memory he calls on to help shape Violet's character so she can be a successful wife:

> Helen, my Helen, how you would have loved and cherished her, and led her to your own precious secret of patience and peace! What is to be done for her? Arthur cannot help her; Theodora would not if she could; she is left to me. And can I take Helen's work upon myself, and try to lead our poor young sister to what alone can support her? I must try – mere humanity demands it.
>
> (124)

Struggling with the role of spiritual guide, John reveals the notion that it should be Violet's new sisters, Helen (if she were still alive) and Theodora (if she were amenable), to help her grow and to comfort her. Her husband is dismissed as unable to do this. Yonge here suggests the responsibility of female relatives in a marriage. Arthur is not capable, so it comes down to John, via the memory of Helen, to help Violet take comfort in religion and to overcome her anxious fears that are overwhelming her health and undermining the happiness of her union with Arthur. It takes a family to raise a wife, especially one so young and unconnected, Yonge seems to say, and the John/Helen combination is a neat compromise of gender roles that allow Violet to submit to masculine influence that is promoting feminine comfort and support. She listens to John, but it is Helen's voice and wisdom that are imparted. John's guidance of his sister-in-law is shown, over the course of the novel, to be invaluable in the shaping of Violet as she becomes a stronger wife and person.

In demonstrating the important of influence and support, and suggesting a marriage is a family affair, Yonge also shows the problematic nature of a marriage that demands such support. Violet has need of strength because her marriage is full of trials, almost exclusively brought about by Arthur's failures as a husband. Certainly, Yonge does not pull punches in *Heartsease* in her portrayal of the difficulties of wifehood. Violet is shown to be naïve and hurried in entering into the marriage; she explains to John 'it all happened so fast, I had no time to understand it' (14). Arthur's initial attraction to Violet is purely physical. He extolls her 'out-of-the-way style – the dark eyes and hair [...] exquisite complexion [...] the form of her face, the perfect oval! [...] her figure, just the right height, tall and taper!' (7), while he suggests that the marriage came about almost against his will. He sums up the courtship with the comment that 'I saw I was in for it, and had nothing for it but to go through with it. Anything for a quiet life' (7). While one might interpret 'it' here as undeniable love for Violet, and the quiet life as one desired by Arthur's own heart, the fact that Violet's father is very involved in pushing the match implies that Arthur's 'it' has more to do with being in a spot he finds too difficult to get out of. Arthur's motives – inability to resist, lust and perhaps apathy – along with the fact that he keeps the marriage secret from his family, do not set things off on the right foot, and his continued debauchery and general selfishness mean that Violet has much to contend with, even though the two are fond of and express love for each other throughout the marriage.

Love and attraction are not enough. Yonge explodes the fantasy of marriage to a richer man as guaranteed happiness and success, portraying the sixteen-year-old pregnant Violet in her first year of wifehood, driven to distraction and dangerous illness by her account books and responsibilities in her husband's household. Because of his embarrassment about her background, Arthur refuses Violet her mother who offers to visit and provide advice, and Violet is cheated by the cook recommended by Arthur's family. As Violet sinks into a combination of depression and undefined but life-threatening complications of labour, she sobs 'Oh, I am very, very miserable! Why did he take me from home, if he could not love me? Oh, what will become of me? Oh, mamma, mamma!' (79). Violet's youth is emphasized here in her calls for her mother, suggesting that marriage at such a young age is another problem. Yonge notes in *Womankind* that women who marry before twenty-one 'lose what is or ought to be a very pleasant and instructive period of life' (80), and Violet's case emphasizes wifehood as a difficult career that requires maturity, training and female support. All that leads to this crisis, down to the details of expenditure with which the reader, like Violet, is inundated, acts as a strong deterrent to marriage, especially to an unknown man from a different social class, at a distance from a girl's own family, before she is really grown up.

Resolution in *Heartsease* does not make up for all the pain of marriage, and Yonge can only suggest that the pain is redemptive. Even after Violet has gotten over her initial difficulties and embraced all her trials in marriage as the cross that brings her closer to Christ, Arthur's dissolute habits and disregard for his familial responsibilities continue to make hers a difficult and unhappy life. Five years into her marriage, Violet's face is described by Theodora: 'The form and expression were lovely as ever; but the bright coloring had entirely faded, the cheeks were thin, and the pensive gentleness almost mournful' (318). Financial troubles continue to be a cause, and Theodora discovers that her brother 'allowed his wife to pinch herself, while he pursued a course of self-indulgence' and that 'it was too plain that Arthur gave her little of his company, and his children none of his attention, and that her calmness was the serenity of patience, not of happiness' (322). Arthur's behaviour is finally changed when he is brought to crisis in illness and taught by his young son to embrace faith and religion, and the book ends with 'what seemed like thorns and crosses [...] all turned into blessings' (478). The majority of the marriage is thorns and crosses for Violet, however, and by no means an idealized or happy time. It works out because she has faith and patience learned from Helen/John, and she uses it to comfort herself when her former ideals of love and marriage are disappointed. Marriage is not presented as an immediate means to happiness, or even the clear and natural path that will lead there eventually; rather, it is a trial that Violet must learn to deal with and suffer through. The focus throughout *Heartsease* on faith and patience is one that goes hand in hand with marriage. Violet would have no need for Helen's lessons if she had not married Arthur, and Theodora does not need to learn to submit, except that her own marriage demands it. Faith and female support make the best of a bad situation in the novel, but marriage is that bad situation.

Published eleven years after *Heartsease, The Clever Woman of the Family* is often recognized as Yonge's most overt engagement with burgeoning feminist attitudes, and though it ends with multiple marriages that appear to put women safely into conventional roles, it also explores alternatives to marriage and critiques and questions hierarchical gender roles within marriage as an ideal state. Twenty-five-year-old Rachel Curtis, the clever woman, is in many ways an exaggerated Theodora Martindale. She is smart, stubborn, proud and in search of a meaningful life. She sees herself as

> [a]ble and willing, only longing to task myself to the uttermost, yet tethered down to the merest mockery of usefulness by conventionalities. I am a young lady forsooth [...] I must not put forth my views; I must not choose my acquaintance; I must be a mere helpless, useless being, growing old in a ridiculous fiction of prolonged childhood, affecting those graces of so-called sweet seventeen that I never had – because, because why? Is it for any better reason than because no mother can believe her daughter no-longer on the lists for matrimony?
>
> (38)

Sturrock suggests *The Clever Woman* 'is a conservative novel centred on a vigorous, unconventional, and independent woman' (Sturrock, 48), deciding that in the end 'The function of marriage and motherhood as resolving the problems of both Rachel and Ermine shows the [...] discomfort at any questioning of domestic values' (66). Certainly Rachel is reformed, after being severely punished for her desire to be something other than a wife. She marries Alick Keith almost against her will, as a means of getting beyond the tragic death of a child for which she is responsible through her misguided attempts at social improvement. Immediately after her engagement, Rachel is

> exceedingly depressed, restless, and feverish, and shrank from her mother's rejoicing [...] Nay, in some moods Rachel seemed to think even the undefined result of the interview [Alick's proposal] an additional humiliation, and to feel herself falling, if not fallen, from her supreme contempt of love and marriage.
>
> (418)

Rachel does get over this depression as she starts to recognize that Alick truly cares for her and she for him, but the immediate dislike of the engagement, especially in contrast with her mother's delight in it, conflicts with traditional depictions of marriage as the ultimate goal for women. Rachel's earlier ideas about marriage simply as a conventional move undertaken to please one's parents are reinforced here, and the engagement almost feels like a further means of punishment. I do not mean to deny the significance of the happy domestic ending where Rachel is a fond and fulfilled wife and mother, which adds to the conservative nature of the novel Sturrock describes, but certainly Rachel's strong objections and questions about women's roles and motives for marriage are heard in the novel. At the very least Yonge acknowledges the difficulties of accepting the role of wife for women like Rachel, presented as admirable in her passion and desire to do good, though she must learn to submit. Again, marriage is more complicated than a simply defined fairy tale, and it involves the expectations of others as much as the woman involved.

Rachel mirrors and complicates Theodora, and her cousin Fanny Temple, a meek, feminine, youthful widow, reflects the role that Violet plays, except that she is spared many of the trials of Violet's marriage and allowed to live happily ever after in an interesting alternative arrangement. When she enters the story, Fanny is twenty-four, mother of seven children, and widowed after an eight-year marriage to General Temple, forty-four years her senior. Though Fanny is a devoted widow, thoroughly affronted by new suitors as disrespectful to the memory of her dead husband, her marriage is represented as questionable. Her cousins are 'electrified by the tidings' (40) that sixteen-year-old Fanny has married the sixty-year-old general who escorted her from England to her father in Africa. Fanny 'feel[s] perhaps the difficulty of writing under changed circumstances' (40), is away from England for the whole of her marriage, and 'all that was known of her was a general impression that she had much ill-health and numerous children, and was tended like an infant by her bustling mother and doting husband' (40). The odd, un-wholesome image of the infant constantly producing infants of her own, with the General playing the role of both husband and father, is one that takes place in the colonies, away from the sight of Fanny's English relatives, suggesting something secretive, questionable, or uncivilized. Husbands were often older than their wives in the period, as Davidoff and Hall point out: 'the young, dependent, almost child-like wife was portrayed as the ideal in fiction, etchings, songs and poetry. Such an image of fragility and helplessness enhanced the potency of the man who was to support and protect her' (Davidoff and Hall, 323). However, the outrageous discrepancy between Fanny and her husband is not usual, and perhaps indicates Yonge's feelings about the ideal of the childlike wife as well.[2]

When widowed Fanny returns, Rachel describes her as experienced, but yet dependent:

> [Her] smile was certainly changed; it was graver, sadder, tenderer [...] and the blitheness of the young brow had changed to quiet pen-siveness, but more than ever there was an air of dependence almost beseeching protection; and Rachel's heart throbbed with Britomart's devotion to her Amoret.
>
> (45)

Like Violet, Fanny is shown to suffer trials related to her marriage in the responsibility and anxiety of raising all her children (six of whom are boys), and in the grief of loss. The idea of Fanny's dependence and need for a knight-protector to lean on is challenged by Fanny's refusal of two male suitors during the course of the novel, and by the determined and heroic part she plays in the discovery and rescue of the children being mistreated in Rachel's social experiment. In spite of this courage and ability, though, Fanny is generally in need of help and guidance, espe-cially in dealing with the products of her marriage. She finds her knight in this regard in governess Alison Williams, who, losing her domestic arrangement with her sister Ermine and niece Rose upon Ermine's mar-riage, becomes very closely involved with Fanny and her children. The disciplinarian Alison becomes a pseudo father to the boys, teaching them to obey where their mother cannot. She also becomes intimate with Fanny, not unlike a husband. Fanny says of Alison that she 'give[s] me strength and hope by her very look. I want to have her for good; I want to make her my sister!' (383) and the two are described as telling 'out their hearts to one another' creating 'a bond [...] that gave the young widow the strong-hearted, sympathizing, sisterly friend she had looked for in Rachel, and filled up those yearnings of the affection [...] [Alison's] life had a purpose, though that purpose was not Ermine!'(383). Fanny and Alison replace sisters and cousins for each other in a relationship that also mimics marriage in its intimacy, in that they are a team of parents to Fanny's children. 'Dear Lady Temple is everything to me' (526) declares Alison. They are not simply sisters, but the significant others in each other's lives. In fact, Ermine describes their arrangement as a marriage, joking to her own fiancé, 'I think you may as well get a license for the wedding of Alison Williams and Fanny Temple at the same time. There has been quite a courtship on the lady's part' (528). Fanny, so terrified at the possibility of remarriage, is given a partner and father-figure for her children without being sacrificed again to the trials of marriage or the possibility of adding to her beloved but burdensome brood. There is no danger of Alison's impregnating her. Compared with her counterpart Violet, Fanny's share of trials seems light. It is as if she gets the trouble of marriage over with early, and then is allowed to live an idyllic life of quiet motherhood in her Aunt's house with Alison to help raise her children and be part of a permanent stable partnership.

Talia Schaffer reads Alison and Fanny as a 'romantic pair' (Schaffer, 100) and suggests that the kind of romance or marriage they represent is replicated in other pairs in the novel, particularly in the two marriages that seem to create traditional resolution in the lives of Rachel and Ermine, who might otherwise be models of independent clever women. She argues that the two major marriages in the novel 'redefine romance as familial rather than erotic, and by so doing, suggest an alternative understanding of family' (Schaffer, 97) and indeed marriage. She concludes the following:

> Whereas the marriage plot shows ardent young suitors eager to wed, but interrupted by various problems, the Yongian marriage plot shows the opposite: reluctant, averse, middle-aged suitors for whom marriage is a terror that is hard to stave off [...] When they finally concede, the marriage re-enacts childhood bliss and the partner fills the asexual role of sibling.
>
> (113)

This sororal romance, as Schaffer terms it, is one that subverts or denies the sexual aspect of marriage, the aspect that is a source of disability and discomfort in Fanny's previous union. The re-imagining of a marriage-like situation to include same sex pairs as well as non-sexual ones is a neat trick on Yonge's part that does away on some levels at least with the imbalance of traditional marriage, allowing for equal partnerships. The relationship between Fanny and Alison might be seen to fit in with the many real-life 'female marriages' that took place during the period, including Yonge's own domestic situation. In her biography of 1903, Christabel Coleridge[3] writes of Gertrude Walter, who lived with

Charlotte from 1873 to 1897: 'she and Charlotte were warmly attached to each other. She called herself playfully "Char's wife," as she played the part of helpmeet in her work [...] There is no doubt her presence did much for Charlotte's happiness, and her help and affection were repaid by the tenderest devotion' (Coleridge, 270–71). Sharon Marcus argues that 'Many nineteenth-century women in what some Victorians called "female marriages" were not seen as challenging [...] Instead, they saw themselves, and their friends, neighbours, and colleagues saw them, as a variation of the married couple' (Marcus, 12). In terms of Victorian understandings of marriage, Marcus suggests 'sexual relationships of all stripes were most acceptable when their sexual nature was least visible as such but was instead manifested in terms of material acts such as co-habitation, fidelity, financial solidarity, and adherence to middle-class norms of respectability' (Marcus, 49). In discussing the possibility of an implied sexual relationship between Fanny and Alison, Schaffer claims it is not there because 'desire quite simply does not interest Yonge, and consequently gets virtually no narrative attention' (Schaffer, 105). Since the propriety of Victorian notions, or at least public discussions, of marriage take sex out of the equation, Yonge's perfectly Victorian denial of it leaves Fanny and Alison – and perhaps Charlotte and Gertrude – with a relationship that lacks nothing that a more traditional union would have. However, sexual desire does enter into *The Clever Woman* (and *Heartsease*, where Arthur's initial attraction to Violet clearly involves physical desire) in the disapproving attitude toward Fanny's marriage to the old General, where perhaps the 'norms of respectability' are violated by the age discrepancy, the advantage taken of the role of escort, and especially the plethora of children produced, children who jealously surround and cling to Fanny so as to inhibit both her words and movements, until Alison is able to take them in hand. It is not that this kind of desire is a mystery to Yonge, but rather that she writes it as a source of trouble for the young wives. The evidence of General Temple's sexual desire and ful-fillment of it with Fanny is apparent, and presented as at least distasteful. That problem is solved by the alternative marriage between two women.

In these two novels, Yonge most prominently shows the burden that marriage is, only suggesting the silver lining as the idea that the bigger the cross one bears, the closer one is to Christ and the more significant the blessing in the end. While to Yonge herself, and she would hope to her readers, this is no small reward, it is not presented as simply worth the sacrifice. It becomes an excuse or way to cover or make up for the failure of imbalanced patriarchal heterosexual marriages. In particular, the alter-natives to marriage imagined by Rachel Curtis in the idea of useful work for women and experienced by Fanny Temple and Alison Williams in their widow/governess marriage offer the means to a satisfying life with-out the disadvantages that come with husbands. Yonge's representation of marriage is one that is conflicted and that insists on harsh realities rather than on ideals of romance and woman's natural role. As a writer with a didactic purpose, suggesting how women might direct their lives, Yonge ironically reveals the problems she sees with traditional marriage in her attempt to present religious faith as solace. Solace and comfort are only required where there is pain, and the thorns as blessings are undermined by the idea that they can be avoided altogether by avoiding marriage or working around it in some way. Yonge's most popular novel, *The Heir of Redclyffe* (1853), involves the courtship and marriages of two sisters, Laura and Amy, to the heirs of Redclyffe. The book is an examination of the characters of the two young men and a lesson in what it takes (faith, of course) to be a good man, but in terms of the women, the happier sister in the end is Amy, not simply because her husband turns out to be the better man, but more substantially because he dies young, leaving her a widow, with a child, in the home of her parents. She says, celebrating that she need not be a young lady any more in the ways expected before her marriage, 'I can go on my own way, attend to baby, and take Laura's business about the school, and keep out of the way of company, so that it is very nice and comfortable' (574). This, I argue, is Yonge's real ideal of happiness, one that suggests that husbands, who create babies and demand submission, are not only superfluous to a happy marriage and life, but actually a detraction from it. Yonge's antifeminist sacrifice of her clever independent women to patriarchal marriages is countered by her realistic depictions of unhappiness in those marriages, and her imagining of alternatives that not only fully embrace the idea of female support and influence, but that also do away with the patriarch altogether.

Notes

1 Keble was a prominent member of the Oxford movement and vicar of Hurseley, Hampshire, where Yonge grew up. His influence on her faith is evident in matters of doctrine, but perhaps most strongly in her lifetime devotion to educating others, through her writing, on the importance of church and faith (Hayter, 16–28).
2 Fanny's upset reaction to Lord Keith's proposal as 'too preposterous to be dreamt of by anyone. At his age too, one would have thought he might have known better' (247) is amusing, but Yonge also points out that even Fanny may have found something preposterous in the larger age discrepancy between herself and her first husband.
3 Coleridge knew Yonge quite well. She saw her as a mentor, worked with her as an editor of *The Monthly Packet* in the 1890s and collaborated with her on several works of fiction.

Works cited

Coleridge, Christabel. *Charlotte Mary Yonge: Her Life and Letters*. London: MacMillan, 1903.

Davidoff, Lenore and Catherine Hall. *Family Fortunes: Men and Women of the English Middle Class 1780–1850*. Chicago, IL: University of Chicago Press, 1987.

Hayter, Alethea. *Charlotte Yonge*. Plymouth: Northcote House, 1996.

Marcus, Sharon. *Between Women: Friendship, Desire, and Marriage in Victorian England*. Princeton, NJ: Princeton University Press, 2007.

Moruzi, Kristine. '"The Inferiority of Women": Complicating Charlotte Yonge's Perception of Girlhood in *The Monthly Packet*' in Tamara S. Wagner ed. *Antifeminism and the Victorian Novel: Rereading Nineteenth-Century Women Writers*, pp 57–76. Amherst, NY: Cambria Press, 2009.

Schaffer, Talia. 'Maiden Pairs: The Sororal Romance' in Tamara S. Wagner ed. *The Clever Woman of the Family'. Antifeminism and the Victorian Novel: Rereading Nineteenth-Century Women Writers*, pp 137–58. Amherst, NY: Cambria Press, 2009.

Sturrock, June. *"Heaven and Home": Charlotte M. Yonge's Domestic Fiction and the Victorian Debate over Women*. Victoria, BC: University of Victoria ELS Monograph Series, 1995.

Wagner, Tamara, S. 'Introduction – Novelist with a Reserved Mission: The Different Forms of Charlotte Mary Yonge'. *Women's Writing*, Vol. 17, No 2 (2010), 213–220.

Wagner, Tamara, S. 'Narratives of Victorian Antifeminism' in Tamara S. Wagner ed. *Antifeminism and the Victorian Novel: Rereading Nineteenth-Century Women Writers*, pp 1–18. Amherst, NY: Cambria Press, 2009.

Yonge, Charlotte M. *The Clever Woman of the Family*. Clare A. Simmons ed. Peterborough, ON: Broadview, 2001.

Yonge, Charlotte, M. *Heartsease or, The Brother's Wife*. London: MacMillan, 1919.

Yonge, Charlotte M. *The Heir of RedClyffe*. London: J.M. Dent, 1909.

Yonge, Charlotte M. *Womankind*. London: Walter Smith & Innes, 1889.

4 'Give me Sylvia, or else, I die'

Obsession and Revulsion in Elizabeth Gaskell's *Sylvia's Lovers*

Marion Shaw

> Obsession: the idea or image that repeatedly intrudes upon the mind of a person against his will and is usually distressing (in psychoanalytic theory attributed to the subconscious effect of a repressed emotion or experience).
>
> —(Oxford English Dictionary)

> Revulsion: The action of drawing, or the fact of being drawn, back or away.
>
> —(Oxford English Dictionary)

Elizabeth Gaskell described *Sylvia's Lovers* (1863) as her saddest book. It has also been less noticed by critics than her other novels and probably less read by the general public. It is, however, more complex and challenging than her other work and though a flawed book it stands high in the register of mature and powerful Victorian fiction. It is a marriage story, a historical novel, a protest work and a study of male obsession. It is with the last of these that this chapter is primarily concerned, with the novel as psychodrama.

Gaskell had dealt with obsession in her earlier novels, in *Mary Barton* (1848) and *Lois the Witch* (1859), for example, and most tellingly in *Cousin Phillis* (1864) where the protagonist shows vivid and nearly fatal physical symptoms of an obsessive derangement caused by disappointment in love:

> I could see the passionate, convulsive manner in which she laced and interlaced her fingers perpetually, wringing them together from time to time, wringing till the compressed flesh became perfectly white [...] her grey eyes had dark circles round them, and a strange kind of dark light in them.
>
> (Gaskell 1982, 121)

Gaskell turned to *Sylvia's Lovers* after finishing her biography of Charlotte Brontë which had introduced her to the 'great waving hills of the Yorkshire moors which seemed to girdle the world like the great Norse serpent [and] to the ungovernable families who lived therein' (Chapple and Pollard, 244). She now planned to write a novel with a more primitive setting than her previous fictions. Anxious to locate her new work in a coastal area she considered North Berwick, Galloway and St Andrews, but settled finally on Whitby on the north-east coast where she and two of her daughters spent a cold, wet, ten-day holiday in late October and early November in 1859. Research for her historical book absorbed her for the next few months. The action of the novel takes place over seven years, from 1793 to 1800, a period rich in events for Whitehaven (Gaskell's name for Whitby) as a whaling town subject to raids by impressment gangs seeking sailors to fight in the naval wars against France. There had also been a riot in 1793 in protest against the raiders, and the leader of the riot was indicted as a felon according to the Riot Act of 1714 and hanged. Gaskell skilfully uses these large historical facts to show her characters caught up in faraway events that they cannot control, yet it is individual human actions and decisions within the context of these events that determine the course of the marriage story and lead to its melancholy end.

Gaskell pondered three titles for her story: *The Specksioneer* (Harpooner), *Philip's Idol* and finally *Sylvia's Lovers*. This last choice positions two men in relation to Sylvia and draws parallels with other Victorian novels in which a woman must choose between two (or more) men. A mistaken choice can be rectified, as in *Middlemarch* (1872) or *Far from the Madding Crowd* (1874), but where this is impossible, as in *Wuthering Heights* (1847), misery and death follow. *Sylvia's Lovers* belongs to the latter group. It is also a return story, a sub-genre dating back to the *Odyssey*, in which a man travels from home and is absent for many years, believed dead but returning to find change in the woman and the circumstances he left. Two of the best-known Victorian versions of the story are Elizabeth Braddon's *Lady Audley's Secret* (1862) and Tennyson's *Enoch Arden*, published in 1864 a year after *Sylvia's Lovers*. Gaskell had used the theme herself to tragic effect in 'The Manchester Marriage' (1858) where a long-lost sailor returns to find his wife married to another man. Return stories had a particular contemporary resonance with readers in the wake of the 1857 Matrimonial Act, which liberalised divorce opportunities and raised ethical and religious questions of whether a woman could be married to two men at the same time. The mid-century was also a time when an increase in trade and emigration meant that men left home as never before, many of them never heard of again. The disappearance of Kinraid and Philip, and their unexpected return, would resonate with Gaskell's readership as surely as during the days of the press gang.

Gaskell's version in *Sylvia's Lovers* creates a love triangle between the young and pretty only daughter of a farming family on the outskirts of Monkshaven, the handsome, gallant specksioneer Charley Kinraid, and Philip Hepburn, Sylvia's cousin who works in a shop in the centre of Monkshaven and is, in Gaskell's words, a 'plain young man' but favoured by Sylvia's mother as steady and reliable as a possible future husband for Sylvia. Sylvia and Kinraid fall in love and vow to marry on his return from a whaling trip, but on his way to join his ship he is seized by the press gang, an action seen by Philip who is implored by Kinraid to tell Sylvia what has happened. Philip's fatal decision is to withhold this message. With her father hanged for inciting riot, Sylvia and her mother fall on hard times and she marries Philip out of expediency. Three years later, Kinraid returns but Sylvia, now with a baby, will not go with him, but she swears she will never forgive Philip for the lie he has perpetuated. He leaves Monkshaven and joins the army where, coincidentally, he saves Kinraid's life at the Battle of Accra. Badly wounded Philip returns home, and after saving his daughter from drowning, he dies, reconciled with Sylvia.

In failing to tell the truth Philip is acting out of character, and he does so because of his obsessive love for Sylvia. Gaskell's text puts his case clearly:

> To Philip she was the only woman in the world; it was the one subject on which he dared not consider, for fear that both conscience and judgement should decide against him, and that he should be convinced against his will that she was an unfit mate for him, that she never would be his, and that it was a waste of time and life to keep her enshrined in the dearest sanctuary of his being, to the exclusion of all the serious and religious aims, which in any other case, he would have been the first to acknowledge as the object he ought to pursue. For he had been brought up among the Quakers, and shared their austere distrust of a self-seeking spirit; yet what else but self-seeking was his passionate prayer, 'Give me Sylvia, or else, I die?'.
>
> (Gaskell 1996, 121)

Gaskell adds a moderating and curiously forewarning comment on Philip by saying that 'his was a rare and constant love which deserved a better fate than it met with'.

The text makes clear that Philip is loved by a woman more suited to him, Hester, his fellow shop assistant, but he is so blinded by his passion for Sylvia that he cannot recognise this, nor can he accept that Sylvia is not attracted to him. Why should he be so enthralled? Freud gave the concept of obsession a specific psychological meaning, that its roots lie in family relationships in childhood, particularly in a boy's relationship with his mother: 'The first object of a boy's love is his mother' (Freud 1959, 212). The text of *Sylvia's Lovers* does not mention Philip's mother until the end when he is dying: 'how she had loved him' and how he would stand by her 'dreaming of the life that should be his, with the scent of the cowslips tempting him to be off to the woodlands where they grew' (Gaskell 1996, 452). Freud interestingly describes the pleasures of infantile sexual life as an

> early efflorescence [which] is doomed to extinction because its wishes are inconsistent with reality [...] That efflorescence comes to an end in the most distressing circumstances [leaving] behind them a permanent injury to self-regard in the form of a narcissistic scar [...] The tie of affection, which binds the child as a rule to the parent of the opposite sex, succumbs to disappointment.
>
> (Freud 1955, 20–21)

As Andrew Brink has observed Freud's most useful contribution to a theory of obsessionality is his bipolar model of the split, ambivalent ego, 'a conflict between two opposing impulses [of] love and hate' (Brink, 19). Freud wrote: 'The necessary condition for the occurrence of such a strange state of affairs in a person's erotic life appears to be that at a very early age somewhere in the prehistoric period of his infancy, the two opposites should have been split apart' (quoted Brink, 19). Philip's obsession with Sylvia is surely his narcissistic scar: 'what else,' asks the text, 'but self-seeking was his passionate prayer, 'Give me Sylvia, or else, I die?' (Gaskell 1996, 121).

Philip's psychological journey begins with his orphaned state. He appears to have no living immediate family and has been brought up by his aunt, Sylvia's mother. It was he who had let her know that Haytersbank Farm was available to rent by her and her improvident husband Daniel. Philip and Sylvia are, then, intimate from her early years and her mother thinks of him as the brother Sylvia might have had as well as a potential husband. His intense concern for her, whereby no other girl or woman will satisfy him, is both fatherly (he is more responsible and sensible than Daniel) and brotherly, but it also has an element of erotic, incestuous passion and this goes some way to account for the intensity of his attraction. As Freud wrote, '[i]ncestuous wishes are a primordial human heritage and have never been fully overcome' (Freud 1959, 214). Such wishes are dramatised in Tennyson's early poem, *The Lover's Tale* (probably written in 1828, published in full in 1879). Julian (the narrator) and Camilla are the children of two sisters: 'The stream of life, one stream, one life, one blood [...] And more than joy that I to her became/ Her guardian and her angel' (Tennyson, 309, 314). In Tennyson's erotic and sensational poem the love between the cousins seems as if to lead to 'the Heavenly-unmeasured or unlimited Love' (Tennyson, 317) of adult consummation, but this is thwarted by Camilla's marriage to another man. Tennyson's poem ends in Gothic excess, and so, to some extent, does Gaskell's novel in the melodramatic rescue by Philip of his rival and later of his daughter from the sea.

The novel's first encounter between Philip and the seventeen-year-old Sylvia is in Foster's shop where she has gone to buy a new cloak. Philip has a 'long face, with a slightly aquiline nose, dark eyes, and a long upper lip, which gave a disagreeable aspect to a face that might otherwise have been good-looking' (Gaskell 1996, 28). His unwelcome presence in the shop signals Sylvia's aversion to him and leads to a contest over what colour cloak she should buy. Philip favours the grey duffle as being more hard-wearing but Sylvia wants and buys the scarlet. The scene introduces two of the opposites that track the marriage story: it takes place indoors whereas Sylvia's habitual environment is the wild moorland, a contest later repeated in the cloistered home Philip provides for her, and her escapes to the heath of her childhood home where 'she was as happy as she ever expected to be in this world' (Gaskell 1996, 327). In psychoanalytic terms she belongs to the pre-symbolic world of childhood and the natural, and to the vivid world of story-telling and the oral tradition. The appeal of Kinraid's oral skills is in sharp contrast to Philip's stilted literacy. In the shop scene Philip is dull and tenacious where she is colourful and wilful. He addresses her as Sylvie, and continues to do so throughout the novel, even though she tells him here 'I don't like to be called "Sylvie"; my name is Sylvia' (Gaskell 1996, 29). He also reprimands her over her contact with a girl belonging 'to the lowest class of seaport inhabitants' (Gaskell 1996, 30) who is passionately rejoicing in the return of a whaling ship. Philip is established in this scene as a repressive figure of authority and control and, as he escorts the weeping Sylvia home, of protection.

But even as he acts as a protective figure he quietly initiates a process of sexual predation: 'Her cousin came up to her on tip-toe, and looked anxiously at what he could see of her averted face; then he passed his hand so slightly over her hair that he could scarcely be said to touch it, and murmured [...] "Poor lassie! It's a pity she came to-day, for it's a long walk in the heat!"' (Gaskell 1996, 34). When they reach her home he moves his chair with 'a harsh screech [...] as he heavily dragged it on the stone floor' so that he can watch her face which she has averted because 'she knew from past experience that cousin Philip always stared at her' (Gaskell 1996, 43).

Philip's passion for Sylvia, which leads him to make the disastrous decision to withhold the knowledge of Kinraid's impressment, is the moral crux of the book. It is a lie of omission rather than commission. Philip's deception begins within minutes of Kinraid's arrest in that he wonders 'how much of a promise he had made to deliver those last passionate words of Kinraid's [...] he doubted if Kinraid had caught his words' (Gaskell 1996, 205). This is followed by the narrative comment that 'the dread Inner Creature, who lurks in each of our hearts, arose and said

"It is well: a promise given is a fetter to the giver. But a promise is not given when it has not been received"' (Gaskell 1996, 205). When he sees the hated Kinraid taken on board the tender he realises that his 'wild prayer to be rid of his rival [...] is granted. God be thanked!' (Gaskell 1996, 205). There is an abysmal contrast between the inner creature of sinful temptation the text invokes and the prayer of Philip's gratitude to God. The text hovers on the possibility of Philip's confession several times, most notably when he learns that Daniel has suggested that the press gang had captured Kinraid. 'Philip spoke, by no wish of his own, but as if compelled to speak. "An' who knows but what it's true?"' (Gaskell 1996, 232). The temptation towards goodness is quickly cancelled by his aunt who says, 'What nonsense, Philip!' and she continues to voice the belief that Kinraid has drowned.

In keeping Kinraid's fate secret Philip in effect kills him and is victorious in his struggle of sexual selection to secure the mate they both desire. Kinraid will return from the dead some three years later, both in dreams and in the flesh, and his return will be the cause of Philip's death. But this is preceded by Philip's success as a lover. Forced into poverty by her father's death and with her ailing mother to care for, Sylvia accepts Philip as future husband and is delivered into his possession, tellingly described in the scene immediately following their engagement: 'she heard a soft low whistle, and looking round unconsciously there was her lover and affianced husband, leaning on the gate, and gazing into the field with passionate eyes, devouring the fair face and figure of her, his future wife [...] Again, that long, cooing whistle. "Sylvie"' (Gaskell 1996, 298), which Carol Lansbury has described as an 'obscene command...' (Lansbury, 97). It also continues the infantilisation of Sylvia into 'Sylvie'.

In the marriage, the spirited Sylvia has become 'stunned into a sort of temporary numbness on most points,' only her father's death and care for her mother concern her (Gaskell 1996, 312). To Philip 'the long-desired happiness was not so delicious and perfect as he had anticipated' (Gaskell 1996, 213). Only in the birth of a baby did Philip 'reach the zenith of his life's happiness' (Gaskell 1996, 321). The failure of this marriage is highlighted in Sylvia's waking dream when 'she stretched out her arms imploringly, and said, in a voice full of yearning and tears, "Oh! Charley! come to me—come to me!"' (Gaskell 1996, 322). Philip's jealousy and anger prompt his harsh rebuke: '[w]hat kind of a woman are yo' to go dreaming of another man i this way, and taking on so about him, when yo're a wedded wife, with a child as yo've borne to another man' (Gaskell 1996, 322). These words haunt Sylvia, causing her 'to shudder as if cold steel had been plunged into her warm living body' (Gaskell 1996, 327), and her words of longing for Charley haunt Philip in the return of 'the old dream of Kinraid's presence [...] night after night it recurred; each time with some new touch of reality' (Gaskell 1996, 328). Sylvia's recourse is to the wild sea coast which is 'my only comfort' and where she is drawn into a sea rescue in which her 'principal feeling was one of gladness and high rejoicing that [sailors] were saved who had been so near to death not half an hour before' (Gaskell 1996, 338). On her return home 'all the despondency of her life became present to her again as she sate down within her home' (ibid).

Kinraid's actual return and the revelation of the lie that Philip has lived are the dramatic climax of the marriage plot and provoke Sylvia to make a double decision: not to go with Kinraid but to stay in her marriage – 'neither yo' nor him shall spoil my soul' she says to the two men – and to make a vow regarding Philip: 'I'll never forgive yon man, nor live with him as his wife again' (Gaskell 1996, 348). She has made this kind of vow on other occasions, notably in her refusal to forgive the man Simpson who had given evidence against Daniel: 'Them as was friends o'father's I'll love for iver and iver: them as helped for t'hang him' (she shuddered from head to foot – a sharp irrepressible shudder!) "I'll niver forgive – niver!"' (Gaskell 1996, 291). When she does reconsider this vow it is too late; Simpson has died unforgiven.

Philip's ensuing journey of self-destruction leads him to war and to his saving of the wounded Kinraid, an act that restores the life he took from Kinraid in his silence about the press gang. It is an unlikely coincidence that he should be on hand when Kinraid is in danger but the two men are bound together throughout the novel and schematically this incident works successfully. They are two aspects of love and of masculinity: the steady, sober man without sexual charm, and the possibly unreliable romantic man of action and allure. Philip's slow journey home is in keeping with his obsessive love for Sylvia, but it has become a kind of punitive martyrdom, of himself and also a desire to present his disfigured self as a reproach and punishment to the wife who vowed never to forgive him. What is disturbing to readers, particularly modern readers, is that Sylvia is living a contented life in a somewhat heterogeneous family of women comprising Alice, Hester, Sylvia and Bella. An extreme act is required to justify Philip's re-introduction into this family scene, the husband and father violently interrupting its matriarchal serenity. Philip's action in rescuing Bella from the sea is a death-inducing action, necessary, both in terms of the characterisation of Philip and also for the resolution of the marriage plot, but it seems somewhat contrived. It is his final act of martyrdom before he can exact forgiveness from Sylvia and in so doing destroy her life. Philip's desire is death, and he obeys the Freudian injunction:

> It seems, then, that an instinct is an urge inherent in organic life to restore an earlier state of things which the living entity has been obliged to abandon under pressure of external disturbing forces [...] the expression of the inertia inherent in organic life. [It is] a truth which knows no exception that everything living died for internal

reasons – becomes inorganic once again – then we shall be compelled to say that *the aim of all life is death*.

(Freud 1955, 36–38 [emphasis in original])

All that remains is to die, and in his death it seems that Philip's obsession with Sylvia will be resolved but this is not quite the case. It is a flaw in the novel that the relationship between them is relegated to the afterlife: 'All will be right in heaven – in the light of God's mercy,' and again '"In heaven", he cried, and a bright smile came on his face,' are Philip's dying words and action (Gaskell 1996, 452–53). But during the death scene he reverts to his infantilisation of Sylvia: 'Little lassie, forgive me now!... try, lassie – try, my Sylvie – will not thou forgive me?' (Gaskell 1996, 448). Philip has come full circle to return to the boy that he was at his mother's knee, self-seeking in his Christian ambition to be like Abraham or David. The scene returns to his mind, 'as very present' the spring time when 'someone had brought in cowslips' – the efflorescence of infantile pleasure – 'and the scent of those flowers was in his nostrils now, as he lay a-dying' (Gaskell 1996, 451). The text struggles to recover itself from this circle of obsession to summon salvation for Philip through Sylvia's, and God's, love and forgiveness.

Philip is not the only case of an obsessive character in *Sylvia's Lovers*. Daniel Robson is obsessed by the press gang and the text traces his fixation from the incident when Sylvia and Philip reach her home after the first instance of a raid. Daniel is an obstinate and opinionated man, something of a 'domestic Jupiter', and having maimed his right hand in escaping from the gang he is easily enflamed by talk of it and more so by its actions. 'He could hardly think of anything else, though he himself was occasionally weary of the same recurring idea [...] the terror of them, which he had braved and defied in his youth, seemed to come back and take possession of him in his age, and with the terror came impatient hatred' (Gaskell 1996, 233). Daniel's obsession is different from Philip's in being externally generated and conforms to an alternative definition as 'the action of any influence, notion or "fixed idea," which persistently assails or vexes, especially so as to discompose the mind' (OED). He will accept no justification of the need for impressment, contesting Philip's view that the government has a right to enlist men for the sake of the country. As Deidre D'Albertis has argued, the novel explores the ways in which the individual is immersed in 'structures of hierarchy and domination, subject to powers of the state and law, which function most effectively by eliciting the consent of the individual in his or her own subjection' (D'Albertis, 104–5). But Daniel refuses consent and his naive defiance of structures – he believes in what 'I, Daniel Robson, think right, and what I, Daniel Robson, wish to have done' (Gaskell 1996, 42) – when harnessed to his hatred of the press gang will result in his death. The trickery of the gang in luring Monkshaven dwellers out

of their houses by the ringing of the fire-bell is the inflammatory beginning, in Daniel's mind and in his action of instigating the riot of which
he becomes the leader, his thoughtless boastful cry, 'If I was as young as
onest a was, a'd have t'Randyvouse down and mak' a bonfire on it. We'd
ring t'firebell then to some purpose' (Gaskell 1996, 240), resulting in the
'hot, lurid mist' where the Mariners' Arms (the Randyvouse) had stood.
In his firing of the Randy-vouse, what seizes him is afterwards 'spoken
as a supernatural kind of possession, leading him to his doom' (Gaskell
1996, 233). Daniel persists in justifying his behaviour, 'saying he would
do it again if he had the chance' as he waits for the trial at York assizes
(Gaskell 1996, 283). His obsession nevertheless damages the lives of his
women folk as much as, if not more than, Philip's by plunging them into
the poverty which only Philip's wealth can rescue them from. Two male
obsessions govern the marriage plot; D'Albertis's 'structures of hierarchy and domination' operate not only on a large, national scale but also
through the personal structures of gendered relationships.

Revulsion is the action of drawing back or away from some disliked or
disgusting thing or person, and Sylvia does this repeatedly in regard to
Philip throughout the book. In many small gestures she turns away from
him and at times her reluctance to become his possession amounts to
'wishing the grave lay open before her, and that she could lie down, and
be covered up by the soft green turf from all the bitter sorrows and cark-
ing cares and weary bewilderments of this life' (Gaskell 1996, 297–98).
But she is trapped in the betrothal, partly by her own fault. Unable
to read – her father refused to send her to school and she has resisted
Philip's attempts to teach her – Philip is the one who signs the tenancy
release forms from the landlord and so she has no control in the removal
of her and her mother. Her waking dream of Charley Kinraid – "Oh!
Charley! come to me—come to me!" – signals both sexual desire for one
man and sexual revulsion towards another. She has indeed borne Philip's
child, as he points out, but the dream creates an uneasy inference that
Philip's sexual actions have revolted her, or at best have left her miserably
unmoved. Her crucial withdrawing from him lies in her words when his
falsehood is revealed: 'I'll never forgive yon man, nor live with him as
his wife again. All that's done and ended' (Gaskell 1996, 348). She joins
other Victorian heroines in resisting male advances, ranging from Jane
Eyre's reluctance to live with St John Rivers as his wife to the most extreme example of Gwendolen Harleth in *Daniel Deronda* (1876) whose
shuddering response to Grandcourt's marital claims will lead eventually
to her culpable involvement in his death. Thomas Hardy, some twenty-
two years later, characterised this kind of response in the modern figure
of Sue Bridehead in *Jude the Obscure* (1895) who does not consider marriage as a profession requiring the obligation 'to be loved on the prem-
ises' (Hardy's Preface). Sylvia is by no means a modern woman but her
repudiation of her marriage, to the disapproval of her mother, Hester

and others of her community after her death, is strikingly justified and in accordance with what we know of her wilful and passionate character.

Sylvia's revulsion from Philip is even more strongly particularised than Kinraid's attraction. But Philip's plainness, the 'disagreeable aspect' of his face, virtually his face altogether, is erased in the fire on board the *Theseus* (Gaskell 1996, 393). When this happens all sexuality is erased, too, and the questions Sylvia asks herself as she contemplates Philip's possible return: 'what would be her duty, if he came again, and once more called her "wife"?' (444) and again, 'for Philip might come back, and then?' (Gaskell 1996, 410) need never be answered. Her belief that Philip has become a spirit 'as come to t'other's help in his time o' need' (Gaskell 1996, 429) renders Philip's future as bodiless, sexless. By the end of the novel Sylvia has lost both lovers, one to marriage, the other to death. The chiming titles of Chapters XX and XLV, 'Loved and Lost' and 'Saved and Lost,' play across the novel to each other and echo Tennyson's famous words in *In Memoriam* (1850), a poem much admired by Gaskell: "Tis better to have loved and lost/Than never to have loved at all' (Section XXII, lines 15–16).

The return scene in Tennyson's *Enoch Arden* reaches a different and evasive conclusion. Enoch, a shipwrecked sailor, comes home after ten years and finds his wife, Annie, married to his best friend, Philip. He goes to the house where they live and looks through the window at the happy (and famous) domestic scene within:

> For cups and silver on the burnished board
> Sparkled and shone; so genial was the hearth:
> And on the right hand of the hearth he saw
> Philip, the slighted suitor of old times,
> Stout, rosy, with his babe across his knees;
> And o'er her second father stoopt a girl,
> A later but a loftier Annie Lee [...]
> And on the left hand of the hearth he saw
> The mother glancing often toward her babe,
> But turning now and then to speak with him,
> Her son, who stood beside her tall and strong,
> And saying that which pleased him for he smiled.
> (Tennyson, 1147–48)

There is no evidence that Tennyson was influenced by *Sylvia's Lovers,* and in his version, Annie does not know Enoch has returned until after he has died in impoverished circumstances similar to Philip Hepburn. When he is dying Enoch says of Annie that she must not come to see him 'For my dead face would vex her after-life' (Tennyson, 1151). Annie is silenced from the poem which ends with the comment that 'the little port/Had seldom seen a costlier funeral' (Tennyson, 1152).

While *Enoch Arden* ends on what at the time and even more so now is thought of as a slightly risible note, at least Annie is left with an ambiguous future and not punished to the same extent as Sylvia. In *Sylvia's Lovers* when Sylvia finally and belatedly learns to read it is the Bible, the most patriarchal of discourses, under the stern eye of Alice Rose, and this is part of the acceptance of her life as a dutiful mother and housekeeper. It also prepares her for her willing submission as Philip's erring wife and then his widow. Her revulsion against Philip has turned into guilt and remorse, and her kissing of 'his poor burnt lips' (Gaskell 1996, 453) is arguably the first voluntary embrace she gives him. Her final words are a capitulation: 'If I live very long, and try to be good all that time, do yo' think, Hester, as God will let me to him where he is?' (Gaskell 1996, 454). There cannot be an answer to this question but after it she, like Annie, is likewise silenced, 'a pale, sad woman, allays dressed in black' (ibid) who does not live long and whose reputation is that of a hard-hearted woman who lived in plenty while her husband died in penury not two stone-throws away. Sylvia, the wilful wench of the red cloak and disorganised curls of her youth, is not only dead but forgotten. Philip is publically remembered by Hester who founds alms-houses 'erected in memory of P. H' (Gaskell 1996, 455).

Gaskell was a Unitarian and although benevolent and liberal in outlook, Philip's crime of omission in not revealing what has happened to Kinraid, of not speaking truth to witness is to a Unitarian deserving of retribution. Philip's crime is his obsessive love for Sylvia and as such is the sin of idolatry: 'I ha' made thee my idol' (Gaskell 1996, 448) he says to Sylvia, echoing the 'wondering idolatry' of his response to his baby daughter (Gaskell 1996, 320). Sylvia's sin is that of lack of charity, the inability to 'forgive those that trespass against us'. It is also the social sin of not being a good wife, in spite of the model before her of her mother's devotion to the reckless Daniel. His obsession ruins his family but there is no reproach from Belle. Both Philip and Sylvia are brought to acknowledge their sins: '[i]f I could live my life o'er again I would love God more, and thee less' Philip says to Sylvia and Sylvia says 'Will He iver forgive me, think yo'? [...] I think I shall go about among them as gnash their teeth for iver, while yo' are where all tears are wiped away' (Gaskell 1996, 448–49). The marriage story is concluded, husband and wife united but in order for this to happen the final chapter moves, as Patsy Stoneman has argued, into an 'alien mystical mode [in which the novel] loses its dialectical impetus and comes to a transcendental standstill' (Stoneman, 103). Well, yes, but Philip dies with the word 'heaven' on his lips and this seems a kind of victory; though it has cost him his life, he has got what he always longed for: Sylvia's complete submission and devotion. Sylvia is left to a miserable widowhood, blamed by 'popular feeling and ignorance of the real facts' (Gaskell 1996, 454) and dying young, her daughter emigrated to Australia, her story all but lost to

Monkshaven. But of course it is not lost; the lady who visits Monkshaven talks to the bathing woman who has another version of what happened. Sylvia's story is what the novel is about and this final section of the final chapter is almost an apology, or, perhaps more accurately, a consolation to readers who mourn Sylvia and the way in which history rolls over her and her like, with no lasting memorial, except, of course for art, particularly the democratic art of the realist novel, which imagines and constructs her story. As Jenny Uglow has written, '[s]peech, songs, and customs lie embedded in the strata of this book as in a rock facing the swirling sea [...] As imagination resurrects the distant, silent people of the past we see their voyage as our own' (Uglow, 528).

Works Cited

Brink, Andrew. *Obsession and Culture: A Study of Sexual Obsession in Modern Fiction*. Cranbury, NJ: Associated University Press, 1996.
Chapple, John Alfred Victor and Arthur, Pollard (eds). *The Letters of Mrs Gaskell*. Manchester: Manchester University Press, 1996.
Freud, Sigmund. 'The Question of Lay Analysis', in James Strachey ed. *The Standard Edition of the Complete Psychological Works of Sigmund Freud*, Vol. XX. London: Hogarth Press, 1959.
Freud, Sigmund. 'Beyond the Pleasure Principle' in James Strachey ed. *The Standard Edition of the Complete Psychological Works of Sigmund Freud*, Vol. XVIII, pp 20–21. London: Hogarth Press, 1955.
Gaskell, Elizabeth. *Cousin Phillis and Other Tales*. Angus Easson ed. Oxford: Oxford World's Classic, 1982.
Gaskell, Elizabeth. *Sylvia's Lovers*. Foster, Shirley ed. London: Penguin Classics, 1996.
Lansbury, Coral. *Elizabeth Gaskell*. Boston, MA: Twayne Publishers, 1984.
Lord Alfred, Tennyson. *The Poems of Tennyson*. Christopher Ricks ed. London: Longmans Green, 1969.
Stoneman, Patsy. *Elizabeth Gaskell*. Manchester: Manchester University Press, 2006.
Uglow, Jenny. *Elizabeth Gaskell: A Habit of Stories*. London: Faber and Faber, 2003.

5 The Spectacle of 'Crowded' Marriage in Ellen Wood's *East Lynne*

Frances Twinn

> I, Isabel Mary Vane, take thee Archibald Carlyle, to be my wedded husband, to have and to hold from this day forward, for better for worse, for richer for poorer, in sickness and in health, to love, cherish and to obey, till death do us part, according to God's holy ordinance; and thereto I give thee my troth. (BCP)

Introduction

> Married. _ On the 1st inst., at Castle Marling, by the chaplain to the Earl of Mount Severn, Archibald Carlyle, Esquire of East Lynne, to Lady Isabel Mary Vane, only child of William, late Earl of Mount Severn.
>
> (Wood, 130)

Thus reads 'the announcement of the marriage in the newspapers' (Wood, 135) of the wedding between the protagonists of Ellen Wood's runaway bestseller, *East Lynne* (1861). Had she been asked about her marriage at the outset Lady Isabel might have replied, 'Well, there were three of us in this marriage, so it was a bit crowded'.[1]

Despite its moralizing Christian message the novel offers a range of possible permutations and exposes the realities of marital union at the time. In this chapter I focus on Isabel and Archibald Carlyle's marriage, which is blown apart by crowding, elopement and infidelity. Wood's fictional voice joins the discourse of change and reform abroad in the mid-Victorian period. Veiled in secrecy, mystery, betrayal and deception, the spectacle of marriage drives the narrative and provides its central theme. As the author trains her omniscient optic lens on the action she uses her considerable literary and technical skills to create illusion, i.e. a disconnect between appearance and reality. If, as Stephanie Coontz contends, 'Victorian marriage harboured [...] hopes for romantic love, intimacy, personal fulfillment and mutual happiness' (Coontz, 177), then Ellen Wood's novel was guaranteed to disappoint. However, unlike Mary Braddon, she refrained from depicting the excesses of an aristocratic female protagonist like Lady Audley who not only committed adultery but added bigamy and murder to her catalogue of transgressions. Instead, Lady Isabel Vane, Wood's transgressive anti-heroine merely elopes, abandons her home and marriage, husband and children to commit adultery with the predatory, serial seducer, Francis Levison, one of those who crowded the marriage. In an attempt to extricate himself Archibald Carlyle divorces Isabel.

The key to Ellen Wood's domestic tale is the Matrimonial Causes Act of 1857, which facilitated divorce for men but not on the same terms for women. Carlyle's swift action to instigate divorce proceedings in the novel is testimony to the effectiveness of the recent reforms.

Entrapment and Escape – The Marriage Plot

Novels in the early part of the nineteenth century foregrounded 'the marriage plot' favoured by Jane Austen and her contemporaries. Their narrative lens was focused on the ritual of courtship leading up to the proposal and often the wedding itself with the expectation of a life lived 'happily ever after'. By the mid-century, when Ellen Wood began her novel writing career, writers were concerned to depict the course of marriage. She joins the other novelists featured in this volume who also represent this shift of narrative focus.

In order to examine the principal marriage in *East Lynne*, a brief appreciation of Archibald's courtship of Isabel is essential to an understanding of their dysfunctional, crowded and fractured union. Ellen Wood's narrative moves quickly through an unconventionally short courtship, engagement and marriage to honeymoon. Archibald Carlyle, an upwardly mobile, middle-class and provincial lawyer buys a small estate from the Earl of Mount Severn, Lady Isabel Vane's father. Under the guise of befriending the ailing feckless earl he courts Lady Isabel. Beguiled by the trappings of an aristocratic home, Archibald is also enthralled by Isabel's 'face of surpassing beauty'; from his perspective, she is 'envisioned' as an angel as if 'from a painter's imagination' (Wood, 11). Subject to his 'male gaze' (Mulvey, 834) Isabel becomes an object to adorn and ornament Archibald's new home. Arguably, he sees her as the trophy wife for his trophy home. As a penniless orphan, when her father dies unexpectedly, Isabel is forced to find a home with her cousin Raymond and his wife Emma. When Archibald, to fulfill his ambitions, proposes, Isabel has little choice but to accept. Unlike the conventional proposal he makes to his second wife later in the novel, Archibald's offer here is indirect, ambivalent and distinctly unromantic. Tentatively, apparently knowing that he is transgressing class boundaries, he asks: May I – dare I offer you to return to East Lynne as its mistress'. Isabel, in a state of incomprehension, responds: 'Return to East Lynne as its mistress?' As an afterthought, Archibald adds '*And* as my wife' (my emphasis) (Wood, 119). This interchange is flooded with sub-text, reinforced by Archibald's body language in the proposal scene. His tentative verbalization indicates the socially transgressive nature of the marriage, and to seal her apparent opposition, 'He not only retained the hand she sought to withdraw, but took the other also', to denote 'the imprisonment of the hands' at the same time, 'his head was bent in devotion' (Wood, 119). This picture reinforces the sense of idolatry because, to Archibald, Isabel was an object of worship. The sense that Isabel is escaping from the entrapment of her cousin Raymond's home for another trap is powerful, too, and as I show characterises all the stages in Isabel's short life. However, there is added spice to this account of Isabel's courtship. At the time of Archibald's proposal there was another suitor for Isabel's hand. At least she imagined that the false, heartless Francis Levison with whom she had fallen romantically 'almost in love' (Wood, 115), would be a suitable husband. However, he ruled himself out. Isabel, therefore, enters marriage, not only carrying the emotional baggage of unrequited love, but also, the self-confessed absence of love for the man to whom she has committed herself.

Oppression and Repression – The Crowded Marriage

Cornelia

By the time Isabel and Archibald return from honeymoon there are 'three of them' in the marriage. Cornelia, Archibald's sister and surrogate mother (his own had died giving birth to him) is in residence as the self-appointed housekeeper and matriarch. If Joyce, Lady Isabel's personal and ultra-loyal maid is to be believed, Cornelia singly, not only puts their marriage in jeopardy, but also is solely responsible for its breakdown. Joyce's revelations in front of Archibald in the immediate aftermath of Isabel's unexplained departure represent the perception of the spectacle from below stairs. Her attack is two-pronged. It highlights that Cornelia's controlling domination of the domestic sphere usurps Isabel's role as mistress of the house *and* its chatelaine. Joyce voices her views unequivocally, addressing Cornelia with the words:

> You have curbed her, ma'am, and snapped at her [...] she has been crossed and put upon; everything, in short, but beaten-ma'am, you know she has! – and she has borne it all in silence, like a patient angel.
>
> (Wood, 279)

Her allusion to an 'angel' echoes Coventry Patmore's popular verse-novel *The Angel in the House* (1854–1862). Immensely popular at the time, the poem applauded the spirit of Victorian womanhood as the self-sacrificing, submissive, saintly wife. His heroine embodies idealised femininity.

Wood, by substituting Cornelia in this role, overturns the paradigm of the domestic goddess. She shows Isabel submissively capitulating in the face of Cornelia's aggression, 'I don't think I know anything about house-keeping [...] Oh! I wish you (Cornelia) would [...] give the necessary orders for today' to the 'butcher' and the 'fishmonger' (Wood, 147).

Not only did Cornelia take possession of the domestic realm, but she also caused tension on the financial front. Joyce's accusation to a totally perplexed Archibald, confirms Wagner's observation of the way in which Wood stresses the financial aspect of Victorian marriage. (See Chapter 10 of this volume.) One of the accusations made by Joyce reflects this view when she says,

> She [Isabel] has been taunted with the cost she has brought to East Lynne and to you. She was forbidden [...] the simplest thing [...] a new dress for herself and an order for 'a new frock for Miss Isabel' was 'countermanded'.
>
> (Wood, 279–80)

This speech endorses Cornelia's view of Isabel as an 'expensive', aristocratic 'girl' (Wood, 131). Cornelia's possessiveness of Archibald and her self-admitted jealousy are reflected in her subjugation of his apparently helpless, passive wife. While Isabel capitulates to Cornelia's attempts to control the household, Archibald, who is 'obedient' to Cornelia's 'will through the force of habit' (Wood, 145) resists and rejects Cornelia's efforts to oversee the purse strings. Archibald, as the financial powerhouse of the marriage, refuses to allow Cornelia to highjack this role when his wife's happiness is at stake. Isabel suffers in silence as her refined sensitivity to the feelings of others prevents her from recounting her domestic woes to her husband. In this gender reversal, one of many in the novel, East Lynne is seen as ruled by a matriarch in the patriarch's shoes. Cornelia is emphatically not 'The angel in the house' but rather, the demon. In this way, Wood cleverly and subtly subverts the ideal of domesticity within the home.

The marriage, crowded on the domestic front, staggers on for another five years cloaked in an atmosphere of disharmony, dysfunction, disturbance and disputation, both above and below stairs. As Tamara S. Wagner acutely observes, Archibald withdraws from the domestic space in pursuit of his profession and appears unaware of the extent of domestic discord at the heart of his own home. By this time Cornelia has become 'the bane of the household' (Wood, 167), and sees Isabel as little more than 'an automaton' (Wood, 167). Isabel, a twenty-year-old ingénue, with little experience of the world beyond her family home is desperate to escape the entrapment of impoverishment and Emma Vane's physical mistreatment and verbal, sexually motivated cruelty. So, she marries for convenience. Ironically, of course, it seems that she has only escaped from one form of captivity to be confronted by another female-dominated domestic prison. Socially transgressive, the marriage between provincial, professional Archibald and a young aristocratic beauty is predicated on idolatrous love and then complicated and jeopardized by a manipulative forty-year-old, confirmed spinster with an ill-temper. Wood's portrait of one-sided (Archibald's) love in a fractured, disintegrating crowded marriage, however, is not confined to the subversive element embodied in Cornelia. When the rivals for the affections of the principal players in the drama enter this already crowded marriage, romance makes an entry into the novel, denoted in part by the language of the 'potboiler'. The next two sections discuss the role of Barbara Hare and Francis Levison as the romantic rivals who overcrowd the Carlyle marriage.

Barbara

The role of female jealousy introduces another tension into the Carlyle marriage. Overheard by Isabel below stairs gossip depicts Barbara, a childhood friend of Archibald, as 'a bowl of poison' (Wood, 158). Isabel, who is perplexed by the reference, seeks clarification from Joyce only to discover Barbara's attachment to Archibald. 'A hot flush passed over the brow of Lady Isabel; a sensation very like jealousy flew to her heart' (Wood, 158). Wood, who wishes to endorse her depiction of Isabel as an already fragile, vulnerable and exposed wife suggests that 'No woman likes to hear that another woman either is, or has been attached to her husband.' A ringing endorsement of the stress that Wood is laying on female jealousy here is made in her iteration of, what for her is, a universal truth, 'here has never been a passion in this world, there never will be one, so fantastic, so delusive, so powerful as jealousy' (Wood, 182).

Barbara is a fixture in Archibald Carlyle's life. The couple assume that many locals consider them destined to marry. Only Archibald seems oblivious to this unspoken understanding. The early part of the novel, punctuated by meetings between Archibald and Barbara, confirms their long-term familial relationship and exposes the way in which the sub-plot feeds into the crowded marriage.

A brief exposition of the sub-plot is essential to an appreciation of the clandestine meetings between Archibald and Barbara that arouse Isabel's suspicions and fuel her jealousy. Richard, Barbara's much-loved brother, has been falsely accused of the murder of Hallijohn, father of Joyce (Isabel's personal maid) and Joyce's sister Afy. Archibald's loyalty to the family, his professional skills and rational approach to life are sought in order to discover the identity of the real culprit. To accomplish this mission the utmost secrecy is called for and only Cornelia is privy to the secret. Even Isabel cannot be trusted in Archibald's view. On the night of the Jeafferson dinner invitation, events reached a dramatic climax. A turning point in the narrative, this occasion became the focus of debate among enthusiastic readers of the novel (Protheroe and Bradley, 6).

Earlier on however, Barbara reveals her passionate love for Archibald on a number of memorable occasions, two of which pre-date and the last, post-dates his marriage. They reveal, not only, the somewhat un-controlled love Barbara has for Archibald and therefore, its implications for sexual jealousy and romantic rivalry in the marriage, but also, the extent of Archibald's one-dimensional character. He is a twenty-seven-year-old man of 'noble presence' who is esteemed and respected in West Lynne. The epitome of the Victorian model of masculinity that invests men with reason and rationality, Archibald appears to possess little emotional intelligence. As a result he seems largely unaware of, and per-haps, even insensitive to, the feelings of others. This flaw in Archibald's character is in direct opposition to Isabel's oversensitivity, and the resul-tant lack of communication between them may in part account for the marital breakdown.

When Archibald replaces a lost chain for Barbara complete with a locket, he is knowingly giving her a love token. He imagines she will place a lock of Richard's hair inside it, but Barbara accepts the gift at face value – that is, as a token of Archibald's affection. A year later, on the eve of his secret marriage to Isabel, Barbara asks him for a lock of his own hair. Underpinned by 'emotion or depth of feeling, the *sort* of feeling that prompted the request', it was met with 'good-natured ridicule' (Wood, 129) because Archibald appears unaware of Barbara's feelings, demonstrating his lack of emotional intelligence. Repressing her disappointment, Barbara contents herself with an imagined cer-tainty of becoming his wife. The culmination of these encounters, at the end of her first wedding visit to the newly married couple, I re-fer to, as Barbara's un-suppressed outburst of passion. Having dined and taken tea, Barbara, treated as Cornelia's guest, is accompanied into the grounds where she plucks a rose and proceeds to destroy it 'leaf by leaf'. The rose is an emblem of romantic love in the 'children's story' of Beauty and the Beast (Wood, 134). Not only that, but it is a subtle inter-textual extension of Cornelia's reference to the fairy tale in a previous exchange with Barbara. When asked if it is a suitable match, Cornelia says of the marriage, '[j]ust as suitable as Beauty and the Beast' (Wood, 135). Barbara's destruction of the rose, petal by petal, is emblematic of her sub-conscious desire to sabotage the union between Archibald and his newly acquired wife. On re-entering the house, Barbara observes the impassioned kisses planted on Isabel's face in exchange for her singing. Not only is her jealousy aroused but also this picture has the effect of cementing the sense that Isabel is the *re-cipient* of Archibald's love. There is no indication of reciprocity from her. Having paid his dues to Isabel for entertainment, Archibald offers to accompany Barbara home.

A significant narrative intervention precedes and sets the scene for what follows. Significant because it seeks to justify but, perhaps, not excuse Barbara's behaviour, it perfectly exemplifies Pykett's 'improper feminine' (Pykett, 16):

> There are moments in a woman's life when she is betrayed into forgetting the ordinary rules of conduct and propriety; when she is betrayed into making a scene.
>
> (Pykett, 163)

Excited, Barbara, her 'heart beat to throbbing' (Wood, 162) takes Archibald's arm just before her 'passionate uncontrol' resulted in convulsive sobs and 'strong hysterics' (Wood, 164). Initially, Archibald affects ignorance, which is followed by a dawning realisation of the truth of her love for him. For once, he is annoyed and vexed as he stammers, 'But my dear Barbara, I never gave you cause to think that I – that I – cared for you more than I did care' (Wood, 164). All the sub-textual nuances of Wood's depiction of their relationship reveal either Archibald's emotional naivety or his disingenuousness, which appear to be subsumed by a cloak of rationality. Their doubts may evaporate on discovering that Archibald was 'a little flattered' as well as 'pained' by her 'revelations. If he was not flattered, then his dismissal of her vow never to marry as 'girlish sentimental rubbish' (Wood, 166) reinforces Wood's sceptical view of her protagonist. Her stylistic craftsmanship is at work in this scene as she complements the language of the potboiling romance with nuanced characterization, narrative intervention and the sustained and powerful gothic image of the 'incubus'.

The reason Ellen Wood is so clever with this thread of discord in the crowded Carlyle marriage is the way in which she uses below stairs gossip to reinforce her message. Wilson's perceptive re-interpretation of the early encounters between Archibald and Barbara, echo Joyce's commentary discussed earlier about Cornelia's crowding of the domestic situation. Of course, these servant's observations about the marriage may not be reliable as they are not impartial narrators. However, they add intrigue and spice and a further narrative dimension to the unfolding complexity of the relationships inside the marriage. From the body language and partially overheard exchanges, Wilson concluded that the meeting on the eve of Archibald's marriage to Lady Isabel was 'a regular love scene' (Wood, 177). Having also seen Barbara's prostration when Cornelia announced news of the wedding followed by Barbara's 'passionate outburst', she feels convinced that: 'If anything happened to my lady, Miss Barbara, as sure as fate would step into her shoes' (Wood, 179). Wilson continues in the hope that nothing untoward will befall Isabel:

> She [Barbara] would not make a very kind stepmother, for it is certain that where the first wife has been hated, her children won't be loved. She would turn Mr Carlyle against them.
>
> (Wood, 179)

Isabel overhears these prescient words, as she lies recovering from the difficult birth of her first-born. She is physically weak, partially delirious and possibly suffering from post-partum depression. On overhearing the conversation she imagines that Archibald has never loved her, 'but his heart had been given to Barbara Hare' (Wood, 180). Confronting Archibald, Isabel echoes Wilson's words 'wildly'; 'when in a storm of tears' she 'bursts' out: 'She would ill-treat my child; she would draw your love from it, and from my memory. Archibald, you must not marry her' (Wood, 180). Faced with expressions of passion, Archibald becomes 'annoyed and vexed' (Wood, 181). He denies love for Barbara, but is unable to admit to his wife that he *was* conscious that Barbara loved him. Isabel at this moment must have felt a knife turning in her heart. As always though, she maintains her silence for fear of humiliation and allows Archibald to imagine that her fears were fantasy; dreams induced by her feverish state. 'But certain it is that Barbara Hare dwelt on her heart like an incubus' (Wood, 183). In a gender reversal, this inter-textual allusion associates the sense of jealous competition between these two women with the nightmare image of an incubus immortalised visually by Henry Fuseli in his painting, 'The Nightmare', exhibited at the Royal Academy in 1782. Immensely popular at the time, 'it was caricatured, emulated and copied' (Myrone, 45) throughout the nineteenth century, so it would have been familiar to writer and reader alike. Cleverly and craftily, Wood reverses the repeated image from the male incubus to the female succubus in order to demonise Barbara in Isabel's eyes and to represent the thread of sexual jealousy that is woven through the warp and weft of the narrative. It serves to highlight the way in which jealousy pervades, and seriously crowds, a conflicted, malfunctioning marriage that, by this stage, features two demons and one angel in the house.

Levison

Cast as a dandified rake, dangerous lover, a second suitor (Lutz 77; Schaffer 7) and desired possibility, Francis Levison and Lady Isabel Vane moved in the same aristocratic circles. Levison was her preferred choice because she imagines herself, 'almost in love with him' (Wood, 115). He, however, once he had learnt of Carlyle's proposal, and undoubtedly alert to Isabel's putative feeling of love for him, ruled himself out due to 'uncertain prospects' (Wood, 122). The memory of her sense of his 'false heartlessness' and the ill-omened, broken cross, her mother's beloved heirloom, hovered in Isabel's peripheral vision as she embarked on marriage to Archibald Carlyle.

However, Levison does not appear again in her life for five years. When 'her eyes fell upon him' in a chance encounter in Boulogne-Sur-Mer 'she found he had never been entirely forgotten' (Wood, 205). It seems to me that this is partly because of the fascination he held for Isabel. This apt word is used repeatedly in connection with Levison, the dangerous lover. 'He was fascinating in manners, in face and in form' (Wood, 15). This episode illustrates how Levison holds Isabel in 'thrall' and begins to crowd the marriage with his physical presence. In her fragile state – she was convalescing after a lingering illness – he draws 'her hand within his arm' as they promenade (Wood, 206). Despite her reservations, he then proceeds to accompany her everywhere and visits her lodgings (permitted in the mornings only). As with Barbara's feelings for Carlyle, with the language of a romance, Wood signifies the underpinning sexual attraction and the growing passion between the two during the six weeks on the French coast. Isabel's heart 'throbs' and 'beats with something like rapture' and she is guilty of 'sinful happiness' (Wood, 214). Isabel found that she could 'no more repress a feeling of attraction towards Francis Levison than she could repress her own sense of being' (Wood, 211–12). Renowned for its exposition of unbridled passion, I am put in mind here of Emily Brontë's Wuthering Heights and Cathy's 'I am Heathcliff' (Brontë, 73). During the visit, Levison declaration of love – 'Isabel, I love you passionately still [...] I loved you until you became the wife of another' – evokes 'the most intense bliss' (Wood, 215) in Isabel's heart. Linguistically, this is contrasted with Isabel's beautifully articulated renouncement of Levison, who has suggested she threw herself 'away upon Mr. Carlyle' (Wood, 215). Isabel's dispassionate description of her 'dear husband' (Wood, 215) as esteemed, respected and beloved is contrasted with her feelings for her seducer. As her 'rebellious heart' 'throbs' with 'sinful happiness' (Wood, 214), Isabel faces a dilemma. Does she remain in a semi-detached, one-sided relationship or does she allow herself to fall for the fascination of Levison? Wood answers this question in an apparently unequivocal and powerful authorial intervention:

> She would have believed it is as impossible for her ever to forsake her duty as a wife, a gentlewoman, and a Christian, as for the sun to turn round from the west to the east.
>
> (Wood, 212)

She feared the temptation of the forbidden 'fruit' (Wood, 213) in the form of Levison, who was forbidden due to her marriage vows, as outlined in the epigraph to this chapter. At this stage, while Isabel *can* contemplate a transgressive act, she rejects it. This intervention would have raised the whole issue of the ideology of marriage. Despite the more liberal law of 1857, it was still virtually impossible for a woman to extricate herself from marital union. Here, Wood anticipates what might happen if Isabel were to abandon her husband, home and family by placing a clue in the text. She cleverly uses the conditional tense, 'she *would have* believed it impossible'(Wood, 212) to make the point. There is a disconnect here between appearance and reality. While her direct address amounts to an instruction to women of seemly behaviour in marriage, she demonstrates what women of the time might actually have contemplated.

Having played with the reader's emotions and prejudices throughout the Boulogne episode, Wood enters the debate with an apparently direct appeal full of sympathy for her protagonist: 'Oh, reader! never doubt the principles of poor Lady Isabel, her rectitude of mind (Archibald), her wish and endeavor to do right, her abhorrence of wrong (marriage vows); her spirit was earnest and true, her intentions were pure' (Wood, 218). What transpires, of course, is that for all her reassurance, Wood shows a flawed, transgressive woman who, given sufficient provocation, cannot live up to the model of 'proper femininity' (Pykett, 16).

In the event, though, it is neither of the romantic rivals who sabotage the marriage but Archibald himself. Admittedly, in character, he does this inadvertently, unknowingly and indirectly, perhaps due to his lack of emotional intelligence. By inviting Levison to stay at East Lynne, Archibald draws the seductive 'dangerous lover' (Lutz, ix) into an already congested domestic space. It is true that while the practicalities of entertaining a houseguest would have rested with the housekeeper, nonetheless, the wife might have been expected to be asked or, at least, told. Isabel's 'first sensation' on learning the news was that 'she has been shown a way into paradise' (Wood, 223), her second, that the visit should be prevented. She does not prevail so Levison arrives and, gradually in a covert manner, ignites Isabel's latent jealousy of Barbara. The information fed back in 'miserably exaggerated' (Wood, 246) form to an 'excited' Isabel fueled the slow, but sure, burn of betrayal. On one occasion Archibald, in order to see Barbara alone at her request, had unashamedly sent Isabel back into the house during an evening stroll in the grounds. 'Never since her marriage had Lady Isabel's jealousy been as excited as it was that evening' (Wood, 252). Throughout Levison's visit these clandestine assignations between Archibald and Barbara take place for the best of intentions: that of securing Richard's acquittal of murder but, patently, they are underlain by Levison's deliberate efforts to play upon Isabel's vulnerability. Both Levison and Isabel effectively become spectators on the periphery of the marriage *partly* reversing the roles of these two members of the dysfunctional scenario. It is, in fact, Barbara and Levison who are the interlopers marginalizing the marital union.

If East Lynne is to Isabel, an 'Eden' and Levison shows her a way to 'paradise', then the power of the inter-textual biblical allusion, is sustained and reinforced by Levison, who 'like a serpent strolling down behind the hedge, watching all his (Archibald's) movements' (Wood, 246), is vigilant in his reporting of these assignations. Wood uses this allusion to demonstrate the almost evil course on which Levison is set to achieve his aim of seduction. The Boulogne episode also references the allusion in its use of images of forbidden 'fruit [...] prolonged intercourse' (Wood, 213) and 'temptation' in order to reinforce the biblical story of the fall of Adam and Eve in the Garden of Eden. Here, Wood is masterly in the way she uses inter-textual allusion subversively. The subtlety of her narrative technique enables her to control the route to the dramatic climax in which Levison triumphs. Almost insanely jealous of Barbara, and goaded and duped by Levison, who fuels the fire by his attempts 'to soothe her with all the sweet and dangerous sophistry of his crafty nature' (Wood, 271), Isabel elopes. Her masochistic action transgresses the law of the land and the Church, renders her a social pariah and exemplar of Pykett's 'improper feminine' (Pykett, 16) and also represents the stereotypical Victorian 'fallen angel'. Idolized by Archibald Carlyle and seduced by yet another 'demon in the house' in the form of a predatory serial seducer, Isabel has toppled off her pedestal.

Before moving on to the fallout from the elopement and subsequent divorce, a word needs to be said about female empowerment. The question arises as to whether Isabel's masochistic act was, at the same time, one of empowerment. As she said of her marriage to Archibald, it was made 'of her own free choice'. Arguably, in an act of unrepressed, emotionally charged rebellion, she *chose* to escape from what had become an intolerably physically and emotionally crowded marriage. So the question remains whether she jumped or was pushed – that is, was it the result of empowerment or oppression? If Afy's testimony is considered, she was 'one of your angels, but, angels go wrong sometimes, you see, they are not universally immaculate' (Wood, 333). Reading between the lines of Afy's support for Isabel, she is implying that Isabel's sexual attraction to, the arguably Byronic, Levison is responsible for her elopement. Wood tries to answer this question in the context of the bleak wretchedness in which Isabel subsequently finds herself.

Retribution and Reconciliation

Isabel's Remorse

Having chosen to elope Isabel has escaped from the prison of a dysfunctional marriage into 'an abyss of horror' (Wood, 283) – that is, another equally unappealing incarceration from which she sensed 'there was never more any escape; never more, never more' (Wood, 283). High in the remote Alps of southwest France with little in the way of company, Lady Isabel is a pitiful sight. Lonely, depressed and virtually abandoned by her lover, she returns to passivity and helplessness.

In one of the most quoted and most powerful authorial interventions in the text, Wood directly addresses the reader. She urges all women to heed her warning about the consequences of transgressing the marriage vows:

> Oh, reader, believe me! 'Lady-wife–mother! Should you ever be tempted to abandon your home, so you will awake. Whatever trials

may be the lot of your married life, though they may magnify themselves to your crushed spirit as beyond the endurance of man to
bear, *resolve* to bear them; fall down upon your knees and pray
to be enabled to bear them: pray for patience; pray for strength to
resist the demon that would urge you so to escape; bear unto death,
rather than forfeit your fair name and your good conscience; for be
assured that the alternative, if you rush on to it, will be found far
worse than death'.

(Wood, 283)

Hard on the heels of that unequivocal exhortation Wood tempers her
universal message by an appeal for sympathy in the case of her protagonist. Wood's support for the transgressor is evident, less for Isabel's action, but more for the 'adder stings' of remorse that set in almost
immediately: 'Poor thing! Poor Lady Isabel...she knew that her whole
future existence... would be one dark course of gnawing retribution'
(Wood, 283).

Having been deceived in her expectation of the marriage that would
have legitimized their son (the manifestation of their adulterous relationship), Levison had also maliciously and deliberately concealed the
news of her divorce. Making the excuse that his family would not countenance marriage to a divorcee, he escaped to England to inherit his
uncle's title and estate.

Doubly duped, a divorcee and social pariah, Isabel was faced with
little choice but to seek employment. So she decided 'to go out as
governess in a French or German family' (Wood, 297), at the time
one of the few options for a fallen aristocratic lady. Ironically it was
precisely this course, so roundly castigated by Wood, that Isabel had
contemplated when she became a penniless orphan. 'She briefly en-
tertained the fantasy of: "Work[ing] for a living! It may appear very
feasible in theory; but theory and practice are as opposite as light
and dark"' (Wood, 104). Fate, then, intervenes in the form of a fatal
railway accident in which her maid and baby son are killed, leaving
Isabel alone with the legacy of life-threatening and life-changing facial
disfigurement.

Transformed from beauty to ugliness, she hides behind a disguise of
high collars, a head 'band of grey velvet', 'a huge cap' and 'blue-tinted
spectacles' (Wood, 611). These spectacles allow her to see the world
clearly because they filter light and intensify blue shades, but help to
conceal her true identity.[2] In a daring and 'wickedly wrong' (Wood,
615) move, she is free to accept the newly vacant post of governess at
East Lynne. So she returns to the children for whom her heart 'yearns'.
'Governesses at East Lynne were regarded as gentlewomen; treated well
and liberally' (Wood, 402) Isabel is provided with 'a room of her own' to
which she can retreat. However, it comes to represent both a sanctuary

and a prison. The 'grey parlour' has if not 'the refinement of its former 'courtly life' (Wood, 66) then all the accouterments of gentility:

> Everything was ready [...] the tea-tray [...] the small urn hissing away, the tea caddy [...] a silver rack of dry toast, butter, and a hot muffin covered with a small silver cover.
>
> (Wood, 402)

This intermediate role in the domestic space of East Lynne provided access to her three offspring as well as companion to Barbara, sometimes, in Archibald's absence. From this position, using her room as a sanctuary, Isabel was able to avoid crowding his second marriage but she became a hovering spectre, a shadow of her former self, spectating from the periphery of Archibald's second marriage. In Isabel's unspoken, but overwhelming, yearning for her children she lavishes toys upon them – for which she was admonished by Barbara – and is over-protective of the sickly William. Her inadvert slips of tongue, at times, also threaten to reveal her identity.

Having watched the spectacle of William's protracted illness and death, it is Isabel's turn to fall ill. Ever sympathetic to her protagonist, who has seen the error of her ways and realises her love for Carlyle, Wood creates one of the most moving literary deathbed scenes of the century. In an act of resolution, closure and, in a sense, escape, the narrator enables Isabel, her face free of the 'disfiguring' spectacles, to reveal her identity to Archibald. She is able to confess her remorse, shame and request forgiveness and reconciliation. In reply, Mr. Carlyle 'suffered his lips to rest upon hers [....] He whispered', the key words of reconciliation, resolution and closure: 'Until eternity' (Wood, 17). Perhaps, like Narayan, many readers would have had tears coursing down their cheeks at this moment (Narayan, 62).

Isabel dies at East Lynne where she was born, where she lived as a married woman and where she felt like a caged bird imprisoned by a lack of communication. She escapes only by death from the relentless feelings of remorse, the trappings of disguise and the threat of revelation to the promise of eternal life reconciled to her husband.

Conclusion

While Ellen Wood scrutinises the lottery of a number of Victorian marriages in *East Lynne* it is the 'crowded' central marriage that drives the narrative. Throughout the novel, Wood has used her strong authorial voice to project her views about the conduct of husband and wife within Christian marriage. However, at the same time, she has *shown* by sub- and inter-textual allusion sympathy for a heroine, who goaded by jealousy, is driven to transgression. However subversive she may wish to be, this cannot be the abiding message of the novel. Having allowed Isabel to die, just before the curtain falls, Wood dramatises a final exchange between Archibald and Barbara, whose dialogue upholds the Christian principles of Holy Matrimony.

Notes

1 Panorama interview with the Princess of Wales, 20 November 1995. BBC 1.
2 My thanks go to Neil Handley, the Museum Director at the College of Optometrists for enlightening me about the use of tinted spectacles in the mid-Victorian period. An hour spent looking at their collection of tinted spectacles gave me insight into what Isabel Vane wore. Neil explained that such spectacles were often used to disguise facial disfigurement as well as for those who were 'light sensitive'. Lady Isabel wore those with sidepieces for extra coverage, as the lenses were quite small.

Works Cited

Book of Common Prayer. Oxford: Oxford University Press, 1861.
Brontë, Emily. *Wuthering Heights*. Ian Jack ed. Oxford: Oxford University Press, 2009.
Chapple, John Alfred Victor and Arthur Pollard eds. *The Letters of Mrs. Gaskell*. Manchester: Manchester University Press, 1966.
Collins, Wilkie *Basil*. Dorothy Goldman ed. Oxford: Oxford University Press, 1999.
Coontz, Stephanie. *Marriage, A History*. London: Penguin Books, 2005.
Law, Graham. 'The professional writer and the literary marketplace' in Jenny Bourne Taylor ed. *The Cambridge Companion to Wilkie Collins*, pp 97–111. Cambridge: Cambridge University Press, 2006.
Lutz, Deborah. *The Dangerous Lover. Gothic Villains, Byronism, and the Nineteenth Century Seduction Narrative*. Columbus: The Ohio State University Press, 2006.
Mulvey, Laura. 'Visual Pleasure and Narrative Cinema' in Leo Brady and Marshall Cohen eds. *Film Theory and Criticism: Introductory Readings*, pp 833–44. New York: Oxford University Press, 1999.
Myrone, Martin. *Gothic Nightmares. Fuseli, Blake and the Romantic Imagination*. London: Tate Publishing, 2006.
Narayan, Rasipuram Krishnaswami. *My Days*. London: Chatto and Windus, 1975.
Nayder, Lillian. *Wilkie Collins*. New York: Twayne Publishers, 1997.
Prothero, Rowland Edmund and George Granville Bradley. *The Life and Correspondence of Arthur Penrhyn Stanley*. 2 vols. London: John Murray, 1893.
Pykett, Lyn. *The 'Improper' Feminine: The Women's Sensation Novel and the New Woman Writing*. London: Routledge, 1992.
Schaffer, Talia. *Romance's Rivals. Familiar Marriage in Victorian Fiction*. Oxford: Oxford University Press, 2016.

6 'Could my hero tell lies?'

Romance and the Marriage Plot in Rhoda Broughton's *Cometh up as a Flower*

Carolyn W. de la L. Oulton

If a sensation novel can be provisionally identified by its use of tropes such as madness, bigamy and murder, it is defined more precisely through its self-conscious treatment of these motifs. Rhoda Broughton's *Cometh up as a Flower* (1867) resonates with other and more famous sensation novels of the decade, including *The Woman in White* (1860) and *East Lynne* (1861), in telling the story of the motherless Nell Lestrange's courtship by one man and reluctant marriage to another, wealthier suitor after a forged letter breaks up her love affair. But the identification of Broughton as a sensation writer depends less on her inclusion of dramatic or criminal episodes than on her tendency to privilege the viewpoint of socially un-rehabilitated and sexually responsive heroines, raising the question of whether her fiction can rightly be considered 'sensational' at all.

This chapter argues that *Cometh up as a Flower* participates in the sensational mode, but that it does so in order to challenge reader response. As Pamela Gilbert observes in her introduction to the text,

> Nell constantly refers to her reading to make sense of her own situation. Often this serves the purpose of foreshadowing or revealing some complexity to the reader that Nell is not yet aware of. Sometimes, also, Broughton uses these references to call attention to the inadequacy of existing literature to address her experiences.
>
> (Broughton, 16)

The appeal of Broughton's style and something of the threat it was seen as posing to female readers is suggested in the association of her work with overtly sensational fiction by writers such as Mary Braddon. As late as 1887 the young novelist Mary Cholmondeley, who was introduced to the Bentley publishing firm by Broughton herself, received a letter from her uncle in which he expressed his horror that she had joined 'the large army of female novelists. The fact is they are a <u>nasty</u>, <u>fusty</u>, <u>frowsy</u> lot, – Braddons and Broughtons & all of them!' (Charles Cholmondeley to Mary Cholmondeley 14 January 1887. Private collection). In linking Broughton to Mary Braddon in this way, the conservative Canon

Cholmondeley may well be thinking of the scandalous *Lady Audley's Secret* (1862) and suggesting that female-authored sensation novels in general are unwarrantably frank in their treatment of the marriage market. Unlike its famous precursor however, Broughton's novel is a fictional autobiography supposedly written by the woman herself, and one which continually disrupts readers' expectations of the sensational mode.

For many, Lady Audley, the most famous of Braddon's heroines, epitomises the threat posed by female characters in sensation fiction. As Michael Diamond helpfully suggests, 'The female characters who foreshadowed the future most strongly were not the villains [...] but the strong, resourceful women who took upon themselves more responsibility than their men ever expected of them' (Diamond, 217). *Cometh up as a Flower* acknowledges but finally resists both these paradigms, as it deploys competing plot lines to frame an account of a heroine who achieves very little, who is by her own account largely uneducated and who is set to die at twenty-two.

As Sanjay Sircar and Linda Conrad have shown, Nell Lestrange revises familiar tropes to frame her own feminist narrative that 'protests against the inherited explanation of Eve as responsible for the Fall, shows [...] that Cinderella may be denied her Prince Charming, and that the Ugly Duckling's new-gained beauty is useless' (Sircar and Conrad, 171). Like many sensation novels, *Cometh up as a Flower* also questions the role of women within marriage. Despite her acknowledged limitations Nell's narrative ably critiques both the courtship or seduction plot, and the basis of conventional marriage for young women of the upper classes. Bored at home, she admits that 'I began to have a morbid longing to do something startling, something that would break the gelid monotony of my existence. In my pretty vacant head [...] I began to cast about what action at once extremely eccentric and extremely naughty I could perform' (Broughton, 159). But rather than adhering to an identifiably sensational formula, this highly allusive text references sensation fiction partly in order to redirect readers' attention to the tragedy of more conventional female experience.

While Nell's relation of her joyous sexuality is problematic – as Shirley Jones puts it, 'Nell knows she should not be saying what she is saying' (Jones, 214) – when she does fall victim it is to a supposedly 'happy' ending and not a seduction as the reader might have expected. Dolly's machinations and Nell's own naïve incompetence, are the catalyst for a series of misunderstandings between her and her lover Major Dick M'Gregor during his leave in her part of the country, as each becomes jealous of the other's supposed encouragement of a rival (Sir Hugh Lancaster and Dolly, respectively). Both Nell and the reader doubt Dick's constancy at certain points, but his ultimate vindication stands as a reminder that formulaic plots (including by extension, happy endings) are simply a convention and not necessarily a reflection of women's experience.

During their second meeting at the Coxes' party, Nell is bewildered when Dick apparently bestows his attention on another woman at the piano, although he abruptly leaves his position when he sees that Nell is leaving, in order to try and arrange a secret assignation. At this point in the narrative he appears suspiciously like a Brontë villain in the Arthur Huntingdon mode. Deprived of the financial means that have allowed the Coxe daughters to enter local society, Nell now has little idea of how to behave in mixed company; in a subtle invocation of the biblical Eve's fall, she openly describes her sexual awakening a few days later as Dick symbolically enters her garden in the absence of her father, and proposes that she ratify a friendship with him:

> It was rather impudent of him, certainly, and I ought to have told him so, I suppose; but as he spoke, the dark gray eyes looked full into mine, with an expression I had never seen in mortal eyes before; an expression that sealed my lips, and sent a sort of odd shiver – a shiver that had nothing to say to cold, through my frame.
>
> (Broughton, 58)

When her father arrives, Dick instantly concocts a story about having been sent with a message by his hostess Mrs Coxe. Nell picks up on the significance of this ready invention, 'A tissue of fibs! listened to by me, with open-mouthed, wide-eyed amazement. Could my hero tell lies?' (Broughton, 71).

The stage seems set for the heroine's inevitable fall, but the reader is dispossessed of this idea, as it becomes clear that Dick's intentions are apparently entirely honourable. By his own account he is prevented from asking Sir Adrian's consent to an engagement only by his absence on a visit to friends. However twice more he will be placed in a position where both Nell and the reader lose confidence in his loyalty, once through his vengeful flirtation with Dolly at the Lancaster picnic when Nell has been manoeuvred into a carriage ride alone with the wealthy Sir Hugh; and again when he fails to write to either Nell or her father after the end of his leave, but does write to Mortimer Coxe to the effect that 'Cork was very jolly quarters, and there were heaps of pretty girls' (Broughton, 252).

While these misunderstandings adhere to a recognisable narrative structure of attraction and loss, the difficulty Nell has in seeing her lover alone stands as a reminder that she knows comparatively little about him, having spent a matter of hours with him over the course of their brief relationship. The early chapters of the novel suggest that the reader is to be presented with a sensational seduction plot, although Nell throws out a clue in her first meeting with her lover that 'There was nothing impudent in his gaze, none of the fervent admiration with which, at a first introduction, the hero in a novel regards the young lady, who at a later period of the story is to make a great fool of, or be made a great fool by him' (Broughton, 39).

The motherless Nell and her older sister Dolly are the last of the ancient but financially straitened Lestrange family, and constant worries about money mean that Nell has not been able to participate in the round of social engagements appropriate to her sex and position. As a result she is in imminent danger of a social as well as, to all appearances, a sexual fall. As Anna Peak points out, the circumscription of her immediate circle (which Nell complains leaves her no one to care about but her father, the man-servant and the sexton) reminds readers 'that isolated circumstances can collapse class differences' (Peak, 842), an impression that is reinforced in Nell's sardonic observation that the Coxes now look down on the Lestranges rather than looking up to them.

Nell's insistence on the right to tell her own story, coupled with her overtly sensual response to her lover, lead the reader to anticipate a series of plot climaxes each of which is ultimately deflated. Nell repeatedly draws attention to the social context of her story, which is suggestive of respectable monotony and a lack of imagination (her own sometimes included), rather than the threat of murder and bigamy: in her account seducers and villains are replaced by well-meaning vulgarians, and even the plotting of her Lady Audley-esque sister Dolly is motivated by practical considerations rather than insane malice. Like her precursor she is 'a practiced con artist, her beauty and manners concealing her capacity for dissipation and deceit' (Faber, 150). But while the calculating Dolly is surrounded with 'a vast network of imagery' linking her to evil practices, underlined by her 'snaky' head and 'coils' of hair (Sircar and Conrad 175), she is finally revealed to be superficial rather than definitively evil. In her conformity to social expectation she also, Lindsey Faber argues, stands for everything Nell must become (Faber, 156).

As both naïve heroine and world weary commentator Nell struggles to find an appropriate means of telling the story of her love for the man who has apparently jilted her, and her dutiful sacrifice of herself in the futile attempt to prolong her father's life, by marrying a rich suitor and paying off the family's creditors.[1] It is never made clear whom Nell believes her reader to be, but her implied audience is quite possibly the experienced consumer of sensation fiction. The early chapters of the novel, including Nell's ingenuous declaration, 'If I went into society, I should like to go to parties where there were no men, only women' (Broughton, 63), apparently foreshadow a sexual fall involving the young and handsome dragoon who tries to lure her into secret meetings and is expelled from her Edenic garden when her outraged father finds him lying on the ground at her feet holding her hand, after only one formal meeting. Significantly even this garden is unstable, part of a heavily mortgaged estate 'with a symbolic graveyard lying just outside it, the first piece of land described in the novel' (Sircar and Conrad, 175).

But while she admits to her own ignorance at an early stage of the novel, Nell makes no decorous apology for relating the story of her life and her forward behaviour is not, as it transpires, a hint that she will fall. In fact, as she re-iterates, Nell is not notably rebellious and she spends much of the novel reluctantly seeking the approval of her manipulative sister rather than struggling with sexual temptation. Her narrative includes satire of the autobiographical as well as interrogation of the sensational mode, as she outlines the class credentials that make her family's adjustment to straitened circumstances so difficult, only to apologise, 'But all this time I am keeping myself waiting by at my own hall-door while detailing my family's genealogy' (Broughton, 41).

Nell struggles to control her story in both senses: the marriage plot she has planned for herself is hijacked when she is outmanoeuvred by Dolly, the superficially 'ideal' woman who stands in for the expected villain of the novel. She is also conscious that she cannot control the interpretation of her story because she will be outlived by Dolly and by her husband. The last pages of the novel reveal that since her marriage Nell has been writing a diary, a permissible because supposedly feminine form of writing which she knows cannot include the story of her own death, 'it is hard, laboursome to me to hold the pencil, but I do not want to leave the story of my poor life incomplete; incompleter at least than the story of all lives must be. Some other hand must put "Finis" I know' (333).

Foreshadowing and undermining the later revelation that she is dying, an early passage rejects the assumption that she would be buried with her ancestors. Nell recalls her own bathetic meditation, 'When my time to make a decent ending has come, I'll have a snug hole grubbed for me right under my old friend the ash (the near one, isn't it?) and there I'll make myself as comfortable as circumstances will permit' (Broughton, 36). Notably Nell is apparently sentimental about her 'old friend' the ash, even as she admits that she cannot be sure on precisely which tree she carved her name ten years earlier. Family memorials feature largely in Nell's meditations at church during her unmarried life at Lestrange, but by the end of the novel the reader accepts that Nell will be buried with her husband's family and not in her own family vault, destined in her turn to become a legendary epitaph disconnected from her actual experience, 'I could see quite plain a new tablet over our pew, in Wentworth's dark old church: I could read the black letters traced distinctly on the white marble' (Broughton, 331).

It is a disenchanted but resigned narrator who is able to comment sardonically on her own romantic fantasies about dying young, a tragedy which as it transpires will provide the resolution to her story. Nell tells her father that she would like to die before losing the capacity for enjoyment: 'I fell a-thinking what an interesting young corpse I should make lying in the big four-poster in the red room, with my emaciated hands folded on my bosom, and a deluge of white flowers about me'

(Broughton, 47). Characteristically Nell anticipates stylised tropes of the dying heroine only in order to subvert them later in the narrative, when she learns that she is dying of consumption. Katherine Byrne has shown that literary fiction 'represented consumption as not contagious, because its value to the novel was based on its existence as a disease of individuals, associated not with contagion but with personal characteristics, behaviour and lifestyle, so that it might function as a cultural signifier' (Byrne, 24). In the final pages of the novel Nell reclaims the discourse of consumption as a vehicle for her own self-expression, 'I am able to watch the steps of my own dissolution. My beauty and my strength are gone from me; they were sorry to go, I think; they went so slowly and I shall not be long after them now' (Broughton, 330). In this clinical observation of her own deterioration from consumption, she retains a sardonic awareness of her position as a woman, aligning her physical decay with the dissolution of earthly identity.

When she remarks at a fairly early stage of the narrative that 'I have lived now more than twenty years, and have seen much of the evil and much of the good (there is a great deal of the latter, after all) that there is in the world' (Broughton, 72), this clue to her age is easily overlooked and the tone is correspondingly difficult to read. Only at the very end of the novel does the reader fully register that this world-weary narrator is barely twenty-two as she waits for her imminent death from consumption, and that she is recounting her early love affair and her own sexual awakening, from the perspective of a passionlessly married woman.

By this stage Nell has come to feel a level of affection for her husband sufficient to make his presence tolerable if not actually welcome, but as Gilbert argues, 'the commodification of the protagonist's body contains her dangerous sexuality in marriage, turning it inward to destroy her own flesh – she dies, appropriately, of consumption' (Gilbert, 114). Byrne argues that both medical and literary writing shows a tension 'between the idea that any diseased body is socially subversive and deviant because unhealthy, and the traditional conception of the consumptive as a spiritually pure, even holy, victim of the White Plague' (Byrne, 27). If one solution to this problem is to present aberrant sinners who atone through illness (Byrne, 28), Nell's detached observation of her own condition and unapologetic stance signal her continued resistance.

Alternately inviting and precluding affective responses, Nell pointedly rejects the reader's assumption about what kind of book they are reading, as she insists that her father means more to her than her lover, and admonishes the devotee of sensational fiction, 'I was not, I think, one of those fiery females, whose passions beat their affections out of the field. And really I don't think that Englishwomen are given to flaming, and burning, and melting, and being generally combustible on ordinary occasions, as we are led by one or two novelists to suppose' (Broughton, 146). Rather than drifting into a seduction of the naïve country girl during his period of leave, Dick intends to write to Sir Adrian Lestrange for his consent to a marriage with Nell.

The sensational elements of the story are further undermined through the motif of the futile sacrifice, when Nell finally agrees to marry Hugh to save her dying father additional anxiety, hoping that she can thereby prolong his life, but protesting to her sister, 'I wonder what can be meaner than selling yourself like a bale of goods or a barrel of beer, as I'm doing. Oh, what do I care how mean I am! What sin is there so big that I would not commit it this minute, and commit it most gladly too, if I could but have him back here this minute in this room' (Broughton, 268–69).

However by her own account, she had been prepared to sacrifice her life's happiness even if it were only for the sake of a few days:

> The doctor said that perfect exemption from all care and anxiety might, probably would prolong my father's life for weeks, nay months; and to win so dear, so inestimably precious a boon as his presence among us, for even a few days longer than I otherwise should have it, I was willing to sacrifice all my future years, willing to give my shrinking body to Sir Hugh's arms, and my abhorring soul into his custody, though both body and soul still clave with desperate ineradicable passion to that other.
>
> (Broughton, 256)

The sacrificial metaphor of burning alive segues into the more clinical terms of medical practice (or possibly vivisection) when Hugh actually proposes, and Nell forces herself to acquiesce, 'The fire glows ruddy in the wide old chimney; the flames go curling, spiring, quivering upwards. I gaze at the steel dogs in the hearth, and await the operation' (Broughton, 258).

It is the most socially adept figure in the novel, the artful Dolly, who precludes a happy ending for Nell. Persuading Dick that Nell intends to marry the wealthy Hugh, she begins an ostentatious flirtation with him herself apparently out of pure malice. This development reinforces the obvious point that Nell's most damaging relations are with other women who have unrestricted access to her in the domestic realm, both before and after marriage. As Gilbert observes, 'Dolly and Nell are refreshingly and believably unpleasant to each other in their daily lives' (Broughton, 22). Like Braddon's Lady Audley, Dolly is compelling as a character less because she is vicious than because, in a narrative double bluff, Nell's charting of her insidious behaviour finally reveals her to be almost exactly as she appears. Broughton departs from the model offered by Lady Audley of a sensational villain who is both murderous and frivolous, to suggest that successful and genuinely respectable women are innately heartless in their trivial approach to human relations.

The reminiscent Nell rejects both conventionally idealised and tragic constructions of her relationship with her scheming sister even before the revelation of her treachery. She admits that she would find it as hard to grieve for Dolly were she to die as she knows Dolly will for her, reflecting that 'I sometimes caught myself wondering whether, in the event of Dolly's death, I should be enabled to cry a little and wear a decent semblance of grief. I hoped I should be, but I misdoubted myself somewhat. I need not have been disquieted. As I write, myself tottering on the verge of that last bed I so tiredly long for, Dolly is in the heyday of health and prosperity' (Broughton, 51).

With predictable irony Sir Adrian dies on the day after her marriage, just as Nell fully realises that 'now I could reach my darling's arms only through the billows of sin or the floods of death' (Broughton, 277). But learning in retrospect that she has been tricked into marrying the wrong man, when she finds that Dolly has forged a letter to Dick and intercepted the actual letters she has written him, Nell still refuses to present her story in sensational or melodramatic terms. She tells the reader that on the contrary, 'It is a mistake to suppose that it is the wicked that make this world such a sad and weary place, it is the good, blundering dunderheads!' (Broughton, 222).

Once again Nell undermines the terms of her own narrative, initially seeming to protest the terms on which women are 'sold' in marriage, only to reveal Hugh's integrity. She writes bitterly that '[h]is arm is round my waist, and he is brushing my eyes and cheeks and brow with his somewhat bristly moustache as often as he feels inclined – for am I not his property? Has not he every right to kiss my face off if he chooses, to clasp me and hold me, and drag me about in whatever manner he wills, for has he not bought me?' (Broughton, 269). Clearly this is not Hugh's intention, as he responds to her obvious abhorrence with an appeal of his own (which she ignores), 'I know I'm not quite the right cut to take a girl's fancy; it would be better you should speak out, while it's time, than that we should make each other miserable for all our lives' (Broughton, 271). But he is denied any tragic role in the narrative when he marries Nell despite her honest admission that she can only try to like him given time, and he apparently remains perfectly satisfied with her polite indifference as his wife.

After her marriage Nell herself realises that she has undergone a transformation, signalled by the loss of her name. Nell Lestrange no longer exists, 'They buried her yesterday in that dull chamber, where Death is holding his carnival among the Lestranges, and have left only a very heavy-hearted Nell Lancaster in her stead' (Broughton, 282). But despite her outward passivity, she figures her subjection as a form of slavery, complaining that 'All Sir Hugh's other servants, if they disliked their situations, or got tired of them, might give warning and leave; but I, however wearied I might get of mine, could never give warning, could never leave. I was a fixture for life. So I said to myself sometimes, and ground my teeth, and snarled like a caged tiger' (Broughton, 292).

Nonetheless the married Nell rejects an entirely tragic role for herself. She increasingly acknowledges that her husband is kind and well meaning, and even that she is becoming quietly fond of him. In an echo of *East Lynne*, the real misery of her new existence is caused by the interference of a female relative, in this case Hugh's appalling mother. Her fantasies of escape are mediated through her reading of light literature, but she satirically undermines the moral tone such narratives are expected to deploy, 'I am buried in an arm-chair in my boudoir, reading a novel. It interests me rather, for it is all about a married woman, who ran away from her husband and suffered the extremity of human ills in consequence' (Broughton, 313).

In this case the cliché of the regretful fallen woman both reminds readers of the plot Nell's narrative has already disrupted, and anticipates her later desire to escape with Dick when she learns that he still loves her. Disrupting the familiar seduction plot for a second time, Dick refuses to take her, replacing her instead in the traditional moral role as he reproaches her, 'you ought to be my good angel. Don't tempt me to kill my own soul and yours!' (Broughton, 300).

Nell initially casts herself as the fallen woman despite having averted such a fate, imagining scenes in which she is driven out of the house by her enraged husband, having confessed the whole story to him. Her ultimate failure to confess complicates the crucial act of mercy in which, having confronted Dolly and threatened to show the letter to both Sir Hugh and Dolly's wealthy suitor, she throws it into the fire instead. This scene constitutes the first significant step in Nell's religious awakening, as she comes to realise that 'I had been clamouring for justice, bare justice. Alas, if bare justice is all I myself get, in that day when the world's long tangled accounts are made up, where shall I be?' (Broughton, 322). Importantly this realization does not fully reconcile the sisters, as Nell disengages Dolly's arms from her neck and rejects her thanks. Refusing the providential declamations of sensation fiction, Nell confides in more muted language that 'Since then, I have been sorry for my sin; at least I have tried to be' (Broughton, 330). Foregrounding her developing religious sensibilities at this point in the novel, she also sustains her sardonic narrative voice. Nell does not in other words define faith and resignation to the divine will in terms of passive acquiescence. Rather her religious development signals both her suffering and increased maturity, as for the first time she begins to register her own actions in terms of personal choice.

This combination of humility and penetrating intelligence frames the discussion of Nell's reading of the Bible as she waits to die. She derives consolation from the idea that 'God was very good and pitying; he was going to release me from the long pain of existence, and through the grave and gate of death I should pass to my beloved' (Broughton, 333). The fact that she has already entered in to the sacrament of marriage with another man, renders this hope theologically controversial. But Nell's invocations of religious striving are the more powerful in these scenes precisely because she brings her personality to bear on the uncertainty she feels, not least in her referencing of heaven as a release from passion, which she both courts and implicitly fears, 'I have been trying (oh, vain endeavour) to picture to myself that land of unpictured, *unpictureable* passionless bliss' (Broughton, 334).

Nell's difficulty in imagining bliss as passionless is characteristically opposed to her insistence throughout the text that she is not herself a passionate or rebellious heroine. 'It has been up-hill, tiring work, and I have often got out of breath, but it is nearly over now' is how she describes her efforts to be a good wife to Hugh after she learns of Dick's death (Broughton, 330). The force of her narration lies in this very contradiction between suffering and the human incapacity to attain tragic status, as she reminds the reader, 'My foolish little tale has been dull enough in the telling, I am afraid; it was not dull in the acting, Heaven knows!' (Broughton, 330).

Nell's strategy of referencing the sensational mode only to collapse it ensures that the reader's suspense is sustained until the end. Indeed it is only with the report of Dick's death that the imagined seduction plot can be wholly discredited. Anti-climax and tragedy compete for dominance, as Nell shows the sheer monotony of a woman's life and the misery of an existence that is seemingly mundane rather than tragic. At the very climax of the novel, Dolly escapes Nell's revenge not just because Nell has attained to a newly Christian sensibility but more obviously, because she has lost interest in this relationship with her conniving sister and therefore feels no interest in preventing her marriage to the wealthy Lord Stockport. In what is surely a comment on the sensational mode, the familiar device of avenging fate is displaced by the heroine's own indifference and recognition of her marginal status.

If then the sensational mode can be understood as the disruption of realism by self-consciously dramatic paradigms, Nell as the first-person narrator frustrates her reader's expectations of the genre, reinstating sensational tropes within the context of an ultimately triumphant domestic realism. In doing so she subtly revises Walter Hartright's famously ironic words 'let Marian end our story', reminding readers that she at least acknowledges, 'Some other hand must put "Finis"' (Broughton, 333). But in acknowledging her own defeat Nell finally suggests that the hidden struggles of apparently conforming women may be dramatic in ways that the more obvious spectacle offered by sensation plots fails to attain.

Note

1 A growing body of work on female life writing strongly suggests that women's accounts of their own lives are contingent on an appeal to a particular context in which they are produced and expected to be read. Carol Mackay argues that life writing by Victorian women is 'always skirting the edge

of propriety by setting in motion the interplay between public and private' (159); Lynn Bloom has shown that ostensibly private diaries can themselves be identified as 'public' documents through their inclusion of features such as narrative structure and an emphasis on topics of interest rather than simple chronology. See '"I write for myself and strangers": Private Diaries as Public Documents' in Suzanne L. Bunkers and Cynthia A. Huff eds. *Inscribing the Daily: Critical Essays on Women's Diaries*, pp 23–37. Amherst: University of Massachusetts Press, 1996.

Works Cited

Broughton, Rhoda. *Cometh up as a Flower*. Peterborough: Broadview, 2010.

Byrne, Katherine. *Tuberculosis and the Victorian Literary Imagination*. Cambridge: Cambridge University Press, 2011.

Collins, Wilkie. *The Woman in White*. Oxford: Oxford University Press, 2008.

Diamond, Michael. *Victorian Sensation, or the Spectacular, the Shocking and the Scandalous in Nineteenth-Century Britain*. London: Anthem Press, 2004.

Faber, Lindsey. 'One sister's surrender: rivalry and resistance in Rhoda Broughton's *Cometh up as a Flower*' in Kimberly Harrison and Richard Fantina eds. *Victorian Sensations: Essays on a Scandalous Genre*, pp 149–59. Columbus: Ohio State University Press, 2006.

Gilbert, Pamela. *Disease, Desire and the Body in Victorian Women's Popular Novels*. Cambridge: Cambridge University Press, 1997.

Jones, Shirley. '"LOVE": Rhoda Broughton, writing and re-writing romance'. In Boardman, Kay and Shirley Jones, eds. *Popular Victorian Women Wirters*. Manchester: Manchester University Press, 2004. 208–36.

Mackay, Carol Hanbury. 'Life Writing' in Linda Peterson ed. *Cambridge Companion to Victorian Women's Writing*. Cambridge: Cambridge University Press, 2015.

Peak, Anna. 'Servants and the Victorian Sensation Novel'. *SEL Studies in English Literature, 1500–1900*, Vol 54, No 4 (Autumn 2014), pp 835–51.

Sircar, Sanjay John and Linda Conrad. 'Rhoda Broughton's *Cometh up as a Flower* (1867): Victorian Best-Seller as Feminist Revisioning'. *AAA: Arbeiton aus Anglistik und Amerikanistick*, Vol 20, No 1 (1995), 171–97.

7 Mystical Nationalism and the Rotten Heart of Empire

The Tangled Trope of Marriage in *Daniel Deronda*

Meredith Miller

> This match with Grandcourt presented itself to him as a sort of public affair; perhaps there were ways in which it might even strengthen the Establishment [...] and was a match to be accepted on broad general grounds national and ecclesiastical.
>
> —(Eliot, 102)

From the earliest episodes of *Daniel Deronda* (1876) George Eliot places marriage within this national context and invites us to view the unions between her various characters in the light of both domestic-national and imperial power. She also makes knowing, meta-fictional gestures towards the novel's use of the marriage plot, as in the epigraph from Molière's *Les Précieuses Ridicules* (1659) that heads Chapter IV. Critics have noted her uses of sensational and/or Gothic effects throughout the novel, and contemporary reviewers noted that the book was a significant stylistic departure from the realism of *Adam Bede* (1859) and *Middlemarch* (1872). In fact, this last of Eliot's novels deploys a determined *bricolage*, using her understanding of the operations of a variety of fictional generic modes purposely for the specific effects of each. This variety of effects is blended to form Eliot's complex intervention in the political relation between psychological identification and ideals of national identity.

The romance plot is unique in its facility for marrying identification, through desire, with ideological intervention. We can render an object of desire as a radical democrat posed against an unfeeling Tory, as Trollope does in *He Knew He Was Right* (1868–9) or render sexual desire as a matter of a free aesthetic communion presented as a socialist ideal, as Gissing does in several works. Like Charlotte Brontë we can render sexual satisfaction as inseparable from the free self-determination of the heroine with whom we are invited to identify. In *Daniel Deronda*, George Eliot uses an intertwined mesh of marriage plots in different generic modes to produce an overall ideological effect that rewrites ideas of nation, empire, culture and gender. At different moments within the novel, characters are presented either as the fixed standard archetypes of the sentimental romance, as the inhabitants of the enervated and over-sensible Gothic bodies common to sensation novels, as classic realist 'types' or as the subjects of the complex and layered psychological prose developing within the sphere of fictional realism. These generic modes are not distinct or unrelated, though they do produce different ideological effects. Each has its specific purpose inside the whole purpose of the novel. As Henry James would do after her, Eliot consciously weaves effects developed within popular genres together with her more writerly psychological prose.

In *George Eliot's Serial Fiction*, Carol A. Martin points out that serialisation allowed for engaged discussions about the form and structure of novels, in which the public often saw themselves as co-creators, licensed to help direct the formation and forward movement of novels. From its first serial publication in 1876, *Daniel Deronda* drew criticism for what readers and critics saw as the lack of integration of its two parts. This carried on well into the twentieth century, and famously culminated in 1948 with F. R. Leavis's presumptuous imaginary rewriting and renaming of the novel as *Gwendolyn Harleth*. It is important to note, however, that other serialised novels were subjected to this same criticism in the 1870s. The *Athenaeum* of July 1876, for example, reviews both *Deronda* and Trollope's *The Prime Minister* (1876). The review calls the 'Jewish scenes' in *Deronda* 'even more wanting in interest' but also criticises Trollope for failing to integrate his two plots (*Athenaeum*, 14–15). Yet it is only for *Deronda* that this common discussion of serialised novels continued to dominate the critical narrative into the twentieth century. The real problem audiences and critics saw with *Deronda* was the Jewishness of its counterplot, and integration is a far more loaded term than Leavis pretends.

Discussions of the serial volumes of *Deronda* in monthly reviews were varied and complex. Henry James' 'Daniel Deronda: A Conversation' (1876) is often read out of context as embodying James's critique of the novel in one of its character voices. In fact, when read in the context of the contemporary reviews, it can be seen clearly as a parody of the variety of positions taken. The appearance of James's parody in the *Atlantic Monthly* in December 1876 demonstrates that contemporary discussions of *Deronda* were especially lively, loaded and widespread. These conversations evidence a remarkably informed reception of the form and effects of various novelistic modes.

R. E. Francillon titled his October 1876 review of *Deronda*, 'George Eliot's First Romance'. The review, which is overwhelmingly positive, argues that the dissatisfaction of Eliot's audience stems from the fact that *Deronda* is not a realist novel. Its status as romance, for Francillon, is located in its characterisations. He writes that, '"Daniel Deronda" is broadly distinguishable from all its predecessors by not dealing with types—with ordinary people who make up the actual world, and with circumstances, events, characterisations and passions that are common to us all' (Francillon, 412). Rather, he argues, *Deronda* should be accorded the status of a high tragedy that depicts idealised figures. Romance, for Francillon, is the window into the larger soul contained within the prosaic stuff of the realist novel: 'Our afternoon tea-tables have been photographed *ad nauseam*: it is time for the cover to be removed, that we may see underneath them. We welcome "Daniel Deronda" [...]' (Francillon, 426). This notion of 'literary photography' signals an emerging understanding of the realist style evolving into naturalism in late-nineteenth-century fiction. In *Deronda* itself, Eliot's narrator refers to the effects of 'what they call literary photographs' in one of her many references to the perceptual gap between fictional representation and material life (Eliot, 146). This gap in perception structures the whole narrative of Gwendolen's courtship and marriage, presented in the first four books of the novel.

Daniel Deronda is structured through what can be read as three intertwined marriage plots: the socially and nationally significant marriage between Gwendolen and Grandcourt, the marginalized and sentimental marriage between Daniel Deronda and Mirah Lapidoth, and the cabalistic marriage of spirit that impregnates Daniel with the soul of Mordecai's religious nationalism. The first of these is presented through a careful blending of psychological realism with effects derived from Gothic sensation fiction. The second, for reasons outlined below, borrows Mirah Lapidoth's character type from sentimental fiction and presents a heterosexual union entirely devoid of any of the questions regarding will and desire which define Gwendolen's narrative. The third writes Daniel and Mordecai's union deliberately through romanticist associations between the visionary consumptive and homosocial bonding, borrowing from Shelleyean depictions of both the mystic and the political radical. Here again, Eliot deploys the effects of the Gothic textual body. This third marriage is synecdochal, writing an imperial 'marriage' between East and West within and through Daniel himself, realised through his dreams of utopian world-building in Palestine.

The first four books of *Deronda* contain a story of courtship and marriage centred on Gwendolen, as well as the story of Daniel's uncertain parentage and his discovery of the lost and suicidal Mirah on the banks of the Thames. While these books contain the usual teleological drive of the marriage plot, they also deploy a series of analeptic loops that enable a depiction of the relation between conscious experience and social reality. In these early books, the mental life of central characters is presented both through a focalised psychological prose and a complicated time structure. Each central scene of action is followed by a lengthy analeptic development of the causes and motivations that lead to that action. The reader is repeatedly invited to look beneath the surface and behind the veil, and is provided with psychological information that enables them to see the blindness of other characters. This blindness, this groping in the social dark, is a central theme of the so-called 'English' episodes in the novel. As the epigraph to Chapter XVI, written by Eliot, puts it,

> Men, like planets, have both a visible and an invisible history. The astronomer threads the darkness with strict deduction, accounting so for every visible and invisible arc in the wanderer's orbit, and the narrator of human actions, if he did his work with the same care, would have to thread the hidden pathways of feeling and thought which lead up to every moment of action.
>
> (Eliot, 121)

Certainly, we can read this as an artist's statement in favour of the new psychological approach to fiction. It is, however, also allied to the thematic of invisibility that structures the novel, and the political critique of ideology that explores the cost in human suffering which is exacted by the proprieties of the social world, the gaps between the real and the ideological.

While we are invited into the drama of Gwendolen's naïve and confident expectations, continuous narrative asides underscore the bleak reality of marriage behind the veil of the public/private divide. These are embedded in a pointed critique of the relation between fiction and material life, as Eliot's narrator tells us of Gwendolen's 'uncontrolled reading' and points out the appalling degree to which realist 'pictures of life' leave her unprepared for the reality of marriage. Gwendolen can see that marriage is disempowering for the women around her, though it also confers social and material security. She views it as

> [a] dreary state, in which a women could not do what she liked, had more children than were necessary, was consequently dull, and became irrevocably immersed in humdrum. Or course marriage was social promotion; she could not look forward to a single life; but promotions sometimes have to be taken with bitter herbs.
>
> (Eliot, 26)

Yet she maintains a naïve confidence in her ability to impose her will upon others, including any prospective husband. Again and again, images and exposition expose the blindness of a young girl on the threshold of marriage. Gwendolen's constitutional belief in the power of her own will, heretofore unchallenged within her small sphere, is set up from the novel's first scene as the vehicle of her unfolding tragedy. Whatever 'peculiar quality' she felt in the air around her suitor, Grandcourt, was

> [n]ot, she was sure, any subjugation of her will by Mr Grandcourt and the splendid prospects he meant to offer her; for Gwendolen

desired every one, that dignified gentleman himself included, to understand that she was going to do just as she liked, and that they had better not calculate on her pleasing them. If she chose to take this husband she would have him know that she was not going to renounce her freedom, or according to her favourite formula, "not going to do as other women did."

(Eliot, 95–6)

Grandcourt's sadism and love of mastery are revealed to the reader through focalized narrative asides during his first conversation with Gwendolen and in Chapter XII where we see him alone with Lush and his dogs (Eliot, 80–81). Grandcourt sees Gwendolen's strong will as an asset in this regard, for 'to be worth his mastering it was proper that she should have some spirit' (Eliot, 115). Thus early on, the reader is shown a disturbing portrait of toxic masculinity. She, however, approaches Grandcourt and Lush with 'no sense that these men were dark enigmas to her, or that she needed any help in drawing conclusions about them' (Eliot, 89). The novel's free indirect discourse is structured so that the reader sees behind a veil to a reality of which Gwendolen is unaware. Eliot invites a double reading of romance inside realism and of the psychological and ideological effects of each upon the other.

Eliot's critique of the institution of marriage is both material and psychological. It is a critique made through an analysis of global capital and national culture, and it is also a cry in defence of the free will of the individual. Chapter IX, in which Gwendolen and Grandcourt are married, is introduced with a wry explanation of the manner in which the wealth of the aristocracy trickles down to local communities and their tradespeople. The narrator then points sarcastically to loftier hopes for the marriage of various daughters before assuring us that marriage 'must be considered as coming under both heads', the pleasures of life as well as its business (Eliot, 65). We are shown an imminent alliance between landed aristocracy and the enormous wealth of the new business class, woven into the fabric of the English economy at every level. That choral crowd at the back of the nineteenth-century realist novel, often referred to as 'the world', the representation of received ideology, does not distinguish this complex economic structure from 'the pleasures' of life, the whims of young men and women and the sober guidance of parents. The critique of marriage throughout these first four books exposes this economic and national interest in the use of young women, and the role that fictional romance plays in reproducing the ideological effect that perpetuates it.

The reverend Gascoigne, Gwendolen's uncle and the acting family patriarch who oversees Gwendolen's prospects, clearly views her in terms of capital investment. Though a good riding horse is a serious expense, he will get her one so that she can be seen to advantage. '"The girl is really worth some expense"' he tells his wife, '"you don't often see her equal. She ought to make a first-rate marriage, and I shouldn't be doing my job if I spared any trouble in helping her forward"' (Eliot, 24). The dialogic epigraph to Chapter X, written by Eliot herself, specifically equates young women with market commodities. In asking what women should be, we ought to consult the tastes of marriageable men, for 'our daughters must be wives' and like 'iron, cotton, wool, or chemicals' they should be shaped to demand (Eliot, 71).

Following a rhetorical tradition begun in the late eighteenth century, Eliot poses her critique of the economic subjugation of European women and their lack of personal liberty through a problematic metaphorical conflation of white women with colonial slaves. In asserting her own right to the exercise of will, Gwendolen reflects dismissively that though other 'people allowed themselves to be made slaves of [...] it would not be so with her'. This equation is Gwendolen's in focalised narration, but the narrator also uses it at one remove to define her more objectively, as the subject of internalised oppression:

> No wonder she enjoyed her existence on that July day. Pre-eminence is sweet to those who love it, even under mediocre circumstances: perhaps it is not quite mythical that a slave has been proud to be bought first.
>
> (Eliot, 72)

A similar equation is conflated with classical and biblical history once Mirah Lapidoth appears as the subject of a very differently constructed femininity. These equations between women and slaves are part of the novel's peculiarly overlapping and paradoxical relationship to colonial ideology. In the first four books, the drama of young women and prominent marriages is set within a very clear critique of violent colonial economies at the same time as it makes an impossible parallel between 'women' and slaves.

The economic situation of Gwendolen's family is given a shadowy connection to plantation slavery at the outset. 'She had no notion how her maternal grandfather had got the fortune inherited by his two daughters; but he had been a West Indian', by which is meant a plantation owner (Eliot, 14). Eliot has set the novel ten to twelve years prior to its composition. This allows her to pose the actions of her characters against the American war and the Jamaican rebellion of 1865, as well as those nationalist wars involving Italian and Austrian states which frame the action of the later books and offset Mordecai's Zionism. Incidental conversations between various characters in Books II and III centre on colonial politics, and these serve as the first frame through which Eliot situates the moral opposition between her two central 'English gentlemen'. Here Grandcourt's sadistic love of mastery is specifically conflated with support for plantation slavery, and Deronda's masculine action tempered with feminine capacity for empathy is specifically associated with the struggle for democracy and self-representation:

> [T]he talk turned on the rinderpest and Jamaica [...] Grandcourt held that the Jamaican negro was a beastly sort of Caliban; Deronda said he had always felt a little with Caliban, who naturally had his own point of view and could sing a good song; Mrs Davilow observed that her father had an estate in Barbadoes, but that she herself had never been in the West Indies; Mrs Torrington was sure she should never sleep in her bed if she lived among blacks; her husband corrected her by saying that the blacks would be manageable enough if it were not for the half-breeds; and Deronda said that the whites had themselves to thank for the half-breeds.
>
> (Eliot, 245)

This combination of real appeals to political sympathy with sarcastic parody of shallow society discourse, so often the mode of Eliot's critique, renders Deronda the moral compass of the novel's world. Many contemporary readers saw him as stiff and lacking complexity, as James's 'Conversation' demonstrates, yet he is clearly intended as the novel's object of identification and desire. Gwendolen's physical attraction to him, her compulsion to seek him out and make him responsible for her anguish, complicates and deepens the understanding of heterosexuality available to the English novel before Eliot. Romantic fiction's specific mechanics of desire, its invitations to reader identification and sexual fantasy, allow Eliot to position our sympathies according to a clearly determined political position. The psychological realism built in focalised narration in Gwendolen's narrative enables a pointed critique of the psychological effects of gender and the blind ideological gap between domestic life and national and imperial power.

Gwendolen, affianced but not yet married, is poised between two gentlemen, drawn spiritually to one and speculating materially on the other. Following the dinner party scene, Gwendolen and Deronda have a discussion about his disapproval of her gambling. In light of her knowledge of the claims of Lydia Glasher, her family's loss through capital speculation and the preceding discussions of industry, colonial slavery and labour resistance, these questions are clearly implicated in Gwendolen's decision to marry Grandcourt. Deronda tells her that there is 'something revolting to me in raking a heap of money together, and internally chuckling over it, when others are feeling the loss of it' (Eliot, 250). Gwendolen kicks her horse and rides away from this understanding, specifically colluding in her own blindness and wilfully pursuing her own material comfort, still assuming that her marriage will not subjugate her will to power.

All of these concerns are raised in microcosm in Chapter XXII of the novel, which relates the story of Catherine Arrowpoint's marriage to the talented Jewish composer Julius Klesmer. This chapter forms an inset narrative that encapsulates all of the novel's concerns in a short secondary marriage plot. This contextual subplot is also the novel's only actual representation of miscegenation, its only implemented blending of a pan-national European Jewish position with the English upper class. The drama, presented analeptically as an interruption in Gwendolen's desperate attempt to initiate a singing career, also involves two opposed suitors between whom Catherine Arrowpoint chooses. Mr Bult, ultimately rejected, has a complex network of colonial interests and 'the general solidity and suffusive pinkness of a healthy English gentlemen on the tableland of life' (Eliot, 178–9). The desired and ultimately won Klesmer appears to Bult to be Panslavist, and energetically objects to 'the lack of idealism in English politics, which left all mutuality between distant races to be determined simply by the need of a market'. He is not a Panslavist he tells Bult, he is a 'wandering Jew'. Catherine terms him 'cosmopolitan' and explains that he 'looks forward to a fusion of the races' (Eliot, 179). Once these two people, each in possession of a strong will, manage to declare their love, the inevitable argument with Catherine's parents ensues. The Arrowpoints tell her that because she will inherit a large fortune it is her duty to marry a man 'connected with the institutions of this country' (Eliot, 183). Once again, marriage is a mechanism for consolidating capital and inscribing national boundaries. Catherine refuses to make the choice Gwendolen makes, instead choosing personal love over social duty, and thus provides a point of sympathy and an ethical compass for the surrounding action. Once married, the Klesmers retreat to the margins of the narrative, whence they occasionally come forward to act beneficently on the central characters.

Susan Meyer writes that, in sending Deronda away and using him to enact Gwendolen's escape, the novel 'purges away resistant female selves and it purges away Jews' (Meyer, 753). Yet the inset narrative of Catherine Arrowpoint's marriage specifically defies such purging, placing intermarriage between a European Jew and a member of England's wealthy elite at the centre of London culture. Both Gwendolen's central drama and Catherine's marriage subplot are set deliberately within the context of empire and capital, both national and global. The novel moves continuously between interconnected registers of conflict, the feminine individual and the national/global. Its portraits of women are pictures of the psychological cost at the level of the individual which underpins national power. At the close of Chapter XI, the narrator sets these two registers explicitly against each other, invoking the American war, the solidarity of suffering textile workers in northern England, new ideas of 'universal kinship' and then asking: 'What in the midst of that mighty drama are girls and their blind visions?' (Eliot, 90). The predictable answer is that they are the vessels that will carry forward the good for which we fight.

Gwendolen's 'blind vision', her inability to see behind the veil of marriage, is very specifically articulated as a failure to perceive the reality of gendered sexual violence. It is here that Eliot begins to employ the textual effects of the Gothic nervous body. Early on the narrative establishes Gwendolen's 'physical repulsion, to being directly made love to' (Eliot, 49). During her engagement, the reader sees Grandcourt's physical advances looming closer as Gwendolen realises only gradually that she will soon have no power to refuse them. The more spirit she has the more pleasure it will be to break her:

> She had been brought to accept him in spite of everything—brought to kneel down like a horse under training for the arena, though she might have an objection to it all the while. On the whole, Grandcourt got more pleasure out of this notion than he could have done out of winning a girl of whom he was sure that she had a strong inclination for him personally.
>
> (Eliot, 237)

The unfolding tragedy of Gwendolen's marriage is her gradual understanding of the physical reality of her loss of power. Driven both by financial necessity and by an unschooled desire for position and comfort, she accepts Grandcourt despite knowing that he has cast aside a 'ruined' mistress and children. Having this knowledge, she is already disgusted by his advances. She considers that perhaps 'other men's lives were of the same kind—full of secrets which made the ignorant suppositions of the women they wanted to marry a farce at which they were laughing in their sleeves' (Eliot, 222). Together with repeated hints that Gwendolen shies from physical affection, this explicit depiction of Grandcourt's sadistic love of mastery of unwilling subjects is revealed to be overtly sexual. Once they are married, Grandcourt makes a sport of angering and then subjecting her. Having deliberately displeased her, Grandcourt regards his wife:

> "She is in a desperate rage," thought he. But the rage was silent and therefore not disagreeable to him. It followed that he turned her chin and kissed her, while she still kept her eyelids down.
>
> (Eliot, 449)

In as clear terms as she is able, Eliot tells us that Grandcourt relishes forcible sexual abuse of his wife. The reality of sexual exploitation and abuse, both hidden and pervasive, is a haunting presence throughout the novel. In *Somatic Fictions*, Athena Vrettos notes Eliot's 'barely disguised' use of tropes from sensation fiction in the construction of Gwendolen's character. She argues that Gwendolen and Daniel are opposed in their relation to, respectively, Reason and Romanticism, and that Gwendolen's hysteria, an expressed fear of the sublime 'works against the broader movement of the text, which reveals increasingly broader intellectual and geographic horizons' (Vrettos, 59–60). Here again the plot is reduced to one, teleological development, essentially to romanticist *bildung*. But reading for closure assumes that Eliot's aim is to produce ideological stability, refuses, in fact, that very romanticist negative capability with which she infuses Daniel's character. While one of these intertwined plots opens out into an imagined frontier, the other closes itself into a domestic nightmare, and this is not accidental. Neither is meant to be subsumed; each is intended to illuminate the cost of the other.

The secrets of sexual power and abuse, and their unspeakable nature, drive the novel's first studied use of Gothic effects. Narrative asides continually hint at domestic violence and tyrannical husbands and fathers, as in the disquisition on abusive patriarchs at the close of Chapter IV, but these are never fully spoken. When Lydia Glasher appears to Gwendolen, carrying the knowledge of sex and its consequences, she comes as an apparition among a circle of standing stones. As the trap of Gwendolen's marriage closes around her, she descends into a nightmare recognisable from sensation fiction, in which her own murderous impulses separate her consciousness from her nervous body. Having exerted tremendous self-mastery, subjugating her own will to the outward social forms of married life, this suppressed will erupts in the form of compulsive thoughts and imagined violence:

> What possible release could there be for her from this hated vantage-ground, which she dare not quit, any more than if fire had been raining down outside it? What release, but death? Not her own death. Gwendolen was not a woman who could easily think of her own death as a near reality, or front for herself the dark entrance on the untried and invisible. It seemed more possible that Grandcourt should die:—and yet not likely.

(Eliot, 456)

These sensational eruptions in Gwendolen's narrative reveal the close relation between the popular Gothic and the development of psychological fiction. By the 1870s Gothic fiction is well known for its exposure of the horrors hidden beneath the surface of domestic life. Here Eliot uses these associations to make the effects of sexual violence in marriage felt, and to expose the psychological effects on women of its repression. The haunting of Gwendolen's marriage by the spectre of Lydia Glasher also embodies this half-hidden understanding.

Gwendolen and Lydia, Grandcourt's legitimate and illegitimate possessions, form one of the novel's many mirrored pairs. They share a dissident and resistant femininity, being each possessed of an excess of will. They are both examples of a new kind of female character, often associated with Thackeray's Becky Sharp, the wilful female. As Stefan Collini argues in *Public Moralists*, will and restraint (the imposition of will upon the self) are concepts that dominate later nineteenth-century conceptions of masculine character (Collini, 99–101). Like Deronda's 'feminine' openness and empathy, Lydia and Gwendolen's possession of strong will disrupts the social order of gender, and disrupts and complicates the heterosexual order of the marriage plot.

Lydia responds to the reality of Grandcourt's disregard much as Gwendolen responds to the reality of her marriage, with a tremendous effort of will exercised upon herself. Each woman confronts her powerlessness by exerting power in the only possible direction, inward: 'This woman [Lydia] with the intense eager look had had the iron of the mother's anguish in her soul, and it had made her sometimes capable of a repression harder than shrieking and struggle' (Eliot, 257–8). This exercise of will is mirrored in the focalised narration of Gwendolen's wedding day in the following chapter, as Gwendolen forcibly represses her fear and doubt 'with a sort of exulting defiance' (Eliot, 264). The scene also echoes the gambling scene that opens the novel where Gwendolen responds to danger with an excess of self-control. Though one woman maintains her marital state until widowhood and one becomes a mistress and social outcast, the substance of their tragedies is the same. Their helplessness is not psychological weakness, it is social and material disadvantage. Inhabiting a dissident feminine will, they suffer more than women of passive character.

The novel's second marriage plot, introduced at the end of Book II, centres on Daniel Deronda and Mirah Lapidoth. Here, for specific reasons, Eliot shifts her generic mode, her prose style and the characterization of her heroine. In sharp contrast to the strong masculine will of Gwendolen and Lydia, Mirah's whole character consists in a yielding, ultra-feminine helplessness. She exists in clear opposition to what we might call the strong feminism articulated through the other female characters in the novel. In her drive to create sympathetic identification with Mirah among her English readers, Eliot reaches for the techniques and characterization of the sentimental novel. It is as if the exercise of will together with Mirah's racialised identity would render her a bigger disruption than Eliot is prepared for. In order to be both Jewish and sympathetic, she must arise out of a tragic narrative even as Gwendolen plunges headlong into one.

From the moment when Daniel rescues her from the Thames, Mirah's story has the style and formal structure of a sentimental narrative, even to its operatic gestures at high tragedy. The sentimental genre determines both her character and the manner in which her story is related. The helpless and uncomplicated femininity of her aspect is immediately established. 'Her little woman's figure as she laid her delicate chilled hands together one over the other against her waist [...] was unspeakably touching' (Eliot, 143). Most significantly, she enters through Daniel's gaze, without any subjective narration, and remains largely without it through the rest of the novel. The sentimental story of her exploitation and distress are related entirely through dialogue, spoken to the good and charming aesthete, Mrs Meyrick. This precludes any psychological depth or layering in focalised prose, providing a style of narration that evokes the epistolary sentimental romances and conduct books of the late eighteenth century. Eliot leaves Mirah no ambiguity.

Here begins a peculiar vacillation in which *Deronda* re-inscribes racial stereotypes even as it resists them. Daniel remains the sympathetic location of ethical tolerance as Mirah, sitting in his boat, tells him that she is Jewish and then asks, '"Do you despise me for it?" "I know many Jews are bad."' Daniel replies, '"So are many Christians. But I should not think it fair for you to despise me because of that"' (Eliot, 143–4). Despite this pose of liberal tolerance, Daniel and the Meyrick women constantly remark on Mirah's 'refinement' in tones of relief. Physical descriptions of her repeat over and over the small delicacy of her features, hands and feet. Mrs Meyrick repeats to her daughters Daniel's assurance that Mirah is 'a Jewess, but quite refined, he says—knowing Italian and music' (Eliot, 148).

Arriving at the Meyrick's house, alienated from her family, bedraggled, depressed and having attempted suicide by drowning, Mirah carries with her the spectre of the fallen woman, then so familiar to readers of periodicals. Eliot is at pains to turn the narrative away from such implications, to further her anti-racist project by establishing Mirah's purity absolutely. While the English Gwendolen can push the boundaries of good feminine character to the limit and still end the novel free and redeemed, the effects of racism confine Mirah to a painfully narrow feminine scope. Her only expression of will is in her stubborn refusal to disown her abusive father.

Mirah's flatness of character is not a secondary effect of the sentimental genre into which Eliot moves here. It is a requirement for redeeming her from all the implications of her culture and situation, a reason for inhabiting that genre in these sections of the novel. Her lack of depth is deliberate, as we can see during the conversation about her which Daniel and Mrs Meyrick have toward the end of Chapter XX. Mrs Meyrick has examined her fully and concluded that: 'It is not in her nature to run into planning and devising; only to submit. See how she submitted to that father' (Eliot, 166). Significantly, her goodness consists particularly in her lack of psychological depth. A theatre director has told her father that '"She will never be an artist; she has no notion of being anybody but herself"' (Eliot, 157). Mrs Meyrick tells Daniel that, 'Her theatrical training has left no trace [...]' and that '"She's just a pearl: the mud has only washed her"' (Eliot, 165). Her purity must consist of lack of artifice. She can be allowed to exist on only one level.

At the same time, there are several references to the common English idea that 'Eastern' women are more oppressed than Englishwomen. The Meyrick girls ask Mirah whether she thinks it 'quite right to you that the women should sit behind the rails in a gallery apart' in the synagogue. Mirah replies that it seems right because it is what she has always known (Eliot, 305). Since the father who took her away to the theatre was profligate and impious, her knowledge of Hebrew and memories of liturgy are all from infancy and are bound up with her mother's physical closeness. They exist in a kind of pre-verbal memory that is one with her being itself. Hence her piety is both religious and filial, and inseparable from her identity. Eliot's *Deronda Notebooks* (1996) demonstrate, alongside her interest in Jewish literature and philosophy, both rabbinical and apostate, a marked interest in questions of Judaism and gender (Irwin). She blends a judgemental sense of Mirah's backward feminine subjugation with a willingness to use that very pliable and yielding character in service to the production of ideological closure in this canonical marriage plot.

The Meyricks' home, where Mirah stays during her months of recuperation, presents an entirely different picture of the domestic from the other family homes in the novel. In keeping with sentimental plot structure, it is the happy, contented and intrinsically moral space in which the heroine finds refuge. The widowed Mrs Meyrick mirrors the unhappy Mrs Davilow, being the picture of cheerful, contented motherhood surrounded by mementoes of her husband. The Meyrick daughters throw the featureless, 'superfluous' Davilow girls into relief, being intellectually curious, aesthetically inclined and possessing faces 'full of speech, as if their minds had been shelled, after the manner of horse-chestnuts, and become brightly visible' (Eliot, 147). They take pleasure in romantic fantasy and excessive displays of sensibility, and thus receive the sentimental character of Mirah with perfect satisfaction. According to Carol Martin, reader responses to Mirah were likewise overwhelmingly positive, at least at first (Martin, 220–2).

Mirah's lack of depth also lends itself to her use as a cipher for the novel's third central marriage, the union of her brother Mordecai with Deronda. Edward Said has pointed out the remarkable absence of any sense of the Palestinian people as Daniel sets off to found his new 'nation' in Palestine. This absence, the sense of the East both as Europe's cultural past and as the geographical blank space in which Europeans can enact a utopian future, is the substance of Eliot's inability to think her way entirely out of imperial ideology. It should also be noted, however, that Jewishness in the nineteenth century is not constructed as it is for us, in strict opposition to an 'Eastern' (Arabic) identity. Semitic identity for Eliot is part of a more fluid orientalist construction of racial, cultural and aesthetic inheritance. Throughout the novel, Eliot deploys references to a non-differentiated Semitic, 'Eastern' culture in her construction of Jewish character. Mordecai is written as Jacob Cohen's 'enslaved Djinn' and Daniel is dubbed 'Prince Camaralzaman' by the Meyrick daughters in several of the novel's many references to the *Thousand and One Nights*. Later they imagine Mirah as Camaralzaman's Queen Budoor. Hans Meyrick imagines Mordecai as 'a Crystal Palace Assyrian with a hat on' (Eliot, 357, 495). This undifferentiated Eastern identity signifies ancientness and cultural inheritance within the imperial narrative of the progress of civilization, but also the other place and space which defines Europe by contrast. It functions as both historical continuance and geographic opposition, which paradoxical blending of effects is the substance of Daniel and Mordecai's 'marriage'. The sharing of spirit across bodies between Daniel and Mordecai will also be a rewriting of Englishness and a blending of East and West in a utopian colonial Zion. The marriage between Daniel and Mirah becomes a secondary facilitator in this latter regard. We might say that Mirah's lack of depth is one with the imagined emptiness of Palestine.

This union between Mordecai and Daniel is the second occasion for Eliot's use of the Gothic body. In Chapter XXXIII, when Daniel first sees Mordecai in the bookshop, Mordecai's body is presented first as a kind of artefact, likened to a statue made of ivory which evokes the history of a racial community, from biblical Exile through medieval mysticism and the Inquisition to the great migration into London's East End. It is a strangely static body, uninvolved in sensation, its pleasures indirect and 'far off'. Immediately it is presented as radically separate from the larger spirit it carries. Mordecai startles Daniel by laying a hand on his arm. When he removes the hand it is 'as if some possessing spirit which had leaped into the eyes and gestures had sunk back again to the inmost recesses of the frame' (Eliot, 288). This spirit, which union with Mordecai will ultimately transfer to Daniel, is collective, historically timeless, and embedded transcendentally in the common body of the everyday.

Just as Catherine Arrowpoint's marriage encapsulates the novel's call for cultural transformation through the will of daughters, the 'philosopher's club' discussion in Chapter XLII balances and complicates all of the novel's central questions regarding heredity, race, nation and cultural inheritance. In an enactment of the lively discussion of cultural inheritance carried on throughout mid-century, culture is presented here as a spiritual transmission that embodies nation. This spirit is the specific haunting to which Daniel is subject, and Mordecai appears as its first ghostly visitation. As a consumptive poet and visionary, Mordecai is constructed specifically so as to invoke romanticist associations with the 'lamp' of Eastern culture and with visionary transformation. His enervated tubercular body, only half-containing the expansive spirit of his culture, enables Eliot's ultimate blending of Eastern and Western culture in the body of Daniel.

While the relation between Mordecai and Daniel is sometimes figured as 'maternal', it is also articulated specifically as a marriage. Mirah is positioned as a vehicle or conduit of this marriage, in a manner we might read through Eve Kosofsky Sedgwick: 'The two men clasped hands with a movement that seemed part of the flash from Mordecai's eyes, and passed through Mirah like an electric shock' (Eliot, 563). Mordecai tells Daniel, 'It has begun already—the marriage of our souls. It waits but the passing away of this body, and then they who are betrothed shall unite in a stricter bond, and what is mine shall be thine' (Eliot, 566).

Once Book V of *Deronda* appeared there was a heated discussion regarding Mordecai's character. Readers and reviewers expressed dissatisfaction with the turn the novel was taking. Many, deploying their knowledge of the conventions of the marriage plot, expected Daniel to marry Gwendolen. There were calls for the discovery that Mirah was Daniel's sister, or even for her death (Martin, 26, 211). Through the critical lens that reads pulmonary tuberculosis as a disease of female, or feminised, characters, the obvious question here would be why isn't Mirah Lapidoth consumptive? The established, almost the canonical, way to resolve the novel's two plots, would be to let Mirah die in as pure a state as she has lived, and to marry Daniel to Gwendolyn. Indeed, once the reading audience realised that Mirah would not turn out to be Daniel's sister, reviews of monthly volumes vocally call on Eliot to kill off Mirah so that Daniel could marry Gwendolyn. (Martin, 26, 256–7) Expressed as an objection to Eliot's subversion of the structure of the romance plot, this was in fact, of course, an objection to her subversion of English desires. It also assumes, as critics have continued to do, that Eliot is producing or ought to produce a unified narrative and a sense of closure which re-stabilises ideology in some manner.

Joseph Jacobs, an outspoken Jewish writer and, as Daniel Novak has pointed out, an acquaintance of Eliot and Lewes, is keen to pose Mordecai both as a tragic figure and as a perfectly possible realist type drawn from the life of the world. Jacobs counters the critical insistence that Jewish characters be relegated to the realm of the low and the comic, making the comparison to Shakespeare and calling the scene in which Mordecai awaits Daniel on Blackfriar's bridge 'Wagnerian'. Jacobs is another critic who interprets Eliot's characters through the realist notion of 'types', arguing that Mordecai is both ideally tragic and realistically possible (Jacobs, 101–111). Sentimental fiction and high tragedy are the continuum on which Eliot builds Mirah and Mordecai. Mordecai's consumption lends itself to just this vacillation. It enables the homo-cultural union between himself and Daniel while at the same time removing, through Mordecai's death and Mirah's passive life, any hint of the homoerotic. Daniel, Mordecai and Mirah form a continuum of feminised characters, possessing the receptivity that allows for the transmission of cultural spirit which is their endpoint. Sander Gilman argues that by 'the nineteenth century, male Jews are seen as feminised' and that this is viewed as the marker of racial inferiority. He also specifically relates this racialised and imperfect masculinity to the perceived prevalence of tuberculosis among Jewish people (Gilman, 60).

Mordecai's consumption is also very clearly allied to the Romantic tubercular masculinity which, through Keats and Shelley became strongly associated throughout the nineteenth century with visionary aesthetics, heightened sensibility and political dissent. Daniel is directly associated with Shelley during the long meditation on his history and psychology which forms Chapter XVI. He is repeatedly described in terms of a dissident feminised masculinity, and contrasted sympathetically with the robust English masculinity associated with positivism and empire. Daniel has 'the stamp of rarity in a subdued fervour of sympathy, an activity of imagination on behalf of others' (Eliot, 132). His study, his meditations on culture and his travels in Germany all associate him with the espousal of German Romanticism in British aesthetic discourse which formed such a strong counter-current to hegemonic masculinity in the period. Stefan Collini describes this structure of feeling in terms of the espousal of Romantic *bildung*: 'an openness to experience, a cultivation of the subjective response, and an exploratory attitude towards one's own individuality' (Collini, 103). Eliot describes Daniel in almost exactly these terms. In order to form the counterpoint to Daniel's dissident English gentlemanliness, both Mirah and Mordecai are rendered even more feminine.

This challenge to the English masculine ideal is one of the unifying threads that runs through *Deronda*'s 'two' plots, and in fact makes them one plot. Two English gentlemen focus these plots, Henleigh Mallinger Grandcourt and Daniel Deronda. Grandcourt is in every way a critique of upper-class masculinity in its legal, social, personal and aesthetic aspects. On the surface he looks well, behaves perfectly and occupies a position of nearly absolute power, yet Eliot quickly pulls aside the curtain and reveals what lies behind this masquerade. Grandcourt has received his inheritance through an entail which unfairly disinherits several young girls. Always behaving perfectly, he has no real sensibility or empathy. Outwardly the image of social propriety, he keeps a hidden mistress with two children towards whom he is cold and indifferent. He is decadent and 'flaccid', informing Lush that the difference between a common man and a gentleman is that rather than kicking his own dogs, a gentleman employs someone to kick his dogs for him. His only feeling or desire is for mastery and, significantly, his sympathies lie with the South in the American War and with white planters in Jamaica.

Daniel Deronda is by contrast an ideal English gentleman to the core. He is always ethical, deeply respectful towards women and impoverished people, thoughtful, intelligent and almost too full of sensibility. He is not, however, hereditarily English, occupies no position of power and has no significant monetary inheritance. In the end his inheritance is revealed to be spiritual, literary and pan-European. Through Daniel, we understand that 'Englishness' is a learned quality, culturally constructed and a matter of choice, or perhaps vocation. Discussing his future with his adopted father, Sir Hugo, Daniel says, '"I want to be an Englishman, but I want to understand other points of view. And I want to get rid of a merely English attitude in studies"' (Eliot, 136). This immediately follows one of many conversations in the novel where characters share opinions on the uses of culture. Taken together these many conversations add up to a complex reflection on cultural inheritance and the formation of those qualities which pertain to race and nation. Daniel as hereditarily Jewish and culturally English, focuses the novel's ultimate call, for a blending of Englishness with 'ancient' cultures of the 'East' in the making of modern nations.

Eliot's various uses of the marriage plot in *Daniel Deronda* are an entwined doing and undoing of ideologies of gender and empire. The novel's two interwoven plots, far from lacking integration, enable a critique of the relation between gender and empire. While each of the two plots demonstrates the ideological limitations of its chosen fictional strategies, together they form a companionate marriage of plots which exceeds the limitations of each. The problem of feminine will and its subjugation exists only for the English women in the novel, chiefly Gwendolen, Lydia Glasher and Catherine Arrowpoint. Neither Gwendolen nor Mirah possesses action or voice, but this is presented as a problem only for Gwendolen, whose psychology erupts in Gothic fashion into the narrative. Like Palestine, Mirah is presented as an empty space, without will of her own and thus available for the reception of British men of action. These problems keep a conflicted discussion of *Deronda* alive, because it is a determined and complex attempt to trouble increasingly racialised constructions of nation and culture.

Susan Meyer argues that Eliot transfers closure from one of these plots to the other, using Daniel to enact Gwendolen's escape. Constructing this transference from one plot to another, Meyer then reads a single narrative resolution, an ideological closure which 'solves the problem of disjunction between the self and the culture by creating an idealized alternative culture' (Meyer, 737–8). But we can only read the novel in this way if we ignore the variety of narrative strategies at work and read its two plots as separate and transferable. Gwendolen's narrative, deploying both Eliot's powerful psychological realism and the effects of the popular Gothic, purposefully undoes the marriage plot and allies that undoing to a critique of national and imperial economies. She does not resolve Gwendolen's plot in the way she does Catherine Arrowpoint's plot because her project relies specifically on undoing the narrative structure of romance, and revealing English marriage as degenerate and pathological. This plot is made to reveal the relation between romantic fiction, national ideology and the lives of English women. Daniel's narrative depicts a radical blending of culture by using the strategies of sentimental fiction to enact a marriage undisturbed by any eruptions of will on the part of its heroine. Together these plots, problematic as they remain, form a pointed critique of ideals of English national and cultural heredity. Eliot married them in this way because she was aware of the specific ideological uses of the marriage plot in its various generic manifestations, and sought to use them against each other. *Daniel Deronda* is very much one novel.

Works Cited

Athenaeum. 'Novels of the Week', Review. July, 1876, 14–15.
Brontë, Charlotte. *Jane Eyre*. London: Smith, Elder, 1847.
Collini, Stefan. *Public Moralists: Political Thought and Intellectual Life in Britain, 1850–1930*. Oxford: Clarendon, 1993.
Eliot, George. *Adam Bede*. Edinburgh: John Blackwood, 1859.
Eliot, George. *Daniel Deronda*. Edinburgh: John Blackwood, 1876
Eliot, George. *Middlemarch*. Edinburgh: John Blackwood, 1872
Francillon, Robert Edward. 'George Eliot's First Romance', *The Gentleman's Magazine*, Oct, 1876, 411–27.
Gilman, Sander. *Health and Illness: Images of Difference*. London: Reaktion, 1995.
Gissing, George. *A Life's Morning*. London: Smith, Elder, 1888.
Gissing, George. *The Crown of Life*. London: Methuen, 1899.
Irwin, Jane (ed). *George Eliot's 'Daniel Deronda' Notebooks*. Cambridge: Cambridge University Press, 1996.
Jacobs, Joseph. 'Mordecai: A Protest Against the Critics', *Macmillan's*, Vol 36 (June, 1877) pp 101–11.
James, Henry. 'Daniel Deronda: A Conversation', *Atlantic Monthly*, Vol 38 (December, 1876), 684–94.
Leavis, F.R., *The Great Tradition: George Eliot, Henry James, Joseph Conrad*. London: Chatto and Windus, 1962.
Martin, Carol A. *George Eliot's Serial Fiction*. Columbus: Ohio State University Press, 1994.
Meyer, Susan. '"Safely to Their Own Borders": Proto-Zionism, Feminism and Nationalism in *Daniel Deronda*' *ELH*, Vol 60, No 3 (1993), pp 733–58.
Novak, Daniel. '"Literary Photographs" and the Jewish Body in *Daniel Deronda*', *Representations*, Vol 85, No 1 (2004), 58–97.
Sedgwick, Eve Kosofsky. *Between Men: English Literature and Male Homosocial Desire*. New York: Columbia University Press, 1985.
Trollope, Anthony. *He Knew He Was Right*. London: Strahan, 1869.
Trollope, Anthony. *The Prime Minister*. London: Chapman & Hall, 1876.
Vrettos, Athena. *Somatic Fictions: Imagining Illness in Victorian Culture*. Stanford, CA: Stanford University Press, 1995.

8 Margaret Oliphant on Marriage and Its Discontents

Joanne Shattock

Widowed in her early thirties, the novelist Margaret Oliphant (1828–97) had much time to reflect on her own marriage, and on the institution, in the course of her long and productive writing life. Her posthumously published *Autobiography* (1899) recalled her early married life, a mainly happy time that was subsequently clouded by the sense of betrayal she felt when her husband, a stained glass designer, deliberately kept the diagnosis of his fatal tuberculosis from her while persuading her to take their young family to Italy in search of a warmer climate. Frank Oliphant's death in Rome in the winter of 1859 left her pregnant with their third child, in debt, and without any obvious means of supporting herself and her children other than by her writing.

Oliphant's output of ninety-eight full-length novels and more than fifty works of short fiction gave her ample opportunity to distil her own experience and her observations of the pressures on women in the second half of the nineteenth century. She was too good a novelist to recreate her own life story transparently in her fiction, but looking at her oeuvre overall there are portraits of less than perfect marriages, of able women married to men of inferior talents, and of women burdened financially by male relations. She also fed into the mix her admiration of independent women, those who like herself had built successful careers without male support and who were the heads of their own households.

In her fiction, written over nearly half a century, she turned a critical eye on marriage, on women coerced by their families to marry for social advantage, on women subjected to cruelty at the hands of their husbands, on women for whom marriage was the be-all and end-all of existence, on others, for whom marriage was a disappointment, and on women dominated by egotistical or selfish husbands. She also presented alternatives, women who whether by choice or necessity, created satisfying independent lives without men. All of these topics have received attention from her biographers and critics.[1]

Oliphant also articulated her views on marriage and women's place within it, on divorce and on other issues related to what became known as the 'Woman Question' in a series of trenchant articles in major journals from the 1850s to the 1880s, decades which saw a number of reforms to the legal position of women. She initiated these articles herself, rather than being commissioned to write them, prompted by a current controversy, a legislative reform, or in some cases, a relevant publication. In this chapter I examine her articles on the 'Woman Question' written over a period of nearly four decades. I then focus on two powerful and little-known novels written in the 1880s, *The Ladies Lindores* (1883) and its sequel, the novella *Lady Car* (1889), which reflect contemporary views on marriage, the impact of recent reforms to women's legal position and the limited power of women to resist societal pressures and the demands of family.

Oliphant and the 'Woman Question'

Oliphant's first foray into contemporary women's issues was written in response to Barbara Leigh Smith's pamphlet *A Brief Summary in Plain Language of the Most Important Laws Concerning Women* (1854). The pamphlet, which was widely circulated, argued for the reform of the laws relating to married women's property. Oliphant had been approached by Mary Howitt to sign a petition organized by Leigh Smith, urging that a bill be put before Parliament, but had hesitated.

Her article, 'The Laws Concerning Women', published in *Blackwood's Magazine* in April 1856, was her response to Leigh Smith and her colleagues, a response that she feared would appear 'unhandsome' if her authorship was known, she told John Blackwood, the magazine's editor (Blackwood Papers 4119, ff. 57, 67). Writing anonymously and adopting a masculine persona, she was lukewarm in her endorsement of the proposed bill. She acknowledged that there might be exceptional circumstances in which married women needed protection, but she disagreed completely with the premise of Leigh Smith's pamphlet, that upon marriage a woman's existence was 'entirely absorbed' in that of her husband. This was 'a mere trick of words'. By their marriage vows husband and wife became one: 'In truth and in nature – with the reality of sober fact and without romancing – these two people set their hands to it, that they are no longer two people, but one person' (Oliphant 1856, 145–6).

Her real target in the article was not the proposed bill to protect married women's property, but the Matrimonial Causes Act that would become law the following year. She was sceptical of the power of legislation to alleviate unhappiness, a common theme in her articles. Moreover she was utterly opposed to divorce where children were involved. 'The law compels no one, either man or woman, to enter into this perilous estate of marriage; but being once within it, it is the law's first duty to hedge this important territory round with its strongest and highest barriers', she began:

> For it is not the question of the wife's earnings or the wife's property which lies nearest the heart of this controversy: there are the

children – living witnesses of the undividableness of the parents [...]
The law can give back to the disappointed wife her *chattels real,*
because the law took them from her. The law can secure to the separated woman an unquestionable right to her own earnings; but the
law cannot secure to her her children. Nature has not made *her*
their sole possessor. God has not given to the mother a special and
peculiar claim. It is hard but it is true. The law might confer upon
her the right to bereave her husband of this dearest possession, as it
now gives him the right to bereave her; but the law can only, by so
doing, favour one unfair claim to the disadvantage of another; for in
this matter right and justice are impossible.

(Oliphant 1856, 147–8)

The only solution in the case of divorce, she suggested, was for the children to become wards of the state.

This was the crux of Oliphant's argument about divorce law reform;
like many of her contemporaries, the issue of married women's property became entangled with the divorce issue. Her position had not altered when she returned to the subject of the Matrimonial Causes Act
'that abominable marriage business', as she referred to it in a letter to
Blackwood, two years later (Blackwood Papers, 4725, f.189). In 'The
Condition of Women', published in *Blackwood's* in February 1858 she
acknowledged that the new act achieved 'theoretical justice' in making
divorce no longer the privilege of the very wealthy, but she regarded divorce as a remedy only 'in cases horrible and extreme':

We can conceive no circumstances, for our own part, which could
make the position of a woman, who had divorced her husband, tolerable to the ordinary feelings of the women of this country. So far
as women are concerned, it must always remain the dreadful alternative of an evil which has such monstrous and unnatural aggravations as to be beyond all limits of possible endurance. We [...] can
suppose, that for women without children the new regulations must
be all that could be desired. But who shall open the terrible compli-
cation of the rights of fathers and mothers? What Solomon shall ven-
ture to divide between the two that most precious and inalienable of
all treasures, the unfortunate child whose very existence stands as a
ceaseless protest of nature against their disjunction?.

(Oliphant 1858, 174–5)

Oliphant returned to the subject of marriage and women's place in it
in 1869, in a review of John Stuart Mill's *The Subjection of Women*
(1869) and of the social reformer Josephine Butler's collection of essays
on *Woman's Work and Woman's Culture* (1869). This time she published her article in the *Edinburgh Review*. Three years earlier, in an

article on 'The Great Unrepresented' in *Blackwood's* she had responded robustly and negatively to Mill's proposal to extend the franchise to single women property owners, a bill that he presented to Parliament in June 1866. As in her earlier article she was respectful of Mill as a philosopher and a dominant figure of the age, but when it came to the argument of his book, that in their subjugation to men women were little better than slaves, she concluded that his judgment had been 'warped by theory', and that it was difficult to reconcile 'the gloomy image conjured up in the philosopher's study' with 'the fresh daylight outside' (Oliphant 1869, 454–5). She challenged his view that to repeal the laws subjecting women to the legal authority of their husbands, and to place both sexes on a footing of external equality would solve all problems. But she acknowledged that the present state of marriage law in England had done 'a great and universal injury' to all women, 'the injury of an insult'. The proposed Married Women's Property Law offered 'a remedy which will cancel the sentimental grievance, and do as much for the real evil as can be done in this life' (Oliphant 1869, 457).

Oliphant also resisted Mill's argument that men and women were equal; the difference in physical strength alone precluded equality. So too did childbearing. 'A woman is a woman, and not a lesser edition of man', she argued. They are 'not rivals nor antagonists'; they are 'two halves of a complete being' (Oliphant 1869, 459). Within marriage they possessed an equality not recognized by Mill: 'the equality of common sacrifices, common self-denials, mutual aids, interposition of the strength of one to succour the weakness of another, of the service of one to recompense the fatigues of another, of perpetual interchange, sympathy and help' (Oliphant 1869, 463).

The one constituency on whose behalf Oliphant supported Mill's argument for higher education, entry into the professions, and even the vote for women, was the class of cultivated, able, mature single women, a group that included widows, of whom she was now one. The latter were often the sole breadwinners in the family and were also householders. These women, she agreed, were entitled to the privileges extended to male householders, whose numbers had been significantly increased with the recent Reform Act of 1867. There was no reason why unmarried women should not enter the professions, medicine in particular, or assume wider public roles, but it was a path that would be followed only by exceptional women:

> Let the women who stand apart from woman's natural existence be it by choice, be it by necessity, be permitted to assume men's privileges if they choose. And what then, oh daughters of Eve? The most of you will still be wives, will still be mothers all the same, will still lie under nature's own disabilities and be trusted with nature's high responsibilities, and have your work to do, which no man is capable

of doing instead of you. Legislation may help the surplus, the exceptional women [...] but for the majority, legislation can do little and revolution nothing at all.

(Oliphant 1869, 473)

Oliphant's position on some aspects of the 'Woman Question' had subtly shifted. She no longer opposed the vote for single women householders. She supported unmarried women's entry into medicine, although she was conscious of the sacrifices and the challenges this would involve. A letter to the editor of the *Spectator* on 7 March 1874, headed 'The Rights of Women' and signed 'M', signalled a further shift in her mood. The letter was prompted by an attack on American women temperance campaigners in the *Pall Mall Gazette*, which she saw as symptomatic of current masculine condescension towards women. She had been antagonistic, she confessed, to much of what had passed under the banner of women's rights, but she had become 'weary of the ceaseless impertinencies which your contemporaries think it right and in good taste to level at all women, because they have, or think they have fit cause of objection against a few'. 'I for one, am so weary of being abused, and set down as an impersonation of absolute folly, inconsideration, and unreason', she continued, 'that I begin to ask myself whether the theories of Mr John Stuart Mill on the subject are really so fantastic and contradictory to experience as I once thought them' (Oliphant 1874, 475, 477). This was a significant admission on her part.

Oliphant published her final article on women's issues, 'The Grievances of Women', in *Fraser's Magazine* in 1880, at the beginning of a decade which would see further public debate on women's rights, and the passing of the second Married Women's Property Act in 1882. In it she further reinforced her sense of the injustice of commonly held views of women and their role within marriage. The 'first, and largest and most fundamental' of all the grievances of women, she argued, was that 'they never have, since the world began, got the credit of that share of the work of the world which has fallen naturally to them and which they have, on the whole, faithfully performed through all vicissitudes' (Oliphant 1880, 220). She was not referring to the professions, but to work in the home, which was acknowledged to be their sphere:

A man's wife is considered to be his dependent, fed and clothed by him of his free will and bounty, and all the work that she does in fulfilment of the natural conditions of their marriage is considered as of no account whatever in the matter. He works, but she does not; he toils to maintain her, while she sits at home in ease and leisure, and enjoys the fruits of his labour, and gives him ornamental compensation in smiles and pleasantness. This is the representation of married life which is universally accepted.

(Oliphant 1880, 224)

She concluded by reiterating that no amount of legislation could redress women's most urgent grievance, the general feeling that 'whatever
women do, in the general, is undervalued by men in the general, because
it is done by women' (Oliphant 1880, 230).

Oliphant made one further intervention, on divorce, in her column
'A Commentary from an Easy-Chair' in the *Spectator* for 25 January
1890, noting a recent trend towards more liberal divorce laws in some
American states, and also in Australia, where it was proposed that men
and women could be separated on grounds of incompatibility alone.
This was owing, she concluded 'to a curious and touching sympathy
with women which has sprung up of late in the minds of men [...] as
if they had newly discovered the additional ills to which women are
subject, and were wonderfully sorry all at once for the sufferings which
they never thought of before'. Such sentiments, she concluded were more
likely in newer nations where women were in the minority and therefore
more 'prized and precious'. These nations would learn from more mature ones, 'that the art of putting up with our troubles is a very fine art,
and, on the whole, better for the human race than lightly shaking them
off: and that to rush in and out of matrimony and lessen the sanctity
of that bond, is a much worse thing than individual vexation, or even,
which is worse, individual misery' (Oliphant 1890, 295).

As a novelist, Oliphant was by no means unique in joining in debates
about the 'Woman Question', but unlike her contemporaries Dinah Craik
and Eliza Lynn Linton, and later Mona Caird, all of whom achieved
recognition, if not notoriety, for their interventions, Oliphant never became a public figure in the debates. Nevertheless her articles are useful in
tracing the gradual shift in her views on married women's right to their
own property, on women's entry into the professions, and on women
householders' entitlement to the vote. She seems never to have changed
her opposition to divorce, except where there were circumstances 'beyond all limits of possible endurance' and even then she preferred a form
of legal separation. Nor did she resolve in her own mind the ultimate fate
of children in a divorce.

The Ladies Lindores

Oliphant's articles confirm that she was attuned to the political issues
of her day which concerned women, the campaigns, petitions and the
ongoing legislative reforms. Her novel *The Ladies Lindores*, written in
1881–2 and serialized in *Blackwood's* from April 1882 to May 1883,
reflects the impact of the Married Women's Property Act of 1870, and
the climate of the 1870s and early 1880s in which so much legislation
affecting women's position in marriage was either enacted or mooted.

The Ladies Lindores, like many of Oliphant's novels, has a Scottish
setting, but it is unusual in that it is set in the present day. The plot

centres on the marriage of Lady Caroline Lindores, the elder daughter of a family of minor Scottish gentry, whose fortunes changed when their father unexpectedly succeeded to the title on the death of his elder brother. The Lindores were living in genteel but straightened circumstances on the continent, where Carry fell in love with Edward Beaufort, a young university don of limited means, who shared her intellectual interests. Their marriage might have taken place, the narrator suggests, if the Lindores' social position had not suddenly changed, causing the new Lord Lindores to use his daughter to improve their position still further by an advantageous marriage.

His choice is Pat Torrance, whose family fortune was built on coal mining, a coarse, brutal and socially ambitious man who sees in 'Lady Car', as he calls her, a wife who will add lustre to his family through her aristocratic lineage and her penchant for intellectual pursuits. Carry begs her father not to force her to marry Torrance, but he is adamant, insisting that it is in her own best interests:

> Before a word had been said she knew her fate, struggling dumbly against it like a creature fascinated and magnetized in the grip of a monster, but without any possibility or hope of escape [...] She felt herself sucked in as to a whirlpool, overpowered, — all her forces taken from her in the giddy rush with which the days and hours were carrying her on.
>
> (*The Ladies Lindores*, ch. 5, 40)

Carry's mother, Lady Lindores, is appalled by her husband's lack of sympathy and deeply disturbed by the revelation of a new side to his character:

> It would be in vain to attempt to describe the struggle that followed; that domestic tragedy would have to be told at length if told at all, and it included various tragedies; not only the subjugation of poor Carry, the profanation of her life, and cruel rending of her heart, but such a gradual enlightening and clearing away of all the lovely prejudices and prepossessions of affection from the eyes of Lady Lindores as was almost as cruel. The end of it was, that one of these poor women, broken in heart and spirit, forced into a marriage she hated, and feeling herself outraged and degraded, began her life in bitterness and misery with a pretence of splendour and success and good fortune which made the real state of affairs still more deplorable; and the other, feeling all the beauty of her life gone from her, her eyes disenchanted, a pitiless cold daylight revealing every angle once hid by the glamour of love and tender fancy, began a sort of second existence alone.
>
> (*The Ladies Lindores*, ch. 5, 50)

Lady Lindores' awakening to her husband's callous disregard for his daughter's feelings is succeeded by a realisation of her own helplessness, as she tells her younger daughter:

'God knows, I would not mind what I did if it was only me. I would fly away with her somewhere – escape from them all. But what would happen? Our family would be rent asunder. Your father and I' — Lady Lindores's voice quivered a little – 'who have always been so united, would part forever. Our family quarrels would be discussed in public. You, Edith – what would become of you? Your prospects would all be ruined. Carry herself would be torn to pieces by the gossips. They would say there must be some reason. God knows, I would not hesitate at any sacrifice'.

(*The Ladies Lindores*, ch. 5, 51)

Caroline's inability to make her father understand her loathing of Torrance and to take a stand against the marriage is mirrored in her mother's ultimate failure to support her. Mother and daughter are similar in temperament, fond of poetry and the arts, interests that are considered feminine by a society that has little regard for them. They are united, too, in their ultimate passivity.

The tensions in the Lindores family are not between the generations but between the sexes. Robin Lindores, now Lord Rintoul, supports his father's determination to secure good marriages for his daughters, considering it men's duty to 'look after the girls' because they are not qualified to choose husbands for themselves. On the other hand he believes that 'a man has a right to please himself as to who he's going to marry' (*The Ladies Lindores*, ch. 47, 346), a conviction that will have its own consequences. He stresses the urgency of finding a suitable husband for his sister Edith, telling his mother: 'She's past her first bloom (and that's mostly the thing that fetches) [...] she's twenty-one, mother'. The spirited Edith, a striking contrast to her elder sister, senses her brother's intentions and asks: 'Did you bring me to London to market? [...] Did you come to set up a booth in Vanity Fair? If you did, you must find other wares' (*The Ladies Lindores*, ch. 13, 109–10).

One of the sub-plots of the novel involves Edith's defiance of her father by refusing to accept an offer of marriage from a Duke's son, an offer which even her mother favours. The stakes in the marriage market for the upper classes are high. Individual feelings are secondary to parental ambition, social status and financial settlements.

The denouement of the story is as shocking as it is unexpected and owes much to the way in which Oliphant structures her narrative. When the novel opens, Carry and Torrance have been married for five years. The circumstances leading to their marriage are revealed in a flashback. Motherhood has brought some solace to Carry but her husband's boorish behaviour and obsessive jealousy have cowed her into a listlessness that borders on illness. When Torrance, somewhat the worse for drink, plunges to his death in a ravine after a quarrel with Rintoul, her response is one of joy: 'Oh, my innocent mother!' she cried. 'Oh, mother! you only know such troubles as angels may have. Look at me! look at me! I am like a mad woman. I am keeping myself in, as you say, that I may not go mad – with joy!' She goes on:

> To think I shall never be subject to all *that* any more—that he can never come in here again – that I am free – that I can be alone. Oh, mother, how can you tell what it is? Never to be alone: never to have a corner in the world where – someone else has not a right to come, a better right than yourself. I do not know how I have borne it. I don't know how I can have lived, disgusted, loathing myself. No, no; sometime else I shall be sorry when I have time to think, when I can forget what it is that has happened to me – but in the meantime I am too happy – too.
> (*The Ladies Lindores*, ch. 29, 223)

The impact of the scene is not in what is said, but in what Carry implies about the nature of their intimate relationship, as Lady Lindores realizes: 'Never in her life had she come in contact with feeling so absolute, subdued by no sense of natural fitness, or even by right and wrong' (*The Ladies Lindores*, ch. 29, 224). Carry's recovery is swift, and is succeeded by a new resolve to stand up to her father, who expects to resume his control over her life. 'I was left desolate when you brought me here—five years – five dreadful years ago', she tells him. 'But now I have neither father nor mother […] I am in my own right; my life is my own, and, my children; I will be directed no more' (*The Ladies Lindores*, ch. 36, 274). Her new-found defiance includes not only her resolve to look after her children herself, but to marry Edward Beaufort, a marriage which her parents think highly inappropriate, given her recent widowhood. 'Don't you think there is a time', Caroline asks her mother, 'when obedience – is reasonable no more?' (The Ladies Lindores, ch. 46, 340).

The Torrance marriage is central to Oliphant's story, but other marriages come under scrutiny, including that of Lord and Lady Lindores, as has been shown. Against his own better judgment, Lord Rintoul proposes to Nora Barrington, whose family have no connections, aware that as the heir he ought to make a more propitious alliance. He cannot see the inconsistency, which his mother points out, of his opposition to Edith's marriage to John Erskine, whose family estate is modest. 'Erskine's a gentleman, but that's all you can say. She will never be anybody if she marries him', he tells her (*The Ladies Lindores*, ch. 47, 349).

The legal and financial aspects of marriage are a constant point of reference in the novel. Torrance cuts a hard bargain in drawing up the marriage settlement because he is angered by Carry's initial refusal of his suit. Later Lord Lindores notes with satisfaction that he had done Carry 'noble justice' (*The Ladies Lindores*, ch. 36, 273) in his will, leaving her in sole control of his estate during her son's minority, without conditions. He nevertheless regards her estate as his to direct, a situation he intends to use to advance himself politically:

> He began to employ and turn to his own advantage the important influence of the Tinto estate, which he, as the little heir's grandfather, was certainly entitled, he thought, to consider as his own. Little Tommy was but four; and though, by a curious oversight, Lord Lindores had not been named as a guardian, he was, of course, in the circumstances, his daughter's natural guardian, who was Tommy's [...] and with Tinto in his hands, as well as Lindores, no man in the county could stand against him.
>
> (*The Ladies Lindores*, ch. 46, 337)

From Carry's revelations to her mother, it is clear that her marriage contained the 'monstrous and unnatural aggravations [...] beyond all limits of possible endurance' that Oliphant identified as the only possible justification for divorce in her 1858 article on 'The Condition of Women'. But until her husband's death Carry gave no hint that her suffering was owing to more than his domineering manner and obsessive jealousy, which were publicly on display. For the purposes of her novel, Oliphant chose an accidental death to end the marriage instead of separation or divorce, perhaps because there were children involved, but more likely because it made it easier to introduce the possibility of a second marriage.

The Ladies Lindores ends with several marriages, presented in contrasting registers. Lord Millefleurs, the heir to an English dukedom, who had pursued Edith Lindores with her parents' encouragement, ultimately defies his father and marries an opinionated middle-aged American lady without a fortune. Edith marries John Erskine, and Lord Rintoul marries Nora Barrington, neither marriage receiving universal approval. Rolls, Erskine's devoted butler, opines gloomily that 'Marriages, in my opinion, is what most shakes your faith in Providence. It's just the devil that's at the bottom o' them, so far as I can see' (The Ladies Lindores, ch. 49, 368).

But the marriage that concludes the novel, and which sets the tone of the ending is that of Carry and Beaufort. In the penultimate chapter, Lady Lindores hesitantly suggests that Beaufort had done nothing to prevent her marriage to Torrance: 'There were things he might have done – he ought to have been ready to claim you before – to oppose your –', but Carry will hear none of it. The chapter concludes with Lady Lindores's reflections:

> What did Carry believe? That her old love would renew for her all the happiness of life [...] that the one dream of humanity, the

romance which is never worn out and never departs, was now to be fulfilled for her? – or that, even into this dream, the canker had entered, the sense that happiness was not and never could be?

(*The Ladies Lindores*, ch. 48, 363)

The marriage takes place in London a year later with only Lady Lindores as a witness. The novel ends with a question posed by the narrator: 'was it a life of hope fulfilled, or of ever increasing and deepening disappointment, which lay before Carry's tremulous feet? They were not the assured feet of a believing and confident bride' (*The Ladies Lindores*, ch. 49, 368).

What resonates with the reader even more than the discordant view of marriage presented in the final chapters is the revelation of Lady Caroline's abusive relationship with her first husband and Oliphant's remorseless scrutiny of the society which condoned such a marriage, where parental ambition, family pride and acquisitiveness outweigh individual feelings and the freedom of women to choose their own husbands.

Lady Car

Oliphant clearly left the way open to write a sequel to *The Ladies Lindores*, but there is no evidence that this was uppermost in her mind in the ensuing six years, years in which she suffered intense personal unhappiness owing to the declining health of her elder son, and the failure of both sons to fulfil the potential she had seen in them. Her work schedule, as usual, was unrelenting. She wrote *Lady Car* in the spring and summer of 1889, squeezing it in, as Josie Billington notes, between completing her biography of John Tulloch (1888) for Blackwood and beginning her novel *Kirsteen* (1890) for Macmillan.[2] The novella was serialised in five parts in *Longman's Magazine* from March to July 1889.

It stands up well to an independent reading, but the reader's experience is undoubtedly enriched by prior knowledge of the characters of Carry and Edward Beaufort, and the circumstances that have led to their late marriage. The reader is made aware of the source of Carry's immense wealth, bequeathed to her by her first husband in trust for their elder son. Shortly after the story opens the couple move into a luxurious new home, the refurbishments of which include an elegant library for Beaufort, in which he can write undisturbed, surrounded by his books. Unusually for Oliphant, the decade in which the story is set is made explicit. We are told that Beaufort has made it clear at the time of his marriage that Carry's own money should remain with her, and that he would play no part in the spending of it. His own small income was sufficient for his personal needs. The narrator adds: 'He lived a fairy life, without any necessity for money, his house kept for him, his living all arranged, everything that he wanted or could desire coming without a thought; but he preserved his feeling of independence by having nothing to do with

its expenditure' (*Lady Car*, ch. 4, 167). In other words, Beaufort makes
an elaborate pretence of allowing Carry to have control of her own personal wealth, which according to the 1870 Married Women's Property
Act would have passed to him automatically on their marriage. It was
only the 1882 Act that entitled married women to the same privileges as
unmarried women, that of retaining their own property after marriage.
Whatever the legal position, Beaufort accustoms himself to the luxurious lifestyle his wife provides.

The great literary career that Carry envisaged for Beaufort does not
develop. He spends his days in desultory reading and going to his London
club. When a new book is published that covers some of the ground that
he intended to write about, he resolves at first to write a stinging review,
and send it 'to Bowles [...] meaning "The Nineteenth Century" of that
day'. The narrator interjects, 'Of course, "The Nineteenth Century"
itself had not yet begun its dignified career' (*Lady Car*, ch. 8, 191), thus
clumsily making it clear to well-informed readers that the story is set before 1877, when the famous monthly review was established. The book
review is not written, and it becomes obvious that Beaufort has neither
the inclination nor the talent for a literary life.

Carry's own life is equally devoid of purpose. Her relationship with
her children is troubled, particularly that with her son Tom, who shows
worrying signs of having inherited his father's boorishness. Beaufort has
some success in curbing his loutish behaviour, whereas the boy treats
his mother with contempt. Much of the critical discussion of *Lady Car*
focuses on what are interpreted as autobiographical elements, namely
Oliphant's own troubled relationship with her sons, whose careers had
not prospered despite their privileged education, and whose increasingly
dissolute behaviour was reminiscent of that of her alcoholic brother
Willie. A visit to St Andrews, where Carry experiences a moment of
spiritual calm in the midst of her worries has echoes of Oliphant's own
experience, also at St Andrews and recounted in her *Autobiography*,
when she too was under strain because of her children.[3]

One crucial episode that critics have overlooked is a scene earlier in
the narrative in which Carry's patience with Beaufort's lack of purpose
snaps, exacerbated by her sense that he has forgotten their shared idealism and commitment to social reform. She links this state of indolence
with his failure to act when her father was forcing her to marry a man
she did not love. Her accusation is unspoken: 'Why did you leave me
to be another man's wife? Why let me be strained, humbled, trodden
under foot? Why expose me to all the degradations which nobody could
impose on you – and why, why?' (*Lady Car*, ch. 7, 187–88). After the
tears and brief illness that follow Beaufort is shocked to perceive a subtle
change in her, which he then dismisses.

Elaine Showalter, one of the first critics to discern in *The Ladies Lindores* and *Lady Car* a more honest portrayal of female emotions than

in most mid-nineteenth-century novels, nevertheless berates Oliphant for making Caroline Lindores 'a perfect lump of female passivity' (Showalter, 178). 'What does Lady Car do with her freedom and solitude?' she asks. 'Educate herself, plan to remain independent, teach her children not to make the same mistakes? Nothing whatever [...] In the sequel we find her remarried, this time for "love", and just as unhappy' (Showalter, 179). One solution open to the novelist, Showalter suggests, was for the heroine to 'stop searching for her happiness in others, and begin trying to generate it through her own accomplishments'. But Oliphant decided otherwise. As a result, 'Lady Car is, in fact, a parasite' (Showalter, 180). This reading of Lady Car's decline and premature death is to ignore her profound sense of disappointment in Beaufort, the seeds of which are hinted at in the end of *The Ladies Lindores* and which becomes a reality in the scene I have alluded to. Beaufort has failed her a second time, in having no ability or apparently no desire to shape his own life, to act when it matters. His is the fatal passivity, not hers. Her disappointment in him is compounded by her growing realisation that her children are becoming more and more like their father, both in appearance and behaviour.

Critics, Showalter included, are right in identifying autobiographical elements in *Lady Car* that contribute to the weakness of the ending. Oliphant's anxiety about her sons, and the impending death of her elder son Cyril contributed indirectly to the sense of defeat which overwhelms Caroline Lindores and leads to her premature death. But nevertheless the novella, together with *The Ladies Lindores*, constitutes a remarkable argument about contemporary marriage and the pressures faced by modern women, pressures that legislative reform could do little to remove.

Conclusion

The impact of Oliphant's two novels, and many others in which marriage features, is reinforced by her articles on the 'Woman Question', in which she supported the reform of married women's property law and recognized that in certain cases, marriages must end in divorce or separation. Nevertheless, as she constantly reiterated, she thought that marriage remained the most likely role for women in the second half of the nineteenth century.

Oliphant was not a campaigner, nor did she anticipate that there would be any response to her articles. Most were unsigned, as was the policy of *Blackwood's Magazine* and the *Edinburgh Review*, but her authorship *was* known in certain circles. Barbara Leigh Smith, later Bodichon, angered by the inference in Oliphant's 1866 article 'The Great Unrepresented' that a petition she organized in support of extending the franchise to single women householders had attracted very few signatures, responded directly in her *Objections to the Enfranchisement of Women Considered* (1866).[4] Her 1880 article 'The Grievances of Women', signed 'M. O. W. O.', was prompted, she confessed in the opening paragraph, by her failure to attend a meeting in London on women's suffrage, primarily because she disliked speaking in public and feared being ridiculed by men.

The theme of that article, men's condescension towards women and their failure to respect their opinions, their talents and their work in the home is reflected in *The Ladies Lindores* and its sequel just as the legislation of the 1870s and 1880s indirectly influenced their plots. Oliphant's views on contemporary marriage are all the more significant because they can be tracked not only through her prodigious fictional output but also in her journalism. She was a writer who was abreast of the women's issues of her day and who made her views known.

Notes

1 See Elisabeth Jay, '*Mrs Oliphant. 'A Fiction to* Herself'. Oxford: Clarendon Press, 1995, esp. Part I, Women and Men, pp 11–138; Valerie Sanders, 'Marriage and the Antifeminist Woman Novelist', in Nicola Diane Thompson, ed., *Victorian Women Writers and the Woman Question*. Cambridge: Cambridge University Press, 1999, pp 24–41; Elsie Michie, *The Vulgar Question of Money. Heiresses, Materialism, and the Novel of Manners from Jane Austen to Henry James*. Baltimore, MD: Johns Hopkins University Press, 2011, ch. 4, 'Margaret Oliphant and the Professional Ideal', pp 142–78.
2 See Introduction to *Lady Car*, ed. Josie Billington, *Selected Works*, Vol 10, *Novellas*. London: Pickering & Chatto, 2013, p xliii.
3 See Introduction, *Lady Car*, pp xxiii–xxv.
4 See the Headnote to 'The Great Unrepresented', *Selected Works*, Vol 1, p 349.

Works Cited

Blackwood Papers, 1805–1900. National Library of Scotland. MSS 4119 [1856], 4725 [1858].
Oliphant, Margaret. 'The Laws Concerning Women', *Blackwood's Magazine*, Vol 79 (April 1856), pp 379–87, rptd *Selected Works* Vol 1, *Literary Criticism 1854–69*, Joanne Shattock ed., 2011, pp 141–56.
Oliphant, Margaret. 'The Condition of Women', *Blackwood's Magazine*, Vol 83 (February 1858), pp 139–54, rptd *Selected Works*, Vol 1, pp 155–77.
Oliphant, Margaret. 'The Great Unrepresented', *Blackwood's Magazine*, Vol 100 (September 1866), pp 367–79, rptd *Selected Works*, Vol 1, pp 349–66.
Oliphant, Margaret. 'The Subjection of Women', *Edinburgh Review*, Vol 130 (October 1869), pp 572–602, rptd *Selected Works*, Vol 1, pp 449–75.
Oliphant, Margaret. 'The Rights of Women', *Spectator*, Vol 47 (7 March 1874), pp 301–2, rptd *Selected Works*, Vol 2, *Literary Criticism 1870–76*, Joanne Wilkes ed., 2011, pp 473–77.
Oliphant, Margaret. 'The Grievances of Women', *Fraser's Magazine*, Vol 101 (May 1880), pp 698–710, rptd *Selected Works*, Vol 3, *Literary Criticism 1877–86*, Valerie Sanders ed., 2011, pp 213–30.

Oliphant, Margaret. *The Ladies Lindores*. Josie Billington ed., *Selected Works*, Vol 24, 2016.

Oliphant, Margaret. *Lady Car*. Josie Billington ed., *Selected Works*, Vol 10, 2013.

Oliphant, Margaret. 'A Commentary in an Easy Chair', *Spectator*, Vol 25, January 1890, pp 116–17, rptd *Selected Works*, Vol 5, *Literary Criticism 1877–87*, Valerie Sanders, Joanne Wilkes and Joanne Shattock eds, 2012, pp 293–95.

Shattock, Joanne and Elisabeth Jay, general editors. *Selected Works of Margaret Oliphant*, 25 Vols. London: Pickering & Chatto/Routledge, 2011–16.

Showalter, Elaine. *A Literature of Their Own. British Women Novelists from Brontë to Lessing*. Princeton, NJ: Princeton University Press, 1977.

9 Mrs Henry Wood's Model Men

How to Mismanage Your Marriage in *Court Netherleigh*

Tamara S. Wagner

Mrs Henry (Ellen) Wood's late novel *Court Netherleigh* (1881) is a provocative Victorian marriage novel that upends the expected plot of married life rendered miserable by the absence of romance or desire. Instead, marriage contracts based on practical considerations are presented as desirable bargains, and unappreciative anti-heroines are punished for wilfully forfeiting packages that include both financial security and male paragons. Wood's model men are members of the rising professional classes whose only weakness is their marriage to an impoverished aristocrat. In *Court Netherleigh*, in fact, Wood reworks, in order to expand on, a dynamic that already underpins her bestselling sensation novel *East Lynne* (1861). This explicit rewriting, I show, clarifies what Wood seeks to dramatise in her marriage novels: how a woman can wreck her marriage for what she subsequently deplores as a worthless, even ridiculous reason. In her late fiction, Wood recurs to her most successful plots with the intention of setting everyday married life firmly in the foreground. With a more muted sensationalism, *Court Netherleigh* instead explores the mundane in detail, and yet ultimately it comes full circle in romanticising the supposedly most humdrum representatives of middle-class Victorian Britain. Wood thereby captures shifting expectations both of ideal marriages and of fiction about marriage.

This chapter re-examines Wood's representation of married life, discussing how she engages with wider debates on middle-class domestic ideals, while self-consciously redeploying narrative conventions. Throughout her fiction, her sensationalisation of everyday domesticity dismantles the popular notion of marriage as a happy ending and narrative closure. Furthermore, her continuous reworking of her most successful novels plays with quickly established literary clichés, while imparting at times contradictory advice about married life. Before I analyse in detail how *Court Netherleigh* presents negative guidelines of how to ruin what is presented as a perfectly suitable marriage, I therefore situate Wood's self-conscious representation of this ideal in the context of changing cultural perceptions and concepts of marriage and the novel of marriage in Victorian Britain. What historians of the family have termed 'companionate' and, more recently, 'familiar' marriage provided Wood with a useful concept for her central contrast between a sexually alluring suitor/lover and the representative of a safe home. However, while this contrast quickly evolved into a literary cliché, Wood provocatively pushed the underlying defence of rational consideration in opposition to romantic expectations further. She did so both by unashamedly bringing the importance of money into the equation and, ironically perhaps, by idealising – indeed romanticising – the middle-class men whom she had so emphatically introduced as dull, practical and altogether typical of their social position.

Romantic marriage indisputably remains a central theme and goal in nineteenth-century fiction. It is a truth universally acknowledged that some of the best-known novels of the time centre on courtship plots that end in a desirable pairing off of the heroine, or heroines, with eligible gentlemen. These narratives, as Jennifer Phegley stresses in *Courtship and Marriage in Victorian England* (2012), 'hinge on the trials and triumphs of love and conclude with satisfying marriages of companionate souls' (Phegley, 1). The most successful of these courtship novels create characters who suitably unite romantic love and rational esteem, and who hence offer a companionate union that also satisfies readers' expectations of romance. In the course of the century, a growing number of novels portrayed and analysed married life instead of culminating in marriage as the final goal. However, despite their overarching criticism of courtship novels' typical narrative trajectory, the majority of novels that presented an 'examination of what happens in a marriage' as 'the major story-line' (Markwick, 127) reinforced the importance of the courtship game by showing how a wrong choice might condemn married life – and, with it, the heroines' chance of happiness – from the start. At the same time, these novels about marriage explicitly cautioned against sanguine expectations of the mundane realities of domestic life and in particular against the concept of romantic love as explored (if not always straightforwardly celebrated) in courtship plots. From Anne Brontë's *The Tenant of Wildfell Hall* (1848) to Wilkie Collins's tellingly titled *Blind Love* (1889), the bulk of novels about the dangers of romantic love dramatises the dire results of letting physical attractiveness outweigh the sage persuasions of relatives or the consideration of practical, financial aspects. As Talia Schaffer pointedly puts it in her breakthrough study *Romance's Rival: Familiar Marriage in Victorian Fiction*, familiar marriage (2016) 'as a crucial literary structure in the Victorian novel' emerged as a counterpart to romantic love (Schaffer, 2). As 'authors were working through fears about marriage', they produced a wide variety of narratives in which 'the main character eventually settles down with the safe suitor, growing past the immature and damaging choice of a charismatic lover' (Schaffer, 12).[1] But if the recent 'recognition of non-romantic marriage' (Schaffer, 26) as a driving force and even an ideal of nineteenth-century fiction has radically changed our understanding of the courtship plot, its significance of the Victorian novel's investigation of marriage itself still needs to be more fully addressed.

In fact, the resulting narrative trajectory – a trajectory in direct opposition to the better-known story of lovers separated by mercenary society – seldom receives any critical attention. This is the trajectory of familiar marriage under threat from romantic expectations, whereby dangerously misleading expectations are often gleaned from popular fiction. The pattern of familiar marriage as the desirable outcome of courtship plots tends to produce such unexpected lovers as the dull, flannel-waistcoated Colonel Brandon, who is a safer match than poetry-reciting Willoughby, in Jane Austen's *Sense and Sensibility* (1811), or the aptly named Mr Grey, who finally triumphs over George Vavasor despite the latter's interesting scar, in Anthony Trollope's *Can You Forgive Her?* (1865). But nowhere except in Wood's novels is there such an insistence on the moral prerogatives of plodding businessmen, such an unflinching prioritisation of financial stability, or such an explicit advertisement of marriage bargains that equate the economic and the moral.

In addition, Wood produces marriage novels that tackle this idealisation of the dull suitor within a detailed analysis of married life. Marriage to the right companion might present a final goal, a solution or even a surprise at the end of a novel that climaxes in wedding bells, but Wood concentrates on the continued negotiations and often the belated reconsiderations after the wedding. In *East Lynne*, she rehearses the juxtaposition of the sexually alluring lover and the worthy, respectable suitor. But by turning the conflict into an adultery narrative, she dramatises more explicitly how romantic expectations could be viewed as a threat. *Court Netherleigh* concentrates on the right appreciation of a good husband. In order to ensure this focus, she ejects the useful figure of the charming lover. Instead, what lures two of the novel's contrasted heroines away from what could have been – and the intrusive omniscient narrator keeps reiterating this – a happy home is extravagant spending, including gambling. The heroines' final goal (and with it, the novel's main theme), therefore, shifts: the central issue is not the choice of the right husband/ lover, but the maintenance of the right home. This underlines Wood's representation of marriage as a rational, practical bargain in which both affection and respect play an ambivalently shifting role. In a peculiar twist, she simultaneously imbues the traditional figure of the dull suitor with a totally different kind of aura. Wood not only insistently depicts the unpromisingly named Mr Grubb as an ideal middle-class husband, but she romanticizes him. Wood's changing marriage novels, I contend, explore the ambiguity with which shifting expectations of marriage were being viewed in Victorian Britain and how popular fiction could at once harness and attempt to redirect these expectations.

Court Netherleigh presents a 'How Not To Do It' of marriage. In contrast to the majority of Victorian marriage novels, it does not involve couples who ought not to have married in the first place. This framework often only has the result of questioning the off-stage courtship plot of prehistories that get frequently rehearsed in the process. On the contrary, the 'much-noted moralising' of Wood's 'intrusive, moralising and gossipy feminine narrator' (Pykett, 115, 118) keeps insisting how well the depicted marriages ought to work. What this novel instead tracks, step by step, is how to ruin a marriage. Wood's text thereby operates as a marriage guide, or conduct book, in reverse. Two paralleled heroines enter into what are described as desirable marriages with model men. But precisely because these fashionable ladies marry for rational, unromantic reasons, they persuade themselves that they can never love their husbands. Admittedly, the clichéd warning resurfaces that rising professional men ought perhaps not to marry the alluring daughters of impecunious aristocrats, even if this ensures entry into aristocratic estate. In fact, even as companionate unions dominated middle-class ideals, it remained a common arrangement to use marriage to cement social mobility. Signalling Wood's ambiguous endorsement of the rising middle classes, both *East Lynne* and *Court Netherleigh* take their titles from Great Houses that become the property of professionals who marry above their class origins. But what is good for the estate does not necessarily guarantee a happy marriage. In *East Lynne*, the underlying cautionary narrative indisputably manages to render Archibald Carlyle a notably problematic character; if *Court Netherleigh* embraces its hero with an almost embarrassing insistence, this also shifts the novel's focus more effectually onto the women's point of view. As the moralising and often sepulchral omniscient narrator keeps stressing, they single-handedly wreck their marriages.

Court Netherleigh rewrites *East Lynne* in parallel marriage plots, in which titled ladies' dissatisfaction with humdrum bourgeois life systematically ruins what Wood suggests would have been good bargains in the marriage market. Yet even as Wood thereby extols bourgeois triumphalism over a decaying aristocracy and appears to affirm a primarily economic evaluation of marriage, she incongruously romanticises the model middle-class husband by continually stressing his 'true nobility – nature's nobility, not that of the peerage' (Wood, 250). The description of Francis Grubb's first appearance in the narrative dwells on his beauty as well as his apparent goodness: 'He is thirty years of age, a tall, slender, noble-looking man, with intellect stamped on his ample forehead, and good feeling pervading his countenance. It is a very refined face, and its grey-blue eyes are simply beautiful' (Wood, 35). We are told again and again, that he 'is one of the best and most admirable of men; a true nobleman' (Wood, 47). As Wood asserts the superiority of the rising middle classes, her highest praise remains an affinity with 'nobility', even if she attempts to redefine this elusive quality in the process.

A brief comparison with *East Lynne* clarifies Wood's double agenda in the later novel. In both narratives, a cross-class marriage is facilitated by the aristocratic fathers' irresponsible extravagance, which has rendered them dependent on their lawyer or man of business. In *Court Netherleigh*, however, Wood renders the resulting bargain much more clear-cut when Grubb asks the impecunious Lord Acorn for his youngest daughter, explicitly in return for settling the father's debts: 'I will take her in lieu of all' (Wood, 38). This almost parodies marriage as a financial transaction. Wood does not leave us in any doubt as to why Adela marries 'the grub' (Wood, 40), as the Chenevix sisters term this rising lawyer among themselves. The importance of a financially comfortable marriage might already form an undercurrent in *East Lynne*. *Court Netherleigh* contains one of the probably most literalised bargains in the marriage market in Victorian fiction. Persuaded by practical considerations, Adela 'bitterly resented the necessity, and from that hour she deliberately steeled her heart against him [Grubb]' (Wood, 50). The reactions are at fault; not the reasons for marriage. Wood does not really criticise the financial transaction or the non-romantic marriage itself, even as she sets out to shock the reader and certainly prepares for Grubb's promised idealisation in a deliberately ambiguous fashion.

The ejection of the seductive adulterer forms the most significant shift in Wood's reworking of a seemingly predictable plot. Amid the otherwise eerily replicated character constellations of *East Lynne*, the stereotyped scoundrel who seduces Lady Isabel in the earlier novel is replaced by Lady Adela's more prosaic transgression, which involves a forged cheque. If this ensures a better focus on what Adela forfeits, her foiled fraud cements the importance of finance in the novel. Simultaneously, Wood plays with her readers' expectations of a sensation novel about marriage. In *East Lynne*, Isabel strives to esteem her husband and learns to love him, when Captain Levison systematically practices on her jealousy. The bulk of the novel details her remorse and in particular her yearning for her lost home and her children, a longing that famously climaxes in her infiltration of her lost home as the children's governess. Wood's ambiguous representation of Isabel's transgressions and their results has significantly continued to puzzle readers. Isabel's 'sadistic' punishment is read either as a warning against sexual desire (Coveney, 136), or as a way of raising sympathy in an ambivalently transgressive text that 'creates space for female sexuality and allows for a critique of conventional feminine roles' (Schaffer, 'West Lynne,' 227).[2] Recent research, moreover, has complicated how Wood's fiction manages to integrate the 'two seemingly conflicting discourses of sensationalism and pious Christianity' (Palmer, 16). While it remains undecided as to whether Wood couched moralising messages in eminently sellable sensational narratives, or whether her 'pious moralism' was 'little more than window-dressing, offering a respectable cover to the pleasures that were to be had in reading of transgressive women' (Flint, 228), it is undeniable that Wood's adaptability was probably her greatest selling point (Riley, 168).[3] In removing the seductive lover, her late novel *Court Netherleigh* is arguably less daring and less sensational than the novel it rewrites. Instead, Wood wants to remove such readerly distractions in order to be able to focus on a marriage that is ruined, not overnight, but slowly, over years of small annoyances, careless behaviour and daily provocations. This already forms an important theme in *East Lynne*, but in the earlier novel, it becomes overshadowed by the seducer's double identity as a sexually charged would-be lover and a murderer.

However, if in removing a seductive villain, Wood allows a much clearer focus on the humdrum realities of daily married life, she illogically also creates a male paragon. In this, she enlarges on a recurrent interest in her fiction, even as Grubb's ultimate transformation at once reinforces and curiously undermines her main point. Archibald Carlyle, the epitome of middle-class professionalism that Lady Isabel deserts in *East Lynne*, is the first in a list of increasingly, indeed impossibly, perfect husbands in Wood's fiction. As literary critics have amply pointed out, Carlyle stars in a 'bourgeois fantasy of ascendancy' and, as such, may 'be read as an endorsement of the new-style hero promulgated by his namesake, Thomas Carlyle' (Jay, xxix). Indeed, 'Archibald exemplifies the masculine ideal, as characters are never tired of exclaiming' (Schaffer, 'West Lynne' 237). Yet several scholars have also pointed out the ambiguities in Wood's representation of middle-class ascendancy. After all, as John Kucich points out, 'Carlyle's self-imposed alienation from his middle-class roots and the way it disorders his relationships with women are the primary causes of the novel's traumatic events' (Kucich, 41). Schaffer goes further in reading Carlyle as an exposé of a fallen man, suggesting that his character challenges affective norms by dividing his attention between his home and his work (Schaffer, 'West Lynne', 227). His professionalism, Schaffer argues, 'threaten[s] spousal harmony and patriarchal authority' because he withdraws too much from domestic space (Schaffer, 'West Lynne', 229). His aristocratic wife notably fails to understand the necessity of work, the division of labour and leisure in middle-class daily life. Wood presents a new understanding and consideration of the mundane realities of the majority of her readers, but she also expresses scepticism about the workability of a male professional life that suggests such a clear-cut divorce from domesticity.

As Wood revises the character of the professional, middle-class husband, she significantly removes any imperfections in order to concentrate more fully on the wife's behaviour. Even if some of the incongruities might have been introduced inadvertently, reflective of prevailing ambiguities among the shifting middle classes at the time, Carlyle is without doubt a flawed character who needs to learn from his mistakes. In his second marriage, for example, Carlyle does not accept his sister's interference in his household. Promoting the emergent nuclear family, he asserts 'that married people are better alone' (Wood 1861, 368). In sharp contrast, Grubb becomes almost annoying in his perfection: 'What a fine, noble-looking man he was! what [sic] a face of goodness and beauty was his! [...] At odd moments this would even strike Adela' (Wood, 151). Since Grubb does everything right, Wood can expand on the wife's mistakes. Refusing to admit that her non-romantic marriage contract has brought her an ideal husband, Adela annoys him daily until she forfeits the hitherto unappreciated bargain.

As a result, *Court Netherleigh* functions much more explicitly and self-consciously as a cautionary narrative that imitates the format of a marriage guide. Wood thereby participates in a fashionable trend in the book market of the time. Although conduct and etiquette books had been popular since the eighteenth century, in the second half of the nineteenth century practical domestic manuals in fictional form were being popularised by such bestselling writers as Mrs (Eliza) Warren. The Victorian age altogether generated an unprecedented proliferation of 'self-help' manuals (named after Samuel Smiles's influential *Self-Help* of 1859). Capitalising on the rapid commercialisation of this self-help format, many popular women writers mixed the genres of autobiographical writing, anecdotal or fictional cautionary tale, and domestic advice manual. With her highly successful *How I Managed My House on Two Hundred Pounds a Year* (1864), which inspired countless offshoots and provoked the parodic *How They Mismanaged Their House on £500 a Year. A Narrative, by 'Mr Warren'* (1878), Eliza Warren famously standardised the much-repeated phraseology of 'how to manage' (Attar, 20; de Ridder and Van Remoortel, 311). Against this background of (often thinly fictionalised) guidebooks about marriage, Wood's marriage novels laid out negative guidelines on how to mismanage a marriage, or to evoke Dickens's running joke on systematic mismanagement in *Little Dorrit* (1857), 'How Not To Do It.'

Although it admittedly seems at first sight a pot-boiler that recycles much of Wood's breakthrough novel *East Lynne*, *Court Netherleigh*, in fact, forms a complex intertextual reworking of the marriage novel as an increasingly popular and important subgenre. At the same time, it reveals shifting attitudes to non-romantic marriage. The novel, in fact, self-consciously reverses readerly expectations of popular fiction about romance and marriage on three counts: (1) in ejecting the seductive, adulterous lover; (2) in substituting gambling and fraud as the seduction, which underscores the significance of finance; as well as (3) in subordinating courtship to marriage as the main theme. As Kelly Hager has suggested, many Victorian novels contain both courtship and 'bad marriage' or 'failed marriage' plots (Hager, 11), but *Court Netherleigh* is particularly ruthless in sidelining courtships. The opening chapters introduce a confusing number of marriageable young men and women whose courtships are either settled fairly quickly to pave the way for a full concentration on their married lives or the characters largely disappear from the narrative. Thus, Robert Dalrymple and Mary Lynn may exemplify 'all the fervency of a first affection' (Wood, 21), but they are only united after Robert's lengthy absence. He returns not only as a deus-ex-machina heir in one of several subplots, but also after a complete character transformation, accomplished offstage, that makes him a deserving husband for Grubb's half-sister, Mary. The main purpose of this marginalised courtship plot is to discuss the importance of money in marriage. Robert indignantly interrupts his father's comment that Mary 'will have money':

> I'm sure I've not thought whether she will or not,' interrupted Robert, quite indignantly. 'Of course not; I should be surprised if you had,' said Mr. Dalrymple, in the satirical tone his son disliked. 'Commonplace ways and means, pounds, shillings and pence, are beneath the exalted consideration of young Mr. Dalrymple. I should not wonder but you would set up to live upon air to-morrow. [...] But when we contemplate the prospect of a separate household, it is sometimes necessary to consider how its bread-and-cheese will be provided.
>
> (Wood, 28)

Wood juxtaposes this inclusion of money matters among the rational considerations involving marriage – defined as the establishment of 'a separate household' rather than the union of two lovers – with Grubb's offer to take Adela 'in lieu' of the money her father owes him. Although Wood suggests that the difference is simply one of degree, at this point it nonetheless seems doubtful how she is going to render 'the grub' the noble paragon she clearly wishes him to be. A close reading, as we shall see, reveals her main agenda: to assert the importance of the right behaviour in marriage rather than in courtship.

Two parallel plotlines exemplify women's financial mismanagement and its impact on their marriage. What Wood perhaps fails to address directly is the then hotly debated question of women's pecuniary rights in marriage. Yet she works in these debates obliquely in illustrating the need for a shared financial responsibility as part of the marriage contract, or 'compact,' as Oscar Dalrymple puts it, after his wife Selina has financially ruined them both through her obsession with finery: 'The compact between us was that you should not run into debt' (Wood, 161). Like Adela, Selina marries to 'escape the trouble' (Wood, 71) of financial ruin at home. Like Grubb, Oscar succumbs to a romantic 'folly': 'Oscar loved her to folly' (Wood, 71). The author is, in fact, almost hilariously self-conscious of the parallelism, regularly apologising that it 'is very inconvenient, as the world knows, to tell two portions of a story at one

and the same time' (Wood, 71), as she shuttles between the interconnected plotlines. Yet the Oscar-Selina plot is a subdued, milder version
of Adela's systematic destruction of her husband's affection. Selina's fascination with dress is moreover scripted as a peculiarly feminine weakness. Nor does she treat her husband openly 'with scorn,' which Adela
'*did so systematically* [emphasis in the original]' (Wood, 68). The appropriate punishment of 'silly Selina,' who 'had no more depth of feeling
than a magpie' (Wood, 169–70), is to spend the rest of her life in genteel
poverty in a dull provincial town, with no new dresses. While Wood
produces a sensational worst-case scenario involving financial crime in
a modern-day setting, the milder version works to bring home the appli-
cability of easily wrecked marriages to the reader.

Adela's crime simultaneously exhibits Grubb's forbearance (and its
limits), exemplifies the infiltration of modern monetary matters into the
home, and, in presenting the marriage novel's climax, effectively reworks
the genre's parameters. Less titillating than Isabel's purely sexual desire
for Levison, Adela's forgery might arguably have been more shocking to
the Victorian reader. If strict compartmentalisation between home and
office is Carlyle's fault, Grubb throws temptation into his wife's way by
bringing his work – including the firm's cheque book – home. That he
drops it in his dressing room is notably caused by a marital dispute about
money over the breakfast table: he needs to change in a rush after Adela
throws a cup of coffee at him – 'a moment of embarrassment for them
both' (Wood, 242) rather than a climactic crisis. But this bizarrely parodic
version of domestic violence prepares for a crime that is coded, in the
text, as male, as deliberate and dispassionate, and as a white-collar crime,
linked to the profession that Adela despises as 'plebeian' (Wood, 52).

It is indeed in a peculiarly parodic rewriting of *East Lynne* that Wood
substitutes financial fraud for adultery. When a family friend's son, employed as a clerk in Grubb's firm, comes to reside with them, Adela – 'out
of sheer ennui at the prolonged cold weather, or in very thoughtlessness, or
by way of inventing another source of vexation for her husband' (Wood,
221) – 'set[s] up a strong flirtation' (Wood, 221) with 'that fantastically
foolish lad, Charles Cleveland' (Wood, 346). The absence of passion or
desire pointedly parodies Isabel's infatuation in the earlier novel. Wood
thereby emphatically rejects this common reason for the breakdown of
marriages in sensation fiction. But if much of the ambiguity in Isabel's
characterisation arises from her transgressive passion, Adela's schemes
are presented as much less excusable. After making Charlie the unwit-
ting instrument in cashing the forged cheque, she lets the misguided boy
go to prison in her stead. Although they manage to cover up the fraud
at the trial (notably through Lord Acorn's use of aristocratic privilege),
Grubb peremptorily arranges a separation. In *East Lynne*, Isabel may
regret her step after nearly a year with Levison and especially after their
illegitimate son's death; Adela's remorse is instantaneous. Wood here

creates a sensational effect, showing how Adela has overstepped the mark. Removing adultery, even parodying the expected plot involving a ruinous flirtation, necessitates a different form of sensationalisation that, in turn, highlights the mundane pitfalls of daily married life. In *East Lynne*, the transgression, the way the heroine oversteps the boundaries of acceptable behaviour, is clear-cut when Isabel elopes. The focus of *Court Netherleigh* is precisely on the intangible, elusive line of demarcation between expandable boundaries and points of no return. Marital misery, in the novel, is the result of seemingly small instances of unpleasantness that, like Selina's cumulative debts, slowly amass.

Wood symptomatically sensationalises separation, reminding us how scandalous and transgressive both informal separation and divorce remained in Victorian Britain. Whereas the majority of debates on divorce and custody laws as well as their best-known representations in fiction (including Caroline Norton's as well as Anne Brontë's writing) evoked such separations as a liberation or solution, Wood charts the ambiguity in prevailing cultural conceptualisations at the time. Even as she capitalises on the sensational potential of broken marriages, she reinforces the conservative idea of separation as scandalous. Not all marriage novels were by definition critical of current social attitudes, including patriarchal norms, idealisations of domesticity, or a condemnation of divorce. In fact, *Court Netherleigh* implicitly attacks the Matrimonial Causes Acts of the century's second half. Written against the background of pressing debates that were to give rise to the passage of the Married Women's Property Law in 1882, a year after the novel's publication, *Court Netherleigh* presents a conservative approach that is usually edited out of literary histories that stress the positive contributions of women writers – and in particular female sensation novelists – to the much-needed reforms on matrimonial and custody acts. The reality was less straightforward, much more complex, often messy and produced a wide range of cultural, including literary, expressions of anxiety.

Wood's treatment of domestic violence and separation forms evidence of this anxiety, while exemplifying how a sensationalist evocation of marital breakdown can work as a moralistic narrative. A useful mouthpiece in the novel, Adela's elder sister Grace revealingly considers divorce worse than wife-beating. As Adela gloats over how contemptuously she treats her husband, Grace retorts: 'If I were Francis Grubb I should beat you' (Wood, 231). Wood thus introduces the theme of domestic violence without tainting her ideal man. But Grubb's way out is clearly more shocking: '"Do not be unkind to her." "Unkind to Adela! No, Grace. Separation, rather than unkindness." "Separation!" gasped Grace, the ominous word affrighting her' (Wood, 239). Social embarrassment is likewise high on the list of Adela's punishments after the cheque fraud. To 'be publicly put away by her husband' (Wood, 325) ought to make – so the moralising narrator keeps insisting – Adela feel 'overwhelmed with shame and remorse' (Wood, 339). In the earlier novel, Isabel is neglected and betrayed by her seducer, disfigured after a railway crash, impoverished and alone before she commits the indisputably most sensational transgression in the novel by infiltrating her former home, incognita. The representation of Isabel's longing for her children is of course the novel's most powerful element, and critics have stressed its context in the custody debates of the time (cf. Thaden 130; Pykett 1994, 136). In *Court Netherleigh*, Wood loses a crucial opportunity when she removes Adela's short-lived baby son somewhat inexplicably from the narrative prior to his parents' separation. Instead, Wood can focus exclusively on Adela's belated recognition of the ideal husband she has forfeited. Building on readers' much-noted sympathy for the transgressive anti-heroine, Wood several times cautions against treating Adela '[a]s though she were a martyr – instead of a silly woman who has wilfully blighted her own happiness' (Wood, 386). But if Isabel has to die, Adela's 'deep humiliation' earns her a second chance – if she promises to be 'very good' (Wood, 470) now.

That Wood trades on her readership's presumed familiarity with her breakthrough novel emerges perhaps most strikingly in two repeated literalised transgressions that eerily repeat Isabel's infiltration of East Lynne. Believing her husband to be absent, Adela visits Court Netherleigh twice. There is a sense that Wood is aware of the deflated sensational impact. The first scene depicting what is, with a somewhat forced sensationalism, termed 'Adela's unlawful presence in the house' (Wood, 404) is indeed a notable failure that only stresses social embarrassment. The repeated transgression then climaxes in a confrontation scene that offers a prime example of Wood's moralising, or in Coveney's terms, 'sadistic' (Coveney, 136), sensationalism. Grubb meets Adela's pleas to forgive her with uncharacteristic coldness. He 'listen[s] in impassive silence' (Wood, 467), raising her from her knees with 'a cold, distant touch, evidently not of goodwill' (Wood, 468). While the novel presents his behaviour as an apt punishment for Adele, it also dramatises her genuine distress. Then unexpectedly, Grubb opens his arms, announcing that they are literally and metaphorically ready to receive her: 'If you do wish to atone for the past, to be my true and loving wife, these arms are open to you' (Wood, 469). Narratively confusing, this twist adjusts Grubb's much-asserted model behaviour and might perhaps offer an answer to ongoing debates about Wood's ambiguous treatment of transgressive women. If *East Lynne* is, as Sally Shuttleworth has put it, 'by no means clear cut in its ideological allegiances' (Shuttleworth, 48), and its 'mixed messages' have notoriously been puzzling 'successive generations of readers' (Jay, xx),[4] *Court Netherleigh* solves the dilemma. Ultimately, Adela's crime, while it is a real crime, is only on paper, and since her remorse is instantaneous, the reader is invited to sympathise with her. The reconciliation may be as implausible as it is sudden, but it is convincingly presented as narratively satisfying. This way Wood can create a flawed anti-heroine who commits shocking transgressions, and yet the reward for her punishment is ironically the ideal marriage that she nearly forfeited. The end of the novel portrays Mr Grubb, now Sir Francis Netherleigh, and his wife at the Christening of the new `infant heir of Court Netherleigh' (Wood, 471), in a double celebration of blissful domesticity and middle-class ascendancy.

As a sensation novel critical of marriage, *Court Netherleigh* might admittedly disappoint, yet the revealing shifts that guide Wood's intertextual reworking of her most famous and successful work clarify some puzzling incongruities in the earlier text and, more significantly still, produce one of the most clear-cut and detailed novels about Victorian married life. By ejecting the expected figure of the adulterous seducer, Wood highlights how the destruction of a marriage need not involve such an obvious transgression. Instead, she dwells on everyday pitfalls. That Grubb is an ideal husband ensures that the main responsibility – and hence the novel's main interest – rests with the female characters. Wood may resort to the sensational device of a cheque fraud in order to justify her model man's temporary repulsion of his wife, but the novel's focus remains on the difficulties of daily married life and how they ought to be managed. In showing what Adela nearly forfeits for good, Wood might arguably go too far. At the end of the novel, 'the grub' is not only in possession of an aristocratic estate; he has also become Sir Francis (oddly enough Captain Levison's name at the end of *East Lynne*). While this punishes Adela more effectively, after all her ridicule of his name, it also obscures one of Wood's major points about ideal middle-class men. The best that such rising professional men seem to offer is the potential to turn into better versions of the aristocrats they replace. But if this trajectory gets somewhat confused in the process of Sir Francis's romanticisation, *Court Netherleigh*'s most important contribution to the genre of the Victorian marriage novel firmly rests in its detailing of 'how not to do it'. It is an admittedly deeply moralistic cautionary narrative that invests everyday behaviour within marriage with a central significance. An implicit criticism of earlier novels about marriage, *Court Netherleigh* may thus be seen as an attempt – however flawed – to produce the ultimate marriage novel.

Notes

1 Schaffer describes familiar marriage as 'a Victorian literary convention that developed out of the eighteenth-century ideal of marrying from rational esteem rather than romantic love. Historians often call this 'companionate marriage' (*Romance's Rival*, 2).

2 Coveney describes Isabel's loss, as she is unable to tell her dying son that she is his mother, as 'the one last, careful, twist of the knife of the sadist masquerading as moralist' (Coveney, 136). Schaffer usefully sums up more

recent assessments of Wood's indisputably ambiguous representation of her transgressive heroine ('West Lynne', 227).
3 Mangham speaks of a 'chameleonic quality' (Mangham, 245); Pykett suggests that there is a 'dialogic relation' that involves 'neither a mixing together of the two nor an assimilation of the one by the other' (Pykett 1994, 67).
4 Jay references several contemporary reviews, including Margaret Oliphant's ambiguous reactions to the transgressive heroine and her uninteresting, if virtuous rival (xx).

Works Cited

Attar, Dena. *A Bibliography of Household Books Published in Britain 1800–1914*. London: Prospect, 1987.

Coveney, Peter. *Poor Monkey: The Child in Literature*. London: Richard Clay, 1957.

de Ridder, Jolein and Marianne Van Remoortel. 'Not 'Simply Mrs. Warren': Eliza Warren Francis (1810–1900) and the *Ladies' Treasury*.' *Victorian Periodicals Review*, Vol 44, No 4 (Winter 2011), 307–26.

Flint, Kate. 'Sensation' in Kate Flint ed. *The Cambridge History of Victorian Literature*, pp 220–42. Cambridge: Cambridge University Press, 2012.

Hager, Kelly. *Dickens and the Rise of Divorce*. Aldershot: Ashgate, 2010.

Jay, Elisabeth. 'Introduction to Mrs Henry Wood' in Ellen Wood ed. *East Lynne*. 1861, pp vii–xxxix. Oxford: Oxford University Press, 2005.

Kucich, John. *The Power of Lies: Transgression in Victorian Fiction*. Ithaca, NY: Cornell University Press, 1994.

Mangham, Andrew. 'Ellen (Mrs Henry) Wood' in Pamela Gilbert ed. *A Companion to Sensation Fiction*. Oxford: Blackwell, 2011. 244–56.

Markwick, Margaret. *Trollope and Women*. London: The Trollope Society, 1997.

Maunder, Andrew. 'Stepchildren of Nature': *East Lynne* and the Spectre of Female Degeneracy, 1860–61' in Andrew Maunder and Grace Moore eds. *Victorian Crime, Madness and Sensation*, pp 59–72. Aldershot: Ashgate, 2004.

Palmer, Beth. *Women's Authorship and Editorship in Victorian Culture*. Oxford: Oxford University Press, 2011.

Phegley, Jennifer. *Courtship and Marriage in Victorian England*. Santa Barbara, CA: Praeger, 2012.

Pykett, Lyn. *The Improper Feminine: The Women's Sensation Novel and the New Woman Writing*. London: Routledge, 1992.

Pykett, Lyn. *The Sensation Novel: From 'The Woman in White' to 'The Moonstone'*. Plymouth, MA: Northcote House, 1994.

Pykett, Lyn. 'Sensation and New Woman Fiction' in Linda Peterson ed. *The Cambridge Companion to Victorian Women's Writing, 1830–1900*. Cambridge: Cambridge University Press, 2015. 133–43.

Riley, Marie. 'Writing for the Million: The Enterprising Fiction of Ellen Wood' in Kay Boardman and Shirley Jones eds. *Popular Victorian Women Writers*. Manchester: Manchester University Press, 2009.

Schaffer, Talia. *Romance's Rival: Familiar Marriage in Victorian Fiction*. New York: Oxford University Press, 2016.

Schaffer, Talia. 'The Sensational Story of West Lynne: The Problem with Professionalism.' *Women's Writing*, Vol 23 (May 2016), pp 227–44.

Shuttleworth, Sally. 'Demonic Mothers: Ideologies of Bourgeois Motherhood in the Mid Victorian Era' in Linda M. Shires ed. *Rewriting the Victorians: Theory, History and the Politics of Gender*. London: Routledge, 1992. 31–51.

Thaden, Barbara Z. *The Maternal Voice in Victorian Fiction: Rewriting the Patriarchal Family*. 1997. London: Routledge, 2013.

Wood, Ellen [Mrs Henry]. *East Lynne*. 1861. Oxford: Oxford University Press, 2005.

Wood, Ellen [Mrs Henry]. *Court Netherleigh*. 1881. London: Macmillan and Co, 1908.

10 "[T]he laws themselves must be wicked and imperfect"

The Struggle for Divorce in Mary Eliza Haweis's *A Flame of Fire*

Laura Allen

A Flame of Fire (1897), written by Mary Eliza Haweis, hereafter shortened to M.E.H, is an undervalued contribution to the radical feminist thought circulating the literary realm at the end of the Victorian period, both in terms of plot and form. It sits comfortably in the genre of 'New Woman' novels, which also demonstrated cynicism towards matrimony. It should consequently be allowed to enter the spotlight of fin-de-siècle women's writing. The novel is intriguing because while it informs the reader of nineteenth-century marriage laws, and legal reform, it also transmutes the author's own personal experiences into fiction. For this reason, what is afforded by the text is an insight into both the legality, and the actuality, of marriage. The novel also subverts the structure of marriage narratives, to suggest that literary portrayals of marriage have become stale and fallacious. Marriage was the cornerstone which many would agree Victorian values were built upon, and therefore narratives would climax with the happy marriage of their protagonists. *Middlemarch* (1872) articulates the plot of antiquated Victorian marriage novels: 'we are not afraid of telling over and over again how a man comes to fall in love with a woman and be wedded to her' (Eliot, 120). In this novel, however, marriage is a catalyst that unveils a host of social issues.

The portrayal of marriage in *A Flame of Fire* is due to the combination of M.E.H's personal experiences with an adulterous husband, and her political feminist views. It is clear that the novel seeks to prove that women are continually suppressed by marriage in a number of ways. The plot is enclosed in a narrative structure not typical of a novel about marriage, in which the heroine, Aglae, begins the novel married. The novel follows the progress, or lack thereof, of the heroine, Aglae, as she enters and subsequently tries to escape from married life, and an oppressive private sphere in which she should have found solace. Aglae lives with her aunt and uncle, the Dorriforths, in picturesque Wales, and owing to their leniency she is free-spirited but naïve. Aglae does not think of marriage until she meets Captain Mildmay, the suitor to whom she immediately becomes engaged. A chance encounter with the enigmatic Henry Quekett ruins the prospects of Mildmay's marriage to Aglae, however. She soon becomes infatuated and breaks off her first engagement to become Quekett's wife instead. What follows are the consequence of this decision. Aglae finds herself trapped in an abusive marriage, and tied to a husband involved in extramarital affairs. In order to escape her brutish husband Aglae makes some unfortunate choices, such as running away with her admirer Charlie Carrington. Through this she is led almost to the point of ruin, but is rescued, through fantastic coincidence, by Mildmay. The pair attempt to find a legal way to separate Aglae from Quekett. Thus, the ways in which marriage laws trapped wives arises and are discussed. The novel also depicts how marital violence is subsequently excused by these unequal laws.

The normality of married life is disrupted by violence, and as such it is suggested that the private sphere was actually an enabler of abuse. In the privacy of the home men were free to act as they wanted with their wives. The very laws that condone this patriarchal authority are highlighted in the narrative. Specifically, the novel brings to the attention of its readers the restitution of conjugal rights and recrimination. Both these elements enforced the sexual double standard of the current marriage laws. These components in the law ensured that a man could control his wife's behaviour; therefore, they were tools of oppression wielded by the patriarch to enforce obedience. First, the restitution of conjugal rights meant, on the surface, that husbands and wives must live together. If one withdrew their society the aggrieved party could appeal to court to have their spouse returned. In reality, this aspect of the law meant that wives were forced to submit their body to their husband's keeping upon marriage, regardless of their desires: 'a husband could not be charged with rape of his wife under the criminal law, so ordering her to live with him for all intents and purposes compelled intercourse if *he* wanted it' (Shanley, 178). Second, the novel highlights how the law enabled the defence of recrimination. This is shown to be another way for husbands to excuse their sexual infidelities through the merest accusation of similar wrongs committed by their wives. Essentially, this defence stated that when there was wrong on both sides divorce would not be granted. As illogical as this defence may seem, Quekett is able to use it to keep Aglae as his wife, which means that she still owes him his conjugal rights. Quekett is backed by these inequalities in the law which enable him to compel Aglae's obedience.

The negative portrayal of Quekett's patriarchal authority is clearly an attack on husbands, and in particular can be read as a way in which M.E.H sought retribution against her own adulterous husband. To read the narrative as a fictional account of the author's life suggests that M.E.H made risky use of her own experiences in the service of feminism. This makes her a very attractive figure, as the details of her married life underscore the fictional rendering of Aglae and Quekett with autobiographical intensity. The novel can be seen as a way in which M.E.H is able to indirectly voice her thoughts through fictional characters, and circumstances similar in some ways to her own. The ways in which Aglae reacts to Quekett can be seen as an imitation of M.E.H's feelings. Quekett possesses an 'extraordinary magnetic power [...] over many persons, especially women' (Haweis, 1897, 160) which originally draws Aglae to him. The power that Quekett possesses is clearly his charisma, which M.E.H's own husband was known to have. Her husband, Hugh Reginald Haweis, or H.R.H as she shortened his name to, was not a particularly attractive man. He was well-known for his dwarfish figure, and M.E.H herself calls him the dear little man in her writings. Yet, at the age of seventeen she was infatuated with him; she writes in her diaries of her delight at meeting with H.R.H, and in similar words the narrator describes Aglae's reactions to Quekett. She recounts in one entry of her thoughts after a visit from H.R.H: 'my wildest dreams realized, what more have I to desire. He had not only been seen by me, not only recognized me in the street & spoken – he has called! – he has talked to me more than to Mamma!' (Haweis, 1865, 26). The exclamation marks and underlining in this entry display the excitement felt by the seventeen-year-old Eliza, which is strikingly similar to Aglae's 'crisis of excited feeling' (Haweis, 1897, 67) elicited by Quekett.

It is contestable therefore that M.E.H was drawing upon her own memories when writing this text. Her marriage was similar to Aglae's in the sense that it began happily; the narrator tells the reader: 'the marriage was made in heaven' with all the 'elements of happiness [...] present' (Haweis 1897, 95), but domestic bliss was later threatened by the husband's adultery. Quekett is indiscreet with his affairs as he meets his lover, Joyce Pringle, in 'very wonderful localities' and is seen 'time and again' (Haweis 1897, 151) by friends. In her biography of M.E.H, *Arbiter of Elegance* (1967), Bea Howe re-counts H.R.H's public dalliances in the company of other women. It is even related that M.E.H was forced to meet one of H.R.H's mistresses, and his illegitimate child: 'M.E.H learnt of the association her husband had formed with her visitor who declared that the child holding her hand was his' (Howe, 240). The betrayal felt by M.E.H is strangely missing from Howe's work, and from her own diaries. Perhaps Aglae reacts in her stead. She is not predictably enraged or distraught, but rather 'calm, cold, mute' (Haweis 1897, 153), after seeing the evidence of the affair with her own eyes. This is certainly a reaction that would fit with M.E.H's own personality. She was a very meticulous and controlled person; hysterics, or unchecked emotion, would not suit her. The novel thus grants M.E.H an opportunity to fill the silent gaps in her personal writings. A letter uncovered by Howe seems to support this assumption. M.E.H writes to her son, Lionel, regarding *A Flame of Fire*: 'I send you the first copy of my "firebrand" [...] I hope it will cause a few apoplectic fits' (Howe, 264). This implies that M.E.H was aware the novel would be read as a fictional account of her own experiences, and fully intended that it should be. There is also a hint that the apoplectic fits she hopes to inspire are those of her husband.

These personal experiences are difficult to disentangle from the narrative of *A Flame of Fire*, and just as M.E.H's private voice influences the plot so does her political one. She was campaigning against the unfairness of the current marriage laws in feminist newspapers and at events in her London home in Chelsea, where many met to discuss suffrage issues. There are two articles that elucidate the issues that seem the most vital to M.E.H; these are 'Will Women Combine?' and 'The Revolt of the Daughters'. In the first article she writes that 'the best work that can be done in England now is to arouse women to take larger views' (Haweis 1891, 566). Evidently, M.E.H wishes to inspire other women to think afresh about their position in society, and this is arguably the chief reason for writing *A Flame of Fire*. Second, her article 'The Revolt of the Daughters' discusses, at length, the ways in which women are inhibited by marriage and child-bearing, to the detriment of their other abilities. She notes that women should be free to pursue other avenues and vocations alongside familial responsibilities: 'a woman's heart may be bigger than a husband and a few children can wholly fill. Her own individuality, her own character, was not intended to be too far subordinated' (Haweis 1894, 436). M.E.H clearly felt that women can, and should, exist as autonomous beings, rather than being defined simply as wives or mothers.

These views conflict with those expressed by her husband, who was also a public speaker, though more experienced in this regard than M.E.H. As a reverend he often gave lectures, and discussed marriage as the very foundation of woman's existence. That two people with such conflicting views lived under one roof no doubt caused tension. One outlet for M.E.H's frustrations could have been her novel, which lambasts this outdated perception of women's position in society. She desires to show that women are being subjected to insidious laws which threaten their autonomy. In her own words: 'I wrote this story to vindicate the helplessness of womankind; and show how completely women, like slaves [...] are often but the natural product of their artificial surroundings' (Haweis 1897, forewords).

The novel diverges from M.E.H's biography in the depiction of Quekett's abuse towards Aglae, but remains firmly in agreement with her political stance. Quekett's penchant for violence foreshadows the abuse found later in Aglae's private sphere. When Aglae is first left alone with him Quekett demonstrates his violent tendencies by stepping on a mouse: '"Good God! a mouse!" said Henry, as his quick eye caught the movement; and quicker than thought, his foot put an end to one thing's agony of suspense' (Haweis 1897, 60). M.E.H, as can be seen in her journalistic writings, was an advocate of animal rights. She campaigned for the fair treatment of cattle and livestock and in one article states that slaughterhouses commit 'obvious inhumanity to sensitive, terrified creatures' (Haweis 1852, 680). It is clear therefore that Quekett's complete disregard for the life of the innocent animal depicts his cruel nature, and marks him as villainous. Surridge states that 'Victorian novelists quite commonly coded marital violence through animal assault' (2005, 102), which M.E.H certainly does. Famous examples of this can be found, for instance, in *Wuthering Heights* (1847) when Heathcliff hangs Isabella's dog (Brontë, 94). More overt still is the way that Bill Sikes mistreats his dog and then later brutally murders Nancy in *Oliver Twist* (1838). One can therefore place M.E.H alongside previous novelists who demonstrate the 'common Victorian assumption that violence to animals correlates with human cruelty' (Surridge, 87). After the incident with the mouse, Aglae, rather unsubtly, admits to her aunt that 'if Mr. Quekett had a wife, I believe he would beat her' (Haweis 1897, 62).

Quekett declares that his reason for killing the small creature is simply because he has a 'great dislike to mice' (Haweis 1897, 61). This leads the reader to fear for Aglae who is continually likened to similar timid animals. Quekett physically detains Aglae, who becomes aware of 'struggling helplessly, and feeling as incapable as a small bird in a vice' (Haweis 1897, 67). When she is in the physically dominating presence of Quekett Aglae becomes small and vulnerable, whereas she had previously been described as 'much larger than life', with lips which 'seemed almost colossal' (Haweis 1897, 13). Aglae, at the beginning of the novel, seems to be a New Woman heroine. Any specific definition of the New Woman is difficult to arrive at, as the term itself is unstable. However, heroines in such fiction were frequently depicted in certain ways: 'by turns: a mannish amazon and a womanly woman; she was oversexed, undersexed, or same sex identified; she was anti-maternal, or a racial supermother' (Richardson & Willis, xii). Aglae is portrayed in contrasting terms in regards to her physicality; at one time she is the Amazon and at another she is timid and weak. The depictions of Aglae as physically small and feeble arise only after her marriage, however. This proves that when women are reduced to wives and mothers their other natural abilities or inclinations are quashed.

Aglae begins her life with many possibilities. She is well read and described as 'an odd girl' which the narrator clearly commends, stating: 'I am not sure that this did not involve the highest praise' (Haweis 1897, 16). Aglae is described as 'odd', a term often linked with the New Woman. Her interest in reading, and disinterest in men, also signals her compatibility with this figure. The potential for Aglae to become a New Woman heroine is ruined once she marries Quekett, however. After she marries, the 'bright and striking' (Haweis 1897, 16) Aglae becomes weak and dreary. Being a wife makes Aglae a passive character, and marriage is likened to a 'grim discontent' which 'sucked vigour out of Aglae's life' (Haweis 1897, 128). Quekett becomes a parasite consuming Aglae's personality: 'every individual fibre of Aglae's nature had its own exhausting and persistent leech' (Haweis 1897, 128). The narrator suggests here that Quekett is absorbing Aglae's individuality; he draws away her uniqueness so that she will become the desirable wife. Clearly the obligations that Aglae must perform as a wife are fatiguing and take away the lustre she possessed as a single woman.

The narrator describes Quekett's mastery over a horse, again using animals to voice problematic issues: 'the horse has always been an unmanageable brute [...] Henry undertook to "break" the creature, and like every other creature that comes into contact with his will, it had to give in' (Haweis 1897, 99). Her aunt immediately connects this with Aglae, stating: 'well, Henry doesn't turn Aglae round his finger' (Haweis 1897, 100). Her assertion is ironic, especially considering that many writers compared wives with 'dogs and horses as beings over which a man has legal and proprietary control' (Surridge, 4). Much like the horse Aglae is also subject to Quekett's will, and much as he 'breaks' the horse's spirit Aglae is altered when she becomes his wife. She is described, before her marriage, as having a 'liberty of speech and action unusual at her age' (Haweis 1897, 14). The freedom with which Aglae is able to act in the home of her aunt and uncle is entirely suppressed in Quekett's household, where she becomes feeble and lethargic. Aglae is rarely seen out of her sickbed once she enters her husband's house. She also loses the outspokenness she previously possessed, and it is said that 'the act of speaking was too much for her' (Haweis 1897, 111) as she is too tired to reveal her husband's abusive actions.

Through Quekett's contact with animals the narrator is able to allude to his actual violent behavior towards Aglae. These allusions serve to shield the reader from a portrayal of the true nature of marital violence, however. Therefore, M.E.H reinforces an aversion that many of her contemporaries shared to directly opening up a discourse on marital violence. The novel's aims to shed light upon the true nature of marriage can be seen to slip away in this instance. The narrator never actually describes the act of violence, but the results are visible on Aglae's flesh. Aglae admits, in tears, to her aunt that 'he has a way of pinching my wrist – when he's angry' (Haweis 1897, 111), which is a rare mention of what Aglae suffers. The violence towards Aglae is therefore written subtly in the narrative as the marks left upon the feminine body are the only evidence of the failed marriage in which she is trapped. Marriage was believed to create a safe space for women in Victorian society, yet this was more and more frequently not the case. As Kate Lawson and Lynn Shakinovsky state in *The Marked Body* (2002) 'domestic violence is thus itself a rupture in a cultural order that stressed the home as a woman's sphere, as the place of her security and her rule' (Lawson and

Shakinovsky, 2). In the first pages of the novel the narrator states that
'woman married is a crowned queen' (Haweis 1897, 3), yet Aglae certainly does not rule husband or household. She is instead subjugated and
defeated by marriage.

That Aglae is, at this point in the narrative, not yet seeking to be
separated from her husband demonstrates how complacent she has become. The law does little to help women beaten by their husbands and
M.E.H therefore suggests that this violence becomes normalized. Aglae
has learned that marriage means suffering, and cannot tell how wrongly
she is being treated. As Tromp states: 'women were therefore often compelled to submit to violence in its myriad forms as a condition of marriage' (Tromp, 39). Aglae later admits that 'I even rather respected him
when he first used to – strike me' (Haweis 1897, 230). This is a daring statement, especially from a Victorian text. Aglae has been made
to believe that husbands have the absolute right to beat their wives as a
show of authority. The novel critiques the powerless position that current marriage laws forced women into upon marriage. It also challenges
assumptions which then prevailed regarding a husband's right to force
obedience from his wife.

Aglae ultimately desires to be divorced from Quekett due to his blatant
disregard for their marriage, exemplified in his affair with Joyce Pringle.
Aglae's complacency means that she suffers physical abuse in silence, yet
to be slighted by Quekett's continual adultery is excessive. The adultery
on Quekett's side would have no bearing on Aglae's right to a divorce, as
the law only made it possible for the husband to obtain a divorce on the
grounds of adultery. The wife, on the other hand, must prove some ag-
gravation such as cruelty to even have a faint hope of gaining a divorce.
Thus: 'in treating men's and women's sexual and reproductive capacities
differently, the law sanctioned the sexual double standard' (Shanley, 80).
Aglae could attempt to use both Quekett's adultery and violence towards
her as the grounds for a divorce, but is unaware of this route. Quekett's
cruelty may prove to not be aggravating enough, however. This route is
also not immediate; it would mean that Aglae would have to return to
her husband's household until she achieves the divorce. She would be
forced to submit to his will until the court allowed her to live separately
from him. Aglae has no desire to return to Quekett, and with no other
options available to her, she makes an error in judgment by fleeing with
her friend, and admirer, Carrington. This action appears scandalous,
and indeed adulterous, but Aglae does not at first recognize what she
has done wrong in the eyes of society. The narrator states that 'she was
actually as reproachless within and without as yourself' (Haweis 1897,
176), but many would not see it this way. Once Aglae begins to understand how this action will seem she has hope that it will force Quekett's
hand: 'no husband would endure to be fettered to such a wife; he would
divorce her for his own sake' (Haweis 1897, 161). In a society which

judged impropriety sternly, being married to such a scandalous wife would indeed be undesirable. Quekett, however, does not behave as the typical patriarch. Indeed, he cares little for the opinions of others, and from the very start his marriage has been open to ridicule: 'he thus gradually Bohemianized his circle, which Aglae had not strength to purify, and "those Queketts" began to be a joke' (Haweis 1897, 115). Out of spite Quekett declares his own adultery, thus putting both himself and Aglae in the wrong. The law of recrimination means that 'crime on one side may claim divorce; but crime on both sides frustrates it' (Haweis 1897, 202). Thus, Aglae has only two alternatives: 'to return to him if he compels you, or to avoid him by concealing yourself', she can choose between 'the life of a fugitive, and the life of a dog!' (Haweis 1897, 202).

Another inequality in the law is highlighted by this; Aglae could be compelled by her husband to return to him as part of her duty as his wife. Thus, M.E.H forces to the reader's attention the unsavory 'restitution of conjugal rights'. That Aglae will be either a 'fugitive' or a 'dog' demonstrates that the law would see Aglae become a social outcast, or the property of a man. These options are equally horrible, as the former means Aglae would be expelled from the society of her family members, and the latter that she would be forced back into the society of her abusive husband. Aglae firmly declares,

> I cannot obtain judicial separation because there is no 'legal cruelty'. I am not entitled to maintenance unless I go back to him [...] I have refused that, therefore now he is proceeding for 'restitution of conjugal rights' [...] *I thought slavery was abolished!*
>
> (Haweis 1897, 257)

Algae's shock at learning that she has no right in law to leave her husband perhaps suggests that many are also unaware of this inequality. Through the likening of marriage to slavery it is possible to ally M.E.H with earlier feminist campaigners, for instance John Stuart Mill. Mill also compared English wives to slaves, yet goes further to suggest that they had even fewer rights, as even the female slave could 'refuse her master the last familiarity' where the wife was forced to the 'lowest degradation of a human being, that of being made the instrument of an animal function contrary to her inclinations' (Mill, 57). Therefore, M.E.H can be seen as a successor to earlier advocates of women's rights. Aglae is also aligned with these protesters: 'You are not the first to complain of the English marriage laws, Aglae, or to suffer from them' (Haweis 1897, 203). The tone of this suggests that little will change, especially as long as people remain ignorant of the inequalities enshrined in the law.

Aglae's fears that Quekett will force her to return to him are ultimately realized. Although he has little desire to keep her as a wife, Quekett views Aglae as his property. His manipulative and controlling personality will not allow her to have her freedom, and thus he claims the support of the law to demand her return: 'I have therefore employed the only means left to me – compulsion. I am backed by the law' (Haweis 1897, 241). Aglae has returned to the house of her aunt and uncle when she is summoned: 'I have come to demand the return of my wife to her own home. I have come to insist upon your detaining her no longer, in the face of the law, decency, and her duty as a mother' (Haweis 1897, 234). Quekett is entitled to recall Aglae owing to her responsibilities, in both the eyes of the law and society, to her child. Quekett would see Aglae forced back into her position as a mother despite her apparent rejection of the role. She discards traditional maternal feelings for her child, believing as she does that it is another version of her tormentor: 'Aglae's shrinking from her husband extended itself to the child [...] the love she had at first felt for it shrank up like a dry flower' (Haweis 1897, 189). The narrative provides little evidence of Aglae caring for her child, and instead shows that after his birth the child becomes 'an instrument of pain' (Haweis 1897, 189). Yet, the law would force Aglae to take up this role once more, regardless of her will, and indeed would allow an abusive husband to make use of such biased legislation in order to control his wife. While M.E.H allows Aglae a voice in which to reject traditionally feminine roles she is continually reminded of her duties; she is unable to escape the role of wife and mother. Hammerton claims that one can see 'husbands, with the backing of a still confident and publicly sanctioned patriarchal authority, going to extreme lengths to enforce obedience' (Hammerton, 108) during this time. Quekett's confidence stems from the patriarchal authority which Hammerton suggests is invested in him, whereas in comparison Aglae is full of apprehension: 'like a hunted deer' (Haweis 1897, 242).

Clearly, M.E.H creates a narrative full of criticisms of current marriage laws. She does, however, praise legal reform, which altered the position of wives. Specifically, such reforms meant that wives would no longer be made, under duress, to live with their husbands. Owing to a real legal case Aglae is liberated from Quekett's constant demand of the restitution of his conjugal rights. The Clitheroe case, named after the town in which the incidents occurred, made it illegal for husband's to imprison their wives under the pretense of 'wifely duties'. In the Clitheroe case it was found that a Mrs. Jackson, after refusing to obey her husband's decree for restitution of conjugal rights, was seized and held in his house. She was released after the court of appeal ruled that her husband should have no right, legally, to detain her. This changed the law substantially, as it meant that the imprisonment of wives was now publically forbidden. As such, the Clitheroe case altered Aglae's position: 'it rendered her 'an honest woman' and 'made it possible for Aglae to return to her aunt's house without fear of arrest' (Haweis 1897, 274). While demonstrating her knowledge of legal cases M.E.H is also able to show that such changes are entirely praiseworthy, and that they will improve the lives of women. Despite remaining married to Quekett at least Aglae can now live separately from him. Aglae represents the helplessness that women would face when the laws which should exist to protect them instead threaten their autonomy. Changes to the law, such as the ruling in the Clitheroe case, would transform and improve the legal situation of wives. Such reform is therefore highlighted in the narrative to show how it is both desirable and necessary to challenge the sexual double standard.

The aims of the novel are clearly to represent marriage in unconventional ways. Aglae does not find domestic bliss as many Victorian heroines before her have done; instead marriage elicits strife and disunity. The narrative further rebels against marriage through its very structure. The *Graphic*'s review of the novel found the narrative to be disorganized and states that the novel's failure is due to the 'inconsequent construction' (*Graphic* 1897). What one reviewer found to be a fault, however, can instead be seen as one of the chief strengths of the novel. The structure of *A Flame of Fire* can be seen as a way in which M.E.H defies the traditional marriage plot. There are a number of ways in which the novel's structure does this. It disturbs perceptions of marriage by denying closure, and shows a resistance to the expectations of a courtship plot. Most notably, it begins rather than ends with Aglae's marriage. The first chapter is entitled 'The Wedding-Day.' Therefore, the novel's central conflict arises not from the heroine's need to find a husband but from her need to escape one. This unusual opening to the novel is highlighted by the narrator, who interjects in a self-conscious fashion that 'some explanation is due to the reader' (Haweis 1897, 9). This strange narrative voice continues throughout, and the narrator seems to be unaware of the heroine's thoughts and actions as variations of 'I cannot tell' (Haweis 1897, 47) and 'I cannot say' (Haweis 1897, 53) are repeated. A reliable and omniscient narrator is not to be found in *A Flame of Fire*, instead there is an erratic, and seemingly detached, one. The novel is therefore filled with uncertainty even in terms of the narration. It is clear that the structure of the novel is meant to reflect the disturbed domestic space in which Aglae is trapped. The strange construction illustrates Lawson and Shakinovsky's concept of 'rupture in a cultural order' (Lawson and Shakinovsky, 2) by betraying the order of marriage novels.

M.E.H designs a deliberately regressive narrative structure, in which Aglae begins the novel married, and therefore the expectations for the novel to conclude with Aglae settled in a happy marriage are quashed from the outset. Aglae's first lover, the gently named Mildmay, was the suitable candidate but sexual attraction to Quekett trumped this logical choice. After Quekett's death Aglae is free to return to the correct storyline; she marries Mildmay and settles in his idyllic 'home-farm' (Haweis 1897, 291). M.E.H seems to offers closure in the novel's final chapter. Aglae is presented as content and safe in her new life: 'when the terrible storm-time of Aglae's life was past, and the joy of rest and happiness lost its almost agonizing novelty, her mind grew calm' (Haweis 1897, 284). The domestic felicity which is suggested by this is promptly snatched from the reader, however. The narrative diverges from the anticipation of a peaceful family life for Aglae, as instead of this the novel ends with the death of one of her children. Her son from her first marriage, Hal, is killed. The penultimate line of the novel is: 'they found only the bull kneeling on the poor pink shell of what had been a brave and noble boy' (Haweis 1897, 294). This is undoubtedly the ultimate shattering of familial bliss. Ironically titled 'The Afterglow' the final chapter therefore leaves the reader bereft of satisfaction. Clearly this ending challenges the customary conclusion of many Victorian marriage novels. It is a way in which M.E.H subtly instils a political statement regarding the false representations of marriage which have come before her. By fracturing the domestic sphere with the death of a child M.E.H dissolves any hopes that the novel will endorse marriage. Through a subversion of the very genre of marriage fiction the novel covertly quarrels with assumptions made in Victorian fictions regarding the experiences of women as wives.

The novel openly judges the subordinate position which the law forced women into, and by challenging literary traditions M.E.H can be seen as equally radical as other New Woman novelists. A Flame of Fire calls for women's place in marriage to be redefined, while suggesting that marriage and motherhood may not be the proper occupation for all women. The themes of the novel arise certainly from its author's own political stance. The time that she spent as a writer for The Woman's Herald, in which she admonished the inequalities of the law that victimised women, no doubt influenced the narrative of her only novel. The same criticisms of society's treatment of women, found chiefly in her journalistic writings, resurface in this novel. A Flame of Fire should be read as a politically charged work, designed to illuminate the inequalities faced by women when they marry. It sheds light on Victorian Britain's social and cultural history, and therefore has documentary value. However, it is the underscoring of the narrative with M.E.H's own personal experiences of marriage that allows a political novel to possess sentiment, and this creates a text that ultimately resonates with the reader on both factual and emotional levels.

Works Cited

Brontë, Emily. Wuthering Heights. Hertfordshire: Wordsworth Classics, 1992.
Dickens, Charles. Oliver Twist. Hertfordshire: Wordsworth Classics, 1992.
Eliot, George. Middlemarch. Hertfordshire: Wordsworth Classics, 1994.
Hammerton, A James. Cruelty and Companionship: Conflict in Nineteenth-Century Married Life. London and New York: Routledge, 1992.

Haweis, Mary Eliza. "A Flame of Fire." *Saturday Review of Politics, Literature, Science and Art*, 1897, pp 122. https://search.proquest.com/docview/9529391?accountid=9869.

Haweis, Mary Eliza. 'Cattle Ships and Abattoirs.' *Westminster Review*, January 1852. https://search.proquest.com/docview/4470648?accountid=9869.

Haweis, Mary Eliza. 'Will Women Combine?' *Women's Penny Paper*, June 27, 1891, p 566. http://tinyurl.galegroup.com/tinyurl/4Wk2o6.

Haweis, Mary Eliza. 'The Revolt of the Daughters.' *The Nineteenth Century: A Monthly Review*, March 1894, pp 430–36. https://search.proquest.com/docview/2649243?accountid=9869.

Haweis, Mary Eliza. *A Flame of Fire*. London: Hurst and Blackett, 1897.

Haweis Papers: Diaries, Memoranda and Letters of Mary Eliza Haweis. 1864–1931. Women's Library, London Metropolitan University, London.

Howe, Bea. *Arbiter of Elegance: A Victorian Biography*. London: Harvill Press, 1967.

Lawson, Kate and Shakinovsky, Lynn. *The Marked Body: Domestic Violence in Mid Nineteenth-Century Literature*. Albany, NY: State University of New York Press, 2002.

Mill, John Stuart. *The Subjection of Women*. London: Longman, 1869.

"New Novels." *Graphic*. 1897. July 10. *British Library Newspapers*. http://tinyurl.galegroup.com/tinyurl/4GFDi8.

Richardson, Angelique and Chris Willis eds. *The new woman in fiction and in Fact: Fin de Siècle Feminisms*. Basingstoke: Palgrave, 2001.

Shanley, Mary Lyndon. *Feminism, Marriage, and the Law in Victorian England*. Princeton, NJ: Princeton University Press, 1989.

Surridge, Lisa. 1994. 'Dogs'/Bodies, Women's Bodies: Wives as Pets in Mid-Nineteenth-Century Narratives of Domestic Violence.' *Victorian Review*, Vol 20, pp 1–34.

Surridge, Lisa. *Bleak Houses: Marital Violence in Victorian Fiction*. Athens: Ohio University Press, 2005.

Tromp, Marlene. 'Throwing the Wedding-Shoe: Foundational Violence, Unhappy Couples, and Murderous Women Author(s).' *Victorian Review*, Vol 39 (2013), pp 39–43.

11 '[T]he chains that gall them' – Marital Violence in the Novels of Florence Marryat

Catherine Pope

"Entirely wanting in womanly reserve and reticence," ('Belle Lettres', 688) is how one reviewer described Florence Marryat's novel *The Nobler Sex* (1892). Correctly sensing the autobiographical nature of the story, the novelist was roundly criticized for making public her sufferings at the hands of two violent husbands. In fact, Marryat's relationship with the press was no more harmonious than her marriages. Throughout a long career during which she wrote sixty-eight novels, Marryat was continually harangued for exposing the darker side of marriage. Her heroines are often escape artists, imagining different possibilities for themselves and presenting readers with compelling alternatives to matrimony.

With a life (1833–99) neatly spanning the Victorian period, Marryat was well placed both to benefit from and to observe the ways in which women's lives were transformed during the nineteenth century. At the time of Marryat's birth, a wife's legal identity was entirely subsumed into that of her husband – she was at best a shadow, at worst a chattel. By the 1890s, women had benefited from momentous changes that granted them a separate identity and greater rights over their bodies and personal property. As I argue, Marryat contributed to the debates that heralded these changes, bringing feminist ideas to an audience they would not otherwise have reached.

In this chapter, I focus on Marryat's treatment of marital violence. Through close readings of three novels – *Her World Against a Lie* (1878), *The Root of All Evil* (1879) and *The Nobler Sex* (1892) – I argue that Marryat went further than any other contemporary novelist by using her literary platform to make a uniquely radical protest against the widespread practice of wife-beating. By considering the critical response to her writing, I also show how attempts to undermine Marryat exemplify the prevailing belief that wives should suffer in silence, rather than challenge the ideology that demanded their subordination.

Grounded on Force: The Victorian Marriage

In *On the Subjection of Women* (1869) John Stuart Mill wrote that relations between the sexes were 'grounded on force' (Mill, 139); women's supposedly submissive nature being a result of physical, rather than intellectual, inferiority. A legal system that upheld a wife's subordinate status suggested that she might require chastisement to keep her in her rightful place. As Elizabeth Foyster explains, 'violence in marriage was not always seen as a deviant behaviour, and could be viewed instead as a feature of a "normal" functioning relationship' (Foyster, 4). The nature of permissible chastisement was an area of contention, however, and this lack of clarity delayed attempts to address the situation. Blackstone's infamous *Commentaries* (1765–69) stated:

> The husband also, by the old law, might give his wife moderate correction. For, as he is to answer for her misbehaviour, the law thought it reasonable to intrust him with this power of restraining her, by domestic chastisement, in the same moderation that a man is allowed to correct his apprentices or children. ... The civil law gave the husband the same, or a larger, authority over his wife: allowing him for some misdemeanours, flagellis et fustibus acriter verberare uxorem[.] [to beat his wife severely with scourges and sticks].
>
> (Blackstone, 417)

The existence of the oft-quoted Rule of Thumb, whereby a husband might beat his wife with a stick no thicker than his thumb, has been rebutted comprehensively by Maeve Doggett (Doggett, 7). However, she also notes that the idea remained influential, notwithstanding its apocryphal nature. Jack Straton has argued persuasively that the Rule of Thumb has served as an unhelpful distraction from more productive debates over women's rights, with some conservatives proclaiming that the mythical status of the term proves the violence it suggests is equally imaginary (Straton, 104).

Sarah Stickney Ellis, arbiter of wifely conduct, was revealingly reticent on the problem in her popular manuals. 'What then, if by perpetual provocation, [the wife] should awaken the tempest of his wrath? We will not contemplate that thought' (Stickney Ellis, 27). Her assumption is that a husband's violence manifests itself only in response to his wife's shrewish behaviour, and the consequences remain unspeakable. This conspiracy of silence persists throughout most literature, proving marital violence to be an unwritable, as well as an unspeakable, act. As I discuss later, attempts to articulate the problem were either elliptical, or roundly denounced by critics.

One of the most prominent voices to acknowledge the extent of wife-beating was historian John William Kaye, who in an article for the *North British Review* decried the treatment of wives in England. Although his argument was powerful in calling for greater equality to make wives less dependent on violent husbands, Kaye also stated unequivocally that 'Men of education and refinement do not strike women'

(Kaye, 235). He allows that such men might inflict psychological damage (as Anthony Trollope was to show powerfully in *He Knew He Was Right* [1869]), but remains confident that the beatings he describes are the sole preserve of the working classes. In Parliament, William Gladstone echoed Kaye's sentiments, but did at least allow a modicum of doubt: 'adultery with cruelty [is] at present a thing *almost* unknown in the higher classes of society' (3 Hansard 147). Even Frances Power Cobbe, whose campaigning journalism was instrumental in changing the law, was unwilling to acknowledge the extent of the problem:

> Wife-beating exists in the upper and middle classes rather more, I fear, than is generally recognised, but it *rarely* extends to anything beyond an occasional blow or two of a not dangerous kind. The dangerous wife-beater belongs *almost* exclusively to the artisan and labouring classes.
>
> (Cobbe, 58)

Perhaps Cobbe's evasiveness was simply an expedient. Would her campaign have succeeded had she tried to convince male middle-class Members of Parliament that they and their friends were potential wife-beaters? Even if this was the case, Cobbe's approach reinforced the misconception, leaving the middle-class wife vulnerable and ignored.

Some of the most compelling evidence to challenge Cobbe's view or position was supplied by the newly established Divorce Court, an institution that exposed middle- and upper-class marriage to unprecedented scrutiny.[1] The results were revelatory. As Hammerton's important survey shows, '48% of petitioners citing cruelty were middle and upper classes' (Hammerton, 105) and, contrary to popular belief,

> among those appearing in the court, upper-class men were as likely as those lower in the social scale to strike their wives with pokers and similar weapons, throw them downstairs, beat them during pregnancy, enforce sexual intercourse after childbirth, and indulge in marital rape or enforced sodomy.
>
> (Hammerton, 276)

While the Divorce Court did extend a means of redress to those with sufficient financial resources, it was only available to husbands and wives whose spouses were guilty of adultery – violent behaviour alone was not sufficient grounds for release from a miserable marriage. Nonetheless, the cases heard by the judges provided incontrovertible evidence that middle-class husbands were not always gentlemen.

Although newspapers delighted in this seemingly endless source of prurient detail, many novelists were too morally squeamish or nervous to exploit it in their fiction. As Kate Lawson and Lynn Shakinovsky write, domestic violence with an origin inside the bourgeois home verges on the edge of the non-narratable, and is thus replete with manifest evasions, silences, and distortions in its representations of both the woman's body and the domestic sphere it inhabits.

(Lawson & Shakinovsky, 6)

There is no absence of domestic violence in the Victorian novel, as studies such as Lisa Surridge's *Bleak Houses* (2005) and Marlene Tromp's *The Private Rod* (2000) reveal. Yet the physical abuse is invariably either oblique, historical, or somehow justified by the victim's behaviour or 'otherness'. Authors who pushed the boundaries of acceptability were soundly punished. Anne Brontë was criticized for producing scenes of 'the most disgusting and revolting species' (Surridge, 75) in *The Tenant of Wildfell Hall* (1848). Most controversial was heroine Helen Graham's denial of her husband's conjugal rights as she slammed the bedroom door in his face, rather than his unreasonable behaviour towards her. Although violence against Helen is implied rather than described, a subplot shows Arthur's friend Ralph Hattersley abusing his wife until she cries. The adverse reaction to this powerful novel possibly explains literary reticence on the issue of marital violence over the next two decades.

Marryat and Wife Torture in England

Florence Marryat, conversely, was prepared to include graphic descriptions of marital violence in her novels. In the same year that Frances Power Cobbe was displaying selective blindness in her refusal to acknowledge the existence of the middle-class wife-beater, Marryat wrote two novels in which she exposed the terrifying reality. By presenting many different types of abuse across all classes, Marryat campaigned for equal marriage – not unions that were grounded on force. As I show, she remained committed to this theme throughout her career, never wavering in the face of sustained criticism from the press.

Marryat intended a shocking description of marital violence in her first novel, *Love's Conflict* (1865). In the original draft, Heroine Elfrida Treherne falls victim to her husband's 'hard rule' (Marryat, *Love's Conflict*, II:308) resulting in the fatal deformity of her baby. Extensive revision by the publisher's reader, Geraldine Jewsbury, ensured the birth defects were instead ascribed to the mother's adulterous thoughts.[2] Marryat had no option but to accept the changes, else her novel would never have been published. By resurrecting Elfrida in a later novel, *A Harvest of Wild Oats* (1877), Marryat was able to retrospectively link the baby's death with its father's violence.

Marryat revisits this theme more overtly in *A Fatal Silence* (1891), the passage of a quarter of a century (and the demise of Jewsbury) allowing a stronger treatment. Heroine Paula is described as 'the mother of Carl

Bjørnsen's idiot child – the child whose brain and body he had blighted by his brutal violence to herself' (Marryat, *A Fatal Silence*, 84). Due to repeated blows sustained by Paula during pregnancy, baby Paulie is born weak, undersized and incapable of speech. His permanently open, yet soundless, mouth marks him as the silent victim of his father's abuse. After Paula flees the marital home and establishes herself as a teacher in a remote village, Bjørnsen torments her further by kidnapping Paulie and exhorting money from her. His physical abuse is compounded by financial exploitation. He is a man who believes he can still treat his wife and son exactly as he pleases. The marital bond confers duties upon the wife, but no responsibilities upon the husband – a recurring theme in Marryat's fiction.

But it was in 1878 that Marryat dealt with these themes most explicitly. This was the year that saw the publication of Frances Power Cobbe's landmark article, *Wife-Torture in England* (quoted above), which is 'widely recognised as the inspiration for the Matrimonial Causes Act of 1878' (Shanley, 165). This act extended the so-called Divorce Act of 1857, allowing abused wives to seek protection orders and alimony without the need to pursue an expensive court case. Mary Lyndon Shanley explains that Cobbe's article 'electrified public opinion' (Shanley, 165) prompting a wide-ranging debate. Part of this debate, I contend, was Marryat's most polemical novel, *Her World Against a Lie*. Through this novel, I argue, Marryat both amplified and challenged Cobbe's arguments, helping educate her readers and also stressing that marital violence was a problem that affected *all* women – not just the working classes.

'The strong-minded asserter of women's rights': *Her World Against a Lie*

Heroine Hephzibah Horton is 'the spirit of a man cased in a woman's body' (Marryat, *HWAAL*, I:4) and has a keen grasp of the law. Frustrated by the absence of women's suffrage, she instead makes it her business to advise wives of their rights and to reform the institution of marriage. Hephzibah herself eventually marries, retaining her own name and choosing for her husband a tiny man she can patronize without fear of him asserting his superior strength. The character is a thinly disguised portrait of the author – almost an avatar.

When Marryat adapted her novel for the stage in 1880, she took for herself the role of Hephzibah, thereby reinforcing her link with the character and her opinions, and also broadcasting her message to a much wider audience. Unfortunately, most of the script has been lost,[3] so it is difficult to know the extent to which the radical elements of the novel were re-created on stage. However, a detailed review of the London premiere suggests the plot was left untouched, with Hephzibah retaining her potency: 'Miss Florence Marryat made a hit as Mrs Horton. The strong-minded asserter of woman's rights was hit off to the life' ('The London Theatres', 6).

Although *Her World Against a Lie* is mainly a vehicle for Marryat's views on married women's property, some of the most memorable scenes concern the physical abuse suffered by heroine Delia Moray at the hands of her alcoholic middle-class husband:

> "[T]o-day, he has beaten my poor child till he is black and blue, and pushed me from the top of the stairs to the bottom. Look at my arm!" she exclaims suddenly, as she pushes up the sleeve of her thin alpaca dress, and shows the angry red and blue mark of a fresh bruise.
>
> (Marryat, *HWAAL*, I:16)

Not content with abusing his wife directly, James Moray ties her to a chair in a locked room and then beats their ill son. The incarcerated Delia is forced to listen to the screams of Willie, who suffers from respiratory difficulties, as he is beaten black and blue by an 'inhuman monster' (Marryat, *HWAAL*, I:96). Delia is completely ignorant of the limited protection offered to her under the law. Her guardian angel, Hephzibah Horton, asks: 'Have you never heard of such a thing as a protection order?' She continues,

> Really, the ignorance of our sex upon matters of general information is astounding! I should have thought it was the interest of every married woman in Christendom to make herself acquainted with the relief the law contains for her. It's little enough, my dear, I can tell you, and would burden no one's brains to get by heart. A protection order, obtained from a magistrate, would render you safe from the assaults of that man to-morrow, and enable you to live in peace, and support yourself and your child.
>
> (Marryat, *HWAAL*, II:24)

Hephzibah goes on to enumerate the benefits of protection orders, also explaining exactly how they operate. This lengthy exposition is clearly designed to enlighten the female reader as much as Delia. A Victorian woman was much more likely to read fiction than to browse a daily newspaper. How else, then, would she learn of a change to the law, unless a man decided to tell her? Marryat uses her literary platform as a means of educating women as to their rights, and advising men of their legal limitations. To emphasize her message, Hephzibah later cites the example of a woman who takes out a protection order against her violent husband and then travels to the United States, where a divorce can be obtained on grounds of cruelty alone.

Her World Against a Lie is part novel, part instruction manual, of-fering female readers the means of both metaphorical and literal escape. Although it is impossible to gauge the impact of such novels, an opinion piece in a Welsh newspaper from 1880 certainly suggests that fiction played a role in enlightening women:

> Until we attended the [women's rights] meeting last Thursday week I was (and I believe many others were) ignorant of certain techni-calities of the law which seem to be especially oppressive to women, and I have lately read a book, written by the well-known novelist, Florence Marryat, 'Her World Against a Lie,' and one of her char-acters, dubbed 'Mrs. Hephzebah [sic] Horton,' in one of her many diatribes against it, painfully enlightened me on certain points of the statute dealing with a subject about which all women feel strongly[.]
>
> (*A. Lady*, 3)

When Hephzibah consults a lawyer on Delia's behalf, he explains that 'there is a difficulty in drawing the line between necessary chastisement and ill-treatment,' (Marryat, *HWAAL*, I:117) adding that the law shows an unwillingness to place any constraints on husbands, preferring to believe them capable of self-regulation. The widespread refusal to accept that marital violence exists in the middle classes is represented by Delia's brother-in-law, William Moray, who banishes her from his respectable suburban villa. When she complains to him of his brother's violence, he responds:

> Really, my dear lady, these little domestic differences can have no interest for a third party. They are so much better kept to one's self.
> "Little domestic differences!" she echoes scornfully. "Would your wife call it a 'little domestic difference' if her arm was bruised as mine is?"
>
> (Marryat, *HWAAL*, II:242)

Here Marryat draws the reader's attention from the general to the par-ticular, inviting them to imagine their own arm in place of Delia's, this shock of proximity a traditional sensation device. After her rapid edu-cation in women's rights from Hephzibah, Delia is finally able to stand up to her husband, asserting 'I don't consider it my duty to submit to be treated like a dog rather than a woman' (Marryat, *HWAAL*, II:221). I argue that Marryat, too, hopes her women readers will also feel more able to confront tyranny.

The critical response to *Her World Against a Lie* was almost unan-imous in its distaste. *The Spectator* detected 'objectionable coarseness' ('Her World Against a Lie', *The Spectator*, 1053) while *Reynolds's*

Newspaper spotted 'glaring crudities of situation' in the stage adaptation ('Adelphi Theatre', 23). Neither elaborated on the specific nature of Marryat's offence. The *Athenaeum*'s reviewer was, however, more forthcoming:

> A worse offence is involved in the description of such a scene as that where James Moray prevents his wife from going to her sick child, whose cry she hears in the next room. There are some human affections so sacred that the attempt to make capital out of them in order to obtain a sensational chapter for an ephemeral novel strikes us as being most repulsive.
>
> ('Her World Against a Lie', *The Athenaeum*, 723)

There is no acknowledgement that Marryat might be drawing her scene from real life or exposing a problem worthy of debate. The reviewer merely bolsters the chorus of voices that refuses to accept the existence of the middle-class wife-beater and insists that such experiences are non-narratable.

Undeterred, Marryat also used her next novel, *Written in Fire* (1878), to expose marital violence in the middle-class home. Emily Hayes, an educated women, dies of consumption, her demise hastened by her husband's physical and mental abuse. Her firstborn child is also 'killed by a passionate blow' (Marryat, *Written in Fire*, I:78) from his hand. The authorial voice pronounces it 'despicable when humility is permitted to merge into humiliation' (Marryat, *Written in Fire*, I:79). Here Marryat argues that the submissiveness demanded of women is the cause of the violence they suffer: by becoming meek and docile, they render themselves worthless. Ominously, their surviving son, Andy, is described as having inherited his father's viciousness, using 'his little sister and his animals to practice upon' (Marryat, *Written in Fire*, I:79). Like many feminists, Marryat perceived unmistakable links between the abuse of women and vivisection, and this became a dominant theme in her fiction.[4]

'A quieting dose': *The Root of All Evil*

In *The Root of All Evil* (1879), Marryat juxtaposes middle- and working-class marital violence. Bonnie Bell, a greengrocer's assistant, is coerced into marriage with costermonger Kit Masters. Before he has even proposed, Kit forces himself upon her, his ardour undampened by her shrieks and frantic struggling (Marryat, *The Root of All Evil*, 14). The authorial voice comments '[c]ommon sense might teach them that the girl who shrinks intuitively from their embrace is hardly likely to prove a passionate and devoted wife' (Marryat, *The Root of All Evil*, 138), and their marriage is predictably unhappy. Kit soon administers a 'violent blow upon the side of [her] head' (Marryat, *The Root of All Evil*, 145), the first of many. When Bonnie seeks her grandmother's sympathy, she is told:

> I suppose you druv 'im beside hisself and 'e just let out at you. You musn't think of sich trifles.[...] You mustn't never go against a man. Allays let 'im 'ave 'is own way, and 'e'll jog on quiet enough
> (Marryat, *The Root of All Evil*, 185)

These are exactly the sentiments expressed by Sarah Stickney Ellis. Having also witnessed the shoemaker's wife 'with her cheek laid open from a blow with a cobbler's awl,' Bonnie realises that marriage means servitude, subordination and harsh discipline:

> To be a wife, she found was to be a sort of servant—at the beck and call of one person only—who must do, not what she liked, but what she was told, or she would be punished for her disobedience.
> (Marryat, *The Root of All Evil*, 186)

The frequency of Kit's violence impairs Bonnie's mental capacity, rendering her 'stupid and dull,' prompting him to 'jog her memory with a stick' (Marryat, *The Root of All Evil*, 186). Her expressions of grief at her grandmother's death provoke a 'quieting dose' from Kit so severe that his mother fears he will end up in jail, just like one of their neighbours, who 'finished his wife by mistake' (Marryat, *The Root of All Evil*, 191). Driven to despair, Bonnie runs away, seeking sanctuary in Putney workhouse. But he soon tracks her down. Although a shadow of her former self, he instantly recognizes her by the 'scream of terror' with which she greets him, her frightened face haunting the matron after he drags her away (Marryat, *The Root of All Evil*, 192). Back home, Kit is told by a neighbour that Bonnie is pregnant, and she warns him that he will be lynched if he lays a hand on his wife. This collective surveillance keeps him in check, at least temporarily. Kit exacts his revenge by selling the baby boy to a rich family for £100. The plot takes a welcome happy turn when Bonnie is reunited with her son, but the reader's joy is short-lived. The baby's constitution has been fatally weakened by his father's mistreatment and he soon dies. This melodramatic storyline grabs the reader's attention by emphasizing the wide-reaching consequences of domestic abuse.

The plight of Bonnie Masters recalls the case of Susannah Palmer, also a costermonger's wife, whose harrowing story dominated the press in December 1868. While her husband had dodged prison after blacking her eyes and punching out five of her teeth, Susannah was sent to Newgate for inflicting a slight cut to his hand in self-defence (Cobbe, 69). When Frances Power Cobbe attempted to secure her release, Susannah 'expressed perfect contentment because her husband could not get at her' (Doggett, 112), mirroring Bonnie Masters's relief at having found sanctuary in the workhouse – the place of last resort for most people. For some women, prison and the workhouse were preferable to marriage, which Marryat often depicts as an equally carceral institution.

This working-class marriage is compared with that of Lord and Lady Chasemore, who are no happier than Kit and Bonnie. Like Kit, Lord Chasemore believes he can do as he pleases with his wife, informing her that she must submit to his control, else he will be obliged to use 'brute force' (Marryat, *The Root of All Evil*, 172–73). Grasping her arm roughly, he snarls 'it is time you learned who is your master!' (Marryat, *The Root of All Evil*, 172). With the benefit of vast wealth, the Chasemores are able to live apart, yet the wife remains under her husband's control. Chasemore's threats and rough treatment of his wife illustrate the prevailing idea that women's behaviour must be regulated by superior strength and coercion. Their supposedly 'natural' sphere requires careful policing. The novel's title of *The Root of All Evil* suggests a plot centred on society's inexorable descent into materialism, but Marryat implies that male brutality is just as damaging – estranging families and dividing communities.

The critical response to this novel confirms societal attitudes. The *Graphic*'s reviewer completely ignores the working-class sub-plot, focusing only on the financial arrangements of the Chasemores and failing to note their abusive relationship ('New Novels', 619). Meanwhile, a reviewer for *The Athenaeum* scorned Bonnie's weakness, presumably implying that she deserved her punishments ('*The Root of All Evil*', 724). These responses were echoes of voices in Parliament and the press which sought to either excuse or disregard the reality of marital violence. Marryat's fictional representations were an unwelcome intrusion of reality.

'A sackful of flies': *The Nobler Sex*

Marryat's final novel on the theme of marital violence was the one that received the harshest criticism – mainly because it was her most avowedly personal story. *The Nobler Sex* (1892) follows closely the documented events of Marryat's life with only a few details – mainly names and locations – changed. Written retrospectively in the first person as Mollie Malmaison, it fulfils George Landow's criteria to be classed as autobiographical:

> [It] must not only present a version, myth, or metaphor or the self, but it must also be retrospective and hence it must self-consciously contrast two selves, the writing 'I' and the one located (or created) in the past.
>
> (Landow, xliii)

Every chapter heading starts with 'I', reinforcing that it is Marryat, rather than the fictional heroine, who is addressing the reader.

William Stopford (modelled on Marryat's first husband) is repeatedly violent toward his wife Mollie (Marryat) and their child Nita. In an early episode, William shoves Mollie violently against a table for refusing the sexual advances of his boss. Her refusal to be bartered ruins her husband's employment prospects. Like James Moray in *Her World Against a Lie*, William also torments his child to indirectly persecute his wife. Misogyny is again compounded by a cowardly attack on the maternal bond. William strikes baby Nita's legs with a riding whip, slashing her legs until they were 'covered with weals' (Marryat, *The Nobler Sex*, 62). Mollie explains how she tried to wrest the whip from him, but

> wrenching his arm away he threw me violently across the threshold which divided the two apartments, where I fell against the bed he had just quitted. I was considerably shaken and my spine was bruised and hurt.
>
> (Marryat, *The Nobler Sex*, 62)

When Mollie succeeds in escaping with Nita, William follows them, expecting her to support him. Mollie seeks refuge with her unsympathetic family, who urge her to return to William and resume her wifely duties. After arguments about money,

> [h]e gave me a blow that sent me reeling down the flight of stairs. I caught at the banisters to try and save myself in falling, and broke off two of them in my hand, and I landed on the mat in the hall with no limbs broken, fortunately, but cut, bruised and bleeding. Although William had often shoved and pushed me about before, and had tied my hands behind my back, and subjected me to various other indignities, this was the first time he had actually assaulted me.
>
> (Marryat, *The Nobler Sex*, 99–100)

'[V]arious other indignities' implies marital rape, a concept absent from British law until 1991. The quote also recalls battered wife Hester Detheridge in Wilkie Collins's *Man and Wife* (1870), who refers obliquely to enduring 'the last and worst of many indignities' (Collins, 270). Mollie seeks protection from the apparently sympathetic David Annesley (based on her second husband), whom she later marries. Unfortunately, he is no improvement on his predecessor, threatening her variously with a chair leg, a truncheon and a carving knife. His attempt to strangle her is prevented only by the intercession of the servants. When David's temper flares again and he accuses Mollie (incorrectly) of adultery, she locks herself in the bedroom. But the door is no obstacle to his violence:

> Without a warning of his intention, Annesley marched straight to the bedside, and, seizing me by the collar of my night-dress, dragged

me out upon the floor, and kicked me before him into the next room, where he flung me upon the bed. I rose to leave him, or call for assistance, but he placed himself before the door. "If you cry out," he exclaimed, "or make a scene about this, I'll kick you all the way downstairs, and out on the pavement just as you are." And then followed the usual execrations and abuse.

(Marryat, *The Nobler Sex*, 300)

The location of the attack – Mollie's bed – again implies marital rape, and she subsequently refers to the incident as 'the last indignity I would suffer at the hands of this man' (Marryat, *The Nobler Sex*, 301). When their masculinity is challenged by Mollie, both William and David respond with the most devastating act of violation: rape.

Mollie, although a strong woman, is a helpless victim of not only her husbands, but also the legal system. She comments, bitterly, 'Let [wives] attempt to rend the chains that gall them, and they will find how little justice there is in England for the woman' (Marryat, *The Nobler Sex*, 141). Towards the conclusion of the novel, a liberated Mollie reflects on the legislative change that has occurred during her (and Marryat's) lifetime:

Woman used to be so entirely and utterly in the power of her master. Thank God for us all that that day has passed away, and that if wives continue to be white slaves, they do so of their own free will. England has never borne a darker blot than the freedom formerly allowed to husbands to torture the unhappy creature they had sworn to cherish. It is sufficient for a quick-witted woman to have noted the ill-concealed chagrin exhibited by the stronger sex, at the passing of the merciful Act of Parliament that in some measure freed their wives from injustice and tyranny, to see how much such a protection was needed.

(Marryat, *The Nobler Sex*, 256–57)

The cumulative effects of the 1878 Matrimonial Causes Act and the 1882 Married Women's Property Act free both Mollie and Marryat herself. These changes came about only because victims and commentators were prepared to demonstrate how greatly reality differed from ideology.

Critics were unwilling, or perhaps unable, to engage with Marryat's arguments. For them, she was a female novelist who had chosen to divulge unsavoury truths that should have remained private. Mollie Malmaison was trivialized by the *Graphic*'s reviewer as 'the helpless victim of morbid impulses,' and the novel likened to 'the dissection of a sackful of flies' ('New Novels', 702). These comments are illustrative of the 'ill-concealed chagrin' Marryat denounces through Mollie – the resistance exerted by conservative forces who wished women to remain subordinate. Of Marryat's sustained attack on the institution of marriage throughout her career, the critic lamented 'a certain angry tone' that had for some time 'injured' her work ('New Novels', 702). A female author must entertain and provide moral nourishment, but certainly not complain.

Conclusion

It is this willingness to complain and to share her own story that makes Marryat an important voice. She insisted that marital violence was both a threat and a reality, refusing the suggestion that she and other victims should suffer in ladylike silence. Her unflinching fictional accounts challenged the idea that women's experiences were unsuitable for public consumption.

As violence alone was insufficient grounds for divorce at this time, the stories of many abused women went unheard. As I have discussed, this led many commentators, even feminists such as Frances Power Cobbe, to conclude that wife-beating was a problem confined to the working classes. By boldly articulating her own experiences, Marryat showed vividly that it did. She challenged the highly influential misconception that the middle-class wife was always *protected* rather than threatened by her husband.

Through her repeated portrayals of middle-class marital violence, rendered more forcefully than by any other author, Marryat helped define its existence. By narrating the non-narratable, Marryat used her fiction to empower women and show how they could resist male oppression, offering strong heroines and practical advice. The furious critical response to Marryat's readiness to make public her sufferings exemplifies the ideology that sought to maintain women's subordinate position. And Marryat's refusal to be silenced attests to the bravery of those women – both real and fictional – who eventually benefited from the changes they demanded.

Notes

1 The 1857 Matrimonial Causes Act, popularly known as the Divorce Act, established the Divorce Court. Under the terms of the act, men could divorce their wives on grounds of adultery alone, whereas a wronged wife had to prove that her husband's adultery had been 'aggravated' by bigamy, incest, sodomy or cruelty. The act, therefore, enshrined the sexual double standard in law. See Shanley (42).

2 For further discussion of these revisions, see the introduction to the forthcoming critical edition of *Love's Conflict* (Victorian Secrets, 2018).

3 The MS included in the Lord Chamberlain's Plays collection at the British Library comprises only a few soot-blackened pages.

4 See *The Dead Man's Message* (1894), *The Blood of the Vampire* (1897) and *An Angel of Pity* (1898).

Works Cited

3 Hansard 147 (13 August 1857), 1538.

A. Lady. 'Feminine Foilbles, Fancies, and Fashions'. *Weekly Mail*, 15 May 1880.

'Adelphi Theatre'. *Reynold's Newspaper*, 20 February 1881.

'Belles Lettres'. *Westminster Review*, July 1892, 687–92.

Blackstone, Sir William, and William Draper Lewis. *Commentaries on the Laws of England: In Four Books*. Vol. 2. 4 vols. Philadelphia, PA: George T. Bisel, 1922.

Cobbe, Frances Power. 'Wife-Torture in England'. *The Contemporary Review* 32 (1878): 55–87.

Collins, Wilkie. *Man and Wife*. Vol. 3. 3 vols. London: F S Ellis, 1870.

Doggett, Maeve E. *Marriage, Wife-Beating and the Law in Victorian England*. London: Weidenfeld and Nicolson, 1992.

Ellis, Sarah Stickney. *The Mothers of England: Their Influence and Responsibility*. London: Fisher, Son & Co, 1843.

Foyster, Elizabeth. *Marital Violence: An English Family History, 1660–1857*. Cambridge: Cambridge University Press, 2005.

Hammerton, A. James. *Cruelty and Companionship: Conflict in Nineteenth-Century Married Life*. London: Routledge, 1992.

'Her World Against a Lie'. *The Athenaeum*, 7 December 1878.

'Her World Against a Lie'. *The Spectator*, 16 August 1879.

Kaye, John William. 'Outrages on Women'. *North British Review* 25, no. 49 (1856): 233–56.

Landow, George P. *Approaches to Victorian Autobiography*. Athens: Ohio University Press, 1979.

Lawson, Kate, and Lynn Shakinovsky. *The Marked Body: Domestic Violence in Mid-Nineteenth Century Literature*. New York: State University of New York Press, 2002.

Marryat, Florence. *A Fatal Silence*. New York: Hovendon Company, 1891.

———. *Her World Against a Lie*. Vol. 1. 3 vols. London: Samuel Tinsley & Co., 1879.

———. *Love's Conflict*. Vol. 2. 3 vols. London: Richard Bentley, 1865.

———. *The Nobler Sex*. New York and London: Street & Smith, 1890.

———. *The Root of All Evil*. London: Richard Edward King, 1879.

———. *Written in Fire*. Vol. 1. 3 vols. London: Tinsley Brothers, 1878.

Mill, John Stuart. *On Liberty and the Subjection of Women*. Edited by Alan Ryan. London; New York: Penguin, 2006.

'New Novels'. *The Graphic*, 20 December 1879.

'New Novels'. *The Graphic*, 10 December 1892.

Shanley, Mary Lyndon. *Feminism, Marriage and the Law in Victorian England*. Princeton, NJ: Princeton University Press, 1993.

Straton, Jack C. 'Rule of Thumb versus Rule of Law'. *Men and Masculinities* 5, no. 1 (1 July 2002): 103–9.

Surridge, Lisa. *Bleak Houses: Marital Violence in Victorian Fiction*. Athens: Ohio University Press, 2005.

'The London Theatres'. *The Era*, 19 February 1881.

'The Root of All Evil'. *The Athenaeum*, 1879.

12 Marriage in Matriarchy

Matrimony in Women's Utopian Fiction 1888–1909

Rebecca Styler

> It is not marriage per se, but the whole social drift with which it is
> at present co-related, that constitutes the evil. We must not look for
> destruction, but for re-birth.
>
> —(Caird, 110)

Utopian fiction flourished in the final decades of the nineteenth century and early decades of the twentieth, when the political scene was
pervaded by a mood of expectancy and a 'widespread perception that
one epoch of history [was] in its decline and another [was] announcing
its ascendency' (Beaumont 2009, 21). This was also the era of the first
organised women's movement, in service to which some female authors
wrote utopian novels embodying a vision of 'emancipated interpersonal
relations' between men and women, grounded in the abolition of sex-
based hierarchies in law and culture (Beaumont 2001, 212). This chapter
considers the characterisation of marriage in a group of feminist utopian texts published between 1888 and 1909 that specifically address
women's societal oppression and envision an alternative society in which
gender relations are radically reconstructed to women's (and it is often argued men's) benefit: Jane Hume Clapperton's *Margaret Dunmore: or, A
Socialist Home* (1888); Elizabeth Burgoyne Corbett's *New Amazonia: A
Foretaste of the Future* (1889); Amelia Mears' *Mercia, The Astronomer
Royal: A Romance* (1895); Florence Ethel Mills Young's *The War of the
Sexes* (1905); and Irene Clyde's *Beatrice the Sixteenth* (1909). Kenneth
Roemer defines a literary utopia as 'a fairly detailed description of an
imaginary community, society or world – a "fiction" that encourages
readers to experience vicariously a culture that represents a prescriptive, normative alternative to their own culture'.[1] These five texts include
fully envisioned societies of the future, alternative worlds glimpsed by
a lost traveller and experimental communities set in the contemporary
moment. They are all in a sense matriarchal: some are explicitly women-
dominated, others that are basically egalitarian nonetheless assume that
it is women who will set the terms of the future based on their moral
superiority, in tune with much feminist rhetoric of the period.[2] They

draw force from the popular myth of origins offered by late-nineteenth-century anthropological descriptions of sympathetic matriarchal societies that, it was argued, universally preceded the dominating structures of patriarchy.[3]

In the late nineteenth century, the central relationship that formed the context for Victorian women's personal, economic and social destinies, and was idealised by traditionalists as 'that faithful union of Two upon which pure and progressive society is built'[4] came under sustained attack. As Shirley Foster shows, mid-Victorian novelists had made oblique moves to 'uncover the miseries of matrimonial bondage', but in the fin de siècle era the institution of marriage became the focus of feminist polemic on a large scale (Foster, 14). It was not so much the idea of a permanent, exclusive heterosexual pairing that was questioned, as the particular legal, economic and cultural binds that made matrimony oppressive to women. The 1890s experienced 'a flood of anti-marriage propaganda' in the 1890s in which writers like George Egerton criticised the institution as little better than legalised prostitution, or as a form of slavery that reduced a woman's status to that of 'the personal body-servant of a despot'.[5] This barrage was instigated by Mona Caird's influential series of journal articles (1887–94), later published as *The Morality of Marriage* (1897), which argued that in its current state, marriage was 'not a thought-out rational system of sex relationship, but a lineal descendant of barbarian usages, cruel and absurd [...] revolting now to all ideas of human justice and of dignity [...] the last citadel of the less intelligent kind of conservatism' (Caird, 57–58). An 1887 article in the *Daily Telegraph* 'Is Marriage a Failure?' elicited 27,000 responses (Bland 1987, 146). Feminist polemicists and novelists presented matrimony as a degrading exchange of sexual and domestic services for economic support and social status that were valuable only because of women's enforced financial dependence on men. While some improvements had been achieved through the 1857 Matrimonial Causes Act, the 1873 Infants Custody Act, the 1870 and 1882 Married Women's Property Acts and expanding professional opportunities in teaching and clerical work which made marriage more of a free choice, there was still much to protest about 'the unequal and undesirable position of married women' even above that of single women (Bland 1987, 146). Women's legal disabilities in relation to divorce, child custody and subjection to men's presumed 'conjugal rights' were all targets. As discussions of 'New Woman' writing show, feminist fiction of the era abounds in depictions of the mental and physical ruination caused by marriages from which women could not escape, forming a barrage of protest against the current conditions on which matrimony was practised.[6]

The drift of these is pessimistic, showing women with progressive views entrapped in an institution that sanctifies primitive male-female relations – as Showalter suggests, these writers were painting the bars of their cage rather than seeing past them to new possibilities (Showalter, 215). Utopian fiction of the same period has a more optimistic strain, painting instead the possibilities of ideal marriage beyond the cage constructed by regressive law and custom. They fulfil the positive aspiration of influential polemicists like Caird who announced that 'To bring the institution of the family up to date is among the next tasks of progressive civilization', a project that was to be achieved by cleansing matrimony of 'patriarchal rights' and establishing it as a fully consensual contract between equals bound not only by affection but by friendship (Caird, 58). As Anne Mellor argues, literary utopias have a dual critical and prophetic function: by portraying 'a potentially realizable world' based on different norms to those that govern the present, the writer can 'define precisely the nature and origin of social ill in the world in which the author lives', as well as offering 'a set of guidelines for social reform' that might determine the future (Mellor, 242–43). Feminist utopias therefore defamiliarise the status quo, and highlight its errors, as well as open the reader's horizons to alternative possibilities on which change could be modelled. As Matthew Beaumont suggests, utopian fiction served as a 'counter-factual thought-experiment' for feminists who could, through their detailed 'realistic' representations of other social models, supply a kind of 'evidence' for the success of non-patriarchal gender relations when no such proof was furnished by any actual social organisation in the past or present (Beaumont 2001, 212). Feminist utopias therefore constituted a genre both of protest, and of aspiration, in which (as Barbara C. Quissell observes) writers were free to express their most radical ideals, undiluted by the compromises demanded by social reality that pressed upon political activists and realist novelists (Quissell, 148).

Criticism on the nineteenth-century novel rarely attends to utopian texts, which tend to be discussed in the separate genre-focused field of utopian studies – perhaps because the polemical 'plainspeaking' of utopian texts does not fit the preferred criteria for literariness of subtlety and ambiguity (Ingram and Patai, 4–5). As Darby Lewes says, these texts are not 'great literature' according to canonical criteria (Lewes, 1). Discussions of feminist utopias of the era of first-wave feminism have suggested that British writers have little to say about marriage in the feminist future. In an argument that has been frequently recapitulated, Nina Albinski contrasts the domestic feminism of US utopian writers, who envisage women's lives transformed by their elevated status within the home and by practical reforms regarding housework and childcare, with British writers' greater interest 'in legal and political changes' to women's condition, above all securing the vote (Ablinski 1990, 51).[7] Albinski cites as typical Florence Dixie Douglas's *Gloriana* (1890), which is all about suffrage with no attention paid to the married state whatever. While the contrast between US and UK utopias holds in general, it an oversimplification worth nuancing. It is true that in all the utopias mentioned above women have equal political agency to men, with the assumption that this is a sine qua non for achieving other feminist reforms, but most of the texts (*Gloriana* aside) offer more ideas than this on how marriage can become acceptable to the emancipated woman. While details vary, they all suggest that the marital relationship cannot be reconstituted in its own sphere sealed from the exigencies of women's legal, economic and political status at large; rather they insist on the interrelation between private and public spheres, home and state, family and collective.

Removing the Pecuniary Motive

The issue given most overt attention is the commercial motive in marriage. Critics saw women's lack of financial independence as the crucial factor that compelled many into marriage, bound them to husbands they did not necessarily love and distorted the dynamic between even affectionate spouses. Mona Caird suggested that marriage functioned as little more than a form of prostitution coated with a rhetoric of religious sentiment, describing women 'selling themselves for a livelihood' in 'the most hypocritical form of woman-purchase'(Caird, 99–100). Feminist utopia writers insist on women's education and professional freedom so that marriage becomes a genuine choice, and a partner can be selected for reasons of fellowship not provision.

The socialist values that pervaded much of British first-wave feminism are evident in texts that are not content simply to equip women to compete with men as individual economic agents, but rather envisage women's equal participation in a collective structure of economic interdependence. In *New Amazonia* (1889), the male guide of the future takes this reform for granted: 'How can women be independent and free, if they have to rely on others to keep them?' he asks in puzzlement of the nineteenth-century time-traveller (Corbett, 147). The state takes the place of the family as provider, owning all services, businesses and welfare sources, removing the need for any individual to depend on another (Corbett, 70–72, 79). A form of maternity benefit is provided in that nursing mothers are 'maintained by the state' (Corbett, 75).

Similar terms are established on a more voluntary and smaller-scale basis in the experimental socialist utopia pictured in *Margaret Dunmore*, whose motto is 'We hold the equal duty of all to labour' in an attempt to abolish the proletarianism of the majority and idleness of the few, but also the financial dependence of women on men (Clapperton, 72). With its emphasis on characters adjusting to socialist living, Clapperton addresses cultural (more than legal) barriers to women, including women's own snobbery about labour and men's pride in their monopoly of the breadwinner role (Clapperton, 4–7). The novel also shows the practical disadvantages of wives' dependence for men as well as women, one male character wondering 'How is a man ever to marry at all, if children are to be taken into account as well as money, social position, and all the rest of it?' (Clapperton, 40). Since the 'associated home' involves women largely working within the home, and men outside of it, Clapperton clearly regards women's financial dependence as a greater problem than the nature of the work they do. As well as addressing the problems of the bourgeois marriage, the novel attends to the impossibility of working-class women holding out for a respectable marriage when their earnings are insufficient to prevent them turning to means to supplement their income that involve them in exploitative dynamics with wealthier men: in an unsentimental treatment of the fallen woman theme, seamstress Ruth's part-time modelling leads to living as her painter's mistress in preference to poverty. Being offered a place in the commune that does not condemn her former behaviour, but recognises its economic under-pinning, liberates her from a relationship in which love is tainted by the commercial motive. Clapperton, like a number of other feminist critics of her time, hence implies the parallel between bourgeois marriage and prostitution, and suggests a cross-class liberation of women from merce-nary marriages through a model of economic interdependence.

Margaret Dunmore is also concerned with the psychological detri-ment to women of economic dependency, which feeds the man's ego and infantilises the woman in a way 'obstructive to a true union' of minds (Clapperton, 17). The narrator is drily satirical about Frank's flattered 'vanity' and 'feeling of male supremacy' when teaching Rose about sci-ence, of which she knows nothing because of being given an inferior education to her brother (Clapperton, 17). Dependent women cannot afford to be assertive and therefore suffer emotional and sexual repres-sion: Vera protests that women cannot be first to declare their feelings (*New Amazonia* and *Mercia* make the same point) and are forced to suffer in silence. In a daring move, *Margaret Dunmore* suggests sexual frustration on the part of women forced to wait for marriage until their husbands can afford to keep them – contravening both the sexual passiv-ity assumed of women in conservative thinking, and the ascetic attitude to sex that is characteristic of the utopia texts and formed a thread in fin-de-siècle feminism.[8] The unreconstructed Joe is rather embarrassed, and unnerved, to recognise that his fiancee would prefer to work because she 'doesn't like waiting'. 'He had an instinct, though he could not have put it into words, that the simple, pure-minded Vera was a little disgraced by her readiness to become wife before masculine urgency required it of her' (Clapperton, 44–45). For Clapperton, women's economic agency becomes a metonym of their personal agency in many dimensions, and the end of their infantilisation. It is men's sense of what they will lose in power that makes them more reluctant to join the collective than their fiancées for whom interdependence involves an expansion, not dimin-ishment, of self since the communitarian model undoes the patriarchal structure of the bourgeois familial set-up.

Not all the utopias adopt this collective vision, for *Mercia* envisions professional equality in purely individual terms, and given that its society is not a democracy but ruled by a patrician few (men and women), it is not the vote but financial independence that is the foundational reform to liberate women. In this scientifically focused society women are doctors, scientists and engineers – traditionally masculine fields of work – and the protagonist is appointed as Royal astronomer in preference to a less able male candidate. As in *Margaret Dunmore*, women's economic equality is argued as a benefit to husbands as well as wives. By 2002, 'A wife ceased to be a kind of encumbrance upon a struggling man, and became a helpmate in a very substantial sense'; wives contributing to the household finances means 'less strain' upon the man, whose longevity increases accordingly (Mears, 21). Reconstructed males feel no threat from women earning up to five times more than themselves – in such cases, 'the bridegroom's good luck might be envied by his companions, but no one thought the worse of either' (Mears, 6). Being 'equal as breadwinners' raises the motives for marriage on both sides from merely material ones (Mears, 9), and women could become 'more exacting' in their requirements of a suitable mate (Mears, 101–2).

Another vital repercussion of women's right to decently paid work is the right to independent vocation that does not have to be surrendered on entering the married state. The utopias refute the conservative commonplace that 'The true woman has no interests separate from those of her home [...] Her highest ambition and her noblest vocation are to be found in that sacred circle', instead demanding that women are to be 'admitted, on equal terms, to the banquet of life' and men must outgrow the petty egoism of being the sole focus of their wives' energies (Caird, 76). While the socialist utopias tend to emphasise women's traditional vocation of sympathetic service extended to a wider community (albeit as a model for men also to follow), others develop the notion of a career, a path of professional fulfilment on parallel terms to that enjoyed by middle-class men. Both *Mercia* and *The War of the Sexes* imagine successful and fulfilled women scientists who expect no compromise of their career when taking a husband. Mercia, the heroic and virtuous protagonist, is 'devoted to her profession' (Mears, 45). When this is threatened by her attraction to her assistant Geometrus (because of an arbitrary ruling that astronomers, male and female, cannot marry and retain their posts) Geometrus chooses to keeps his romantic feelings hidden rather than 'ruin her life' by making her choose between marriage and the work she loves, as well as its good income (Mears, 105). Neither regards marriage and colleagueship as mutually exclusive: 'they two could labour together' (Mears, 107).

The right to an independent vocation is the primary message of the parodic utopian novel *The War of the Sexes*, a comedy in which a misogynistic nineteenth-century professor of science finds himself in a future world in which men have become extinct, and women reproduce parthenogenetically (with chemical assistance) – a destiny argued in all seriousness as the goal of evolution by anti-male feminists such as Frances Swiney. (See, for example, Swiney's 1906 *The Cosmic Procession, or The Feminine Principle in Evolution* which forecasts and celebrates such an eventuality.) Through the experience of being the sole living vestige of 'a lower order of being' (Young, 39), the Misognynist (as the protagonist is consistently called) is educated through role reversal, powerless in a world where men fulfil none of women's needs – he is variously demeaned and lionised as a curiosity. Seeking a wife for protection and respectability, he proposes to the independent Miss Harward, also a scientist, who mocks his egocentric assumptions about the role she would play in his life: 'I could help you with your work, and discuss your theories intelligently with you across the breakfast-table. Occasionally, perhaps, you would take an interest in my little aims, but you would be relieved if I didn't expect you to do it too often' (Young, 226–27). In a world where he is powerless to set his own terms, his humbling is achieved through becoming a laboratory assistant to Miss Howard (ironically in her project to devise a means to chemically preserve his remains for posterity as a biological curiosity), and finally announcing he is willing to give up his own work to marry the woman he has learned to regard as a friend and colleague first, and a lover second (Young, 242–43). The novel does not view a manless society as the ideal but makes its point through use of a festive comedy structure: the lesson learned in the subversive dream-world brings a reformed perspective to reality. When the professor wakes to find himself back in nineteenth-century reality, he sees the possibility of 'friendship' with the real Miss Harwood, who is widely recognised as 'quite as great a genius' as him (Young, 295, 259), and promises in his proposal to 'stand on a level with [her]', rather than place her 'on a pedestal' through condescending chivalry. That both *Mercia* and *The War of the Sexes* envisage husbands and wives sharing a common vocational interest makes a case for intellectual fellowship as the new basis for marriage, rather than distinct and complementary roles.

Divorce

The 1857 Matrimonial Causes Act had enabled women for the first time to seek a divorce, but not on equal terms to men. While a husband could sue for adultery, a woman had to prove in addition to adultery another form of abuse (including cruelty, desertion, incest), with the implied double standard regarding male and female infidelity. A theme in much criticism of this inequity was a woman's right to ownership of her body, in objection to marital sex that was frequently non-consensual, and its consequent endless childbearing, in a culture which upheld husband's 'conjugal rights'.[9] A bill to equalise divorce for women and add desertion as a grounds went before Parliament in 1892, but failed. Several of the utopia texts present a world in which divorce is not only equally accessible to women and men (achieved in 1923), but easily and inexpensively, and in addition for the grounds of incompatibility alone (grounds not recognised in UK law until 1969). In *New Amazonia*, the marriage contract becomes a 'purely civil one, dissolvable almost without cost, upon one or other of the parties to it proving incompatibility or unfaithfulness on the part of the other' (Corbett, 74), and since the state provides for children, women are at no risk of becoming burdened with their financial support. In *Mercia* too, marriage is 'a serious civil contract' unclouded by religious rhetoric: divorce is permitted for adultery and incompatibility, 'on equitable principles' for the sexes, with people's happiness in mind rather than a culture of blame or accusation (Mears, 99–101). With its characteristic lack of reverence for parental attachment, children are divided up between the separated parents, and the husband obliged to contribute to his ex-wife's maintenance if her earnings are not sufficient for her needs.

Margaret Dunmore makes an implicit plea for divorce through an example of a couple whose love seems on the wane, a situation presented with no sense of fall or failure but as a consequence of the vicissitudes of human affection and desire. When Rose's husband Frank appears to be falling in love with another inhabitant of the collective home, she does not want them to be 'the bondmen of a luckless and helpless matrimony', and although her original feelings are unaffected she tells him 'you are not to blame' (Clapperton, 162). While the situation is perhaps rather close to the image of a patient wife forbearing with her husband's infidelity, Rose's suggestion of a divorce is presented as an act of empowerment and self-respect, a refusal to live in a loveless marriage. While many Christian socialist utopias of the era – including ones written by women – were often quite conservative in their apportioning of gender roles (such as Marianne Farningham's *1900? A Forecast and a Story* [1892], and C. A. Scrymsour Nichol's *The Mystery of the North Pole* [1908]), Rose claims that 'Christianity' is on her side. She quotes John Milton (who was usually the butt of nineteenth-century feminist criticism for his representation of a subordinate Eve): 'It is a less breach of wedlock to part with wise and quiet consent betimes, than to foil and profane that mystery of joy and union' (Clapperton, 167). She asserts the right to seek a divorce herself, and not wait for his instigation, renouncing her legal status as his 'property' to keep or dispose of as *he* wishes (Clapperton, 167). None of these texts present a couple actually using their divorce rights – Frank recalls his deeper love for Rose, as does a temporarily troubled husband in *Mercia* – but they evoke divorce to suggest that its easy availability enhances marriage by obliging husbands in particular to earn their wives' continuous goodwill, since they can no longer rely on the law to oblige them to stay.

Being a Wife: Housework and Motherhood

It is true that the British utopian texts are less focused than contemporaneous American ones on the practical, everyday matters that constituted many married women's lives, such as housework, childbearing and childrearing. However, they do not ignore these matters entirely, and offer some suggestions, most of which involve support from sources outside of the home. Essentially, these fictions aim to break away from a model that aligns domestic labour inevitably from wifehood, although some traditional class and gender attitudes linger in the way they apportion this work. Edward Bellamy's seminal socialist utopia *Looking Backward* (1888), which launched the fin-de-siècle wave of literary utopias in America and Britain, envisaged housework being done in factory-style laundries and kitchens, rendered efficient and less burdensome by the application of technology that had industrialised other manual processes in the nineteenth century. *New Amazonia* follows suit to a degree, since electricity is harnessed to fuel 'warming, lighting, cooking' (Corbett, 152), and the narrator finds it a particular 'treat' to see how electric machinery solves 'the greatest problem which my own countrywomen are beset with, viz., how to minimise the labour and discomfort which with us so invariably attend washing days' (Corbett, 156). Laundry and clothes-making are undertaken outside the home in Domestic Aid Societies, which can also be booked to offer home services, and which employ 'skilled workpeople' of both sexes whom the narrator confirms are state-trained, well-paid and highly respected and who choose the work because it suits them (Corbett, 156–58). Nonetheless, there is a hierarchy of intellectual and manual labour that smacks of lingering class divisions in their designation as 'working classes' and in the state's close supervision of their labour routines (Corbett, 156, 158). In *Mercia* similar class inflections linger, as well as the assumption that this is essentially women's work. The intellectual woman is freed to pursue a profession by outsourcing housework to 'the woman-servant'; gender is reconfigured only in as far as the husband oversees 'housekeeping' (presumably to book the woman-servant's services) if his wife is indisposed (Mears, 7). The servants' burden is lightened by electrical appliances, their status raised, and their wages sufficient to 'run a home, husband, and children on her own account' (Mears, 8). Despite these utopias conforming to the 'middle-class world-views' typical of the genre in this era,[10] both authors at least insist that the work should be well-paid, respected and made less onerous through deploying the latest technology.

   Margaret Dunmore is more egalitarian in its treatment of who does the housework, working towards the possibility that men might undertake it cheerfully in a completed utopia. As in other matters, the novel addresses the emotional trials of womanhood in the bourgeois isolated home, arguing the 'care and weariness' incurred ordinarily by domestic labour for a wife who spends long hours alone at home (Clapperton, 160). Communal housework is not only more efficient, but more fun: 'instead of weary monotony, a breeze of healthful activity and excitement pervades the household' (Clapperton, 89). Although traditional gender assumptions to some extent continue with women seeming to do most of the housework, leading Sally Ledger to criticise Clapperton's failure to fully work through her feminist principles (Ledger, 37), this is in fact presented as a transitional phase rather than the commune's destiny. The matter of whether housework is innately gendered is a subject for debate among the inhabitants, one man arguing that 'The pen is no more manly than the needle ... If a man liked to sit all day at a desk, why should he not like to sit at a table darning stockings?' (Clapperton, 92–93). With work being chosen according to personal preference and ability, this man makes his contribution through cleaning. One man who does insist such work is intrinsically 'feminine' later 'flung his notions of sex-distinctions in work to the wind' to nurse his wife rather than leave it to someone else (Clapperton, 125). The egalitarian principle that children must do their own housework instead of having servants (or mothers) do it for them, suggests the potential for fuller gender reconstruction in the next generation: 'the boys have to darn their own stockings and sew on their own buttons' (Clapperton, 178). This manifests at a practical level the text's general sense that the era of rigid sex-determined roles is over, and progress will be achieved through men and women living out a 'broad humanity' and following their individual inclinations (Clapperton, 194–95).

Reproduction is treated with great wariness in the fin-de-siècle utopias, responding to the widespread feminist complaints about women's bondage to continual childbearing, and a developing view that heedless motherhood was socially irresponsible in view of economic constraints and a burgeoning population. Integral to the 1890s marriage debates were discussions about forms of birth control (widely used among the middle classes by the end of the century), and calls to end women's sexual ignorance prior to marriage (Cunningham, 6–7). As Lucy Bland shows, late-century feminists often took ascetic views towards sex, hostile to free unions, extra-marital sexual relations and artificial means of birth control since they feared these options would increase male control – they demanded a change in male sexual behaviour far more than liberty of sexual expression for women (Bland 1987, 163–64). The only intervention Mona Caird is willing to advocate is abstinence, voicing a hope that the male sexual instinct will gradually diminish as humanity evolves to a higher state (Caird, 222–28). It was not until the publication of Marie Stopes' innovative marriage manual, *Married Love* (1918), that female sexual desire became a public topic. The utopian texts universally assume regulation of reproduction and subsume discussion of sex into a concern for limited family size – only *Margaret Dunmore* considers it in any positive way as integral to marital fellowship and affirms women's expression of desire as an aspect of their emancipation (as shown above). In an atmosphere that distrusted natural instincts as the guides to a progressive civilisation, the family is subject to regulating discourses and is less inevitably regarded as the 'nursery of virtue' for the next generation. Maternal instinct has little positive function in the utopian texts, which prioritise freeing women from the obligations and ties of maternity, and framing reproduction as a civic, not familial, function.

While *New Amazonia* ensures marriage is egalitarian, this condition of life is clearly disparaged in comparison with singleness: 'Our laws and social economy hold out wonderful premiums for chastity!' boasts the guide (Corbett, 113), stating that New Amazonians generally 'prefer honour and advancement to the more animal pleasures of marriage and reproduction of species' (Corbett, 114). Married women are denied public office on the grounds that 'perfect clearness of brain, and the ability to devote oneself exclusively to intellectual topics' are compromised by descent into the immediate and sensual experience of marriage and motherhood (Corbett, 114). *New Amazonia* places the provision and education of the child in the hands of the state, often referred to as 'the Mother' (Corbett, 75) and regulates family size ruthlessly according to 'Malthusian doctrines', criminalising anyone who has more than four children (Corbett, 75). There is no respect for parental attachment and little patience with sexual desire, as adulterous women are also criminalised, though punished less than the male party (in a reversal of nineteenth-century practice) suggesting he is inevitably the instigator (Corbett, 115). Most troublingly, the state's parenting extends into eugenic control, since deformed and illegitimate children are destroyed as degenerate undesirables, a practice given religious sanction by the theosophical claim that they are being released from corporeal imprisonment to evolve in a higher spiritual sphere (Corbett, 121); this demonstrates the eugenicist feminism common to much New Woman writing which made 'improvement' of the race a maternal responsibility.[11] As Alexis Lothian notes, the narrator-visitor's horrified reaction to these policies leaves us uncertain as to whether New Amazonia is meant to be entirely utopian, or in part a warning about the consequences of handing over reproductive functions to the control of a utilitarian state.[12]

Mercia also absolves women of most of the responsibilities of motherhood, albeit in a more libertarian framework. There is a cultural pressure for small families, assisted by education in 'the functions of reproduction' which 'enabled women to fill more intelligently the positions of wife and mother' – suggestive of birth control (Mears, 9). Horror is voiced at the memory of large Victorian families. Sentimental ideas of maternal influence become focused on 'the formation of the pre-natal mind' before birth through a woman's activities and thoughts during pregnancy (Mears, 12ff), rather than in long years of childrearing, which is outsourced to (female) professionals in another outworking of the text's bourgeois feminism (Mears, 50). Distaste for the physical aspects of maternity is voiced in the novel's wishful thinking on childbirth. A number of feminist utopias share Caird's logic that difference between the sexes in physical size and strength was 'not aboriginal' but created by restrictions on women's engagement in sports from childhood, and them being crushed into corsets; (Caird, 67) in emancipated societies, women are bigger and stronger, giving the Amazonian trope a literal future reality (see *Mercia*, *New Amazonia*, and *Gloriana*). *Mercia* optimistically argues that with greater strength and elasticity, a woman can endure childbirth with relative ease and recover quickly: 'in the space of a week she was fully restored and able to resume her social, household or professional duties, as if nothing had happened' (Mears, 49). Furthermore, evolved women have lost the capacity to breastfeed, so that 'the mother was equally free as the father in the matter of nursing, if she elected so to be' (Mears, 50). Mears wants to remove as far as possible not just the cultural, but also biological, characteristics that mark women out for childbearing so she can claim the same freedoms as men.

Margaret Dunmore presents sexuality and motherhood with more approval, but still suggests both should be regulated in the communitarian context. Family size is limited voluntarily through sexual abstinence, and delayed until the husband feels ready for fatherhood (Clapperton, 127). The novel strongly attacks the nuclear family structure as the cradle of civilised society, arguing that it is quite the opposite, since it fosters a narrow tribalism that furthers one's own child competitively at the expense of others. One member of the commune reflects: 'The English home is not what he thought it. Within its narrow bounds, in an atmosphere of class prejudice, dominancy, sometimes selfishness and pride, a noble or altruistic humanity can scarcely be reared. The home itself must evolve' (Clapperton, 58–59). Collective parenting is shown as the way to develop a child's altruistic consciousness, drawing on a 'breeze of parental emotions' (Clapperton, 127) and benefiting from the specialist input of various adults that is overseen by the Education Committee. A by-product of this is that the intergenerational hierarchy is much levelled, as children become active contributors and citizens in this social microcosm, calling adults by their first names and 'tak[ing] part in household work from the earliest possible age' (Clapperton, 132). The resultant child's 'affections are collective rather than individual' by habit, seed of a more altruistic humanity (185). Clapperton does not show women struggling to adjust to this relinquishment of attachment, but suggests the benefits to mothers, first because the sharing of childcare relieves her of constant responsibility and loneliness (Clapperton, 174), and second because women's equal role in the Education Committee (as on the overall household council) grants women more influence over their children's upbringing than was the reality in traditional homes where their much-vaunted authority was undermined by patriarchal domestic, legal and educational structures. Motherhood is empowered, then, only if it becomes a less exclusive attachment and is exercised for the good of the civic body.

Decentring the Heterosexual Bond

British feminist utopias question the pre-eminence of marriage as the location of women's highest personal and emotional fulfilment, recontextualising it alongside other modes of fulfilling relationship. (The exception is *Mercia* in which marriage becomes elevated to mystical proportions in a union between Mercia and the ruler of self-governing India that represents a meeting of feminine and masculine principles, West and East, in a theosophically inflected orientalist fantasy.) The conjugal monopoly on women's affections is under attack as another dimension of patriarchal dominance.

As is evident from the discussion above, some utopias envisage enhanced participation in the human collective as ethically superior to the confining focus on one partner, and service to humanity in a network of mutual obligations as less demeaning than dancing attendance on a solitary lord of the home. While in New Amazonia intimacy of any sort seems to vanish in cool co-operation and deference to the state, *Margaret Dunmore* envisages an expansion of 'home' that foregoes conjugal exclusivism. Emotions progress by the same logic as economics, in that the 'wealth of love is a simple necessity' to be shared on egalitarian terms, in which 'a selfish monopoly on the part of husband or wife is intolerable' (Clapperton, 195). While in the classic bildungsroman the protagonist's maturation is confirmed by matrimony, Clapperton shows characters growing out of exclusive pairings into a richer social consciousness, a development she suggests is something of a painful retraining for men, but a welcome relief for women. Vera escapes the 'hours of dreary solitude' and 'moods of depression' characteristic of wives left alone in the traditional home while the husband spends long hours at work, to experience 'an extraordinary animation' in the commune in which she transforms into 'an active, bustling little wife, whom her husband seemed hardly to know' (Clapperton, 116, 118). The diminutive is unfortunate, but the point is made that women thrive on more social stimulation and become their own person. The husband has to unlearn his centrality in his wife's existence, losing the expectation that 'the little woman would be all his own' through a domestic routine which has Vera heading off to sociable breakfast preparations, after which 'a few moments could generally be spared for young wives to be with their husbands' (Clapperton, 118). Joe's jealous 'tone of possessive authority' is denounced as a token of 'unfit survival' in the more broadly bonded humanity of the future (Clapperton, 119), just as parents have to surrender possessiveness towards their children. What is more, living in community gives Vera more points of reference from which to assess her husband, and she learns to criticise him, to his initial horror. But, ever optimistic about people's capacity to evolve, Clapperton shows his consequent growing respect for his wife's hidden capacities: 'he recognised that a simple innocent girl may have depths that he could not fathom', which he 'revered' (126). Clapperton shows with a mixture of amusement and sympathy men's growing pains as they adjust from an ethos of ownership and authority to one of fellowship and mutuality with their wives, arguing that ultimately this will be of benefit to both.

Margaret Dunmore presents other close friendships supplementing marriage, as both wives and husbands have emotional and intellectual needs met by others in the commune. A widespread complaint in feminist polemic was the way in which 'Mrs Grundy' style proprieties pressurised all forms of male-female intimacy towards marriage, a tendency that Clapperton's unmarried protagonist describes as 'disgusting' (Clapperton, 4) and undermines by pursuing a platonic friendship with a married man based on their common interest in chemistry. Through long evenings spent in the laboratory 'A quick understanding between the two was established. To both, their fellowship in work became a source of keen and lasting enjoyment' (Clapperton, 152). It is clear that Margaret's companionship affords Frank intellectual stimulation that is lacking in his (nonetheless warm) relationship with his wife Rose, who has to school her jealousy into an appreciation of her husband's abilities and interests that are not shared with her, another facet of spouses recognising their partners as individuals not just adjuncts to themselves: 'In discussion with Margaret, [Frank's] speculative faculty showed all its vigour, his reasoning powers their full swing' (Clapperton, 158). Characteristically, Clapperton suggests men are slower to adapt from old modes of relationship, showing Frank's feelings slipping towards the romantic, yet his great dismay since he still loves Rose. After delicate renegotiations, Margaret suggests that as men improve their self-awareness, in a 'habit of introspection', they will be able to have women as friends as well as wives (Clapperton, 170). The novel aspires to a richer intersubjectivity in which, as Margaret says, 'we all, unconsciously, absorb one another' and help each other 'to grow' (Clapperton, 169), within and beyond marriage. What the novel shies away from (as perhaps too threatening) is an example of a married women enjoying friendship with a man. By focusing on the reconstruction of husbands, and the liberty of single women to enjoy male companionship, the novel leaves married women's heterosocial capacities unexplored.

Women's close female friendships, which the novel suggests normally come to an end on marriage (Clapperton, 3) have room to flourish as husbands are schooled out of their possessive habits: 'there were long summer evenings when Rose and Ruth sat apart in the garden, and Frank generously relinquished his wife's society and occupied himself else-where' (Clapperton, 151). However, close female friendships are shown in some utopias as an alternative to the heterosexual bond that fulfils or surpasses the emotional fulfilment offered by union with a man. As a compensation for not finding a worthy husband, Margaret enjoys an intense romantic friendship with Miss José, meeting whom she describes as an 'era' in her life and a sharing of souls (Clapperton, 2). Margaret's delight in collective living is due in large part to her being able to live intimately with her female friend: 'I knew no one of the opposite sex whose presence thrilled me as Miss José's did, or with whom I would have cared to live' (Clapperton, 159). The setting of the commune brings such a relationship onto the same continuum as marriage, as a specially bonded pair contextualised by rich community inter-relationships.

The replacement of husbands with women reaches its epitome in *Beatrice the Sixteenth,* in which a traveller stumbles on a parallel world whose inhabitants are all female. It is not presented as a vision of future humanity, but (like in Swift's *Gulliver's Travels,* 1726) as an alternative society which prompts the protagonist-narrator to make comparisons with her own world, finally choosing to stay in Armeria. The novel effec-tively deconstructs the idea of gender roles altogether since sex ceases to be a category of difference in a world where only one exists. A striking defamiliarisation is achieved in the novel by the technique of delaying identification of its inhabitants as female, merely noting an absence of sexual difference among its unbearded, androgynously dressed people whose mixture of activities evade masculine/feminine characterisations and blur the boundary between public and private worlds (Clyde, 78), There are no gendered pronouns to describe 'he' or 'she' – people are just individuals who fulfil roles as governors, educators, traders, artists, and soldiers according to preference and ability. (However, as in other middle-class utopias, class distinctions prevail in the apportioning of housekeeping to well-treated slaves.) By the time the narrator recognises her companions as women, the term is empty as a category of gender differentiation. As Daphne Patai suggests, this defamiliarising technique 'has an extraordinary effect on the reader's imagination, straining to place these beings within social paradigms which absolutely require gender specifications', and sets woman as the standard for the human being (Patai, 66–67). The narrator's guide struggles to comprehend the narrator's description of 'Two complementary divisions, each finding its perfection in the other', responding that 'I cannot see how perfection is to be attained, except in one's own spirit' (Clyde, 78). Therefore, a heterosexual pairing has no meaning as an economic unit, nor as a con-text for childrearing which is done in an informal communitarian way. Motherhood is, in a sense, avoided, for children are adopted from neigh-bouring countries through war (the militarism of the original mythic Amazonians is present) and are not attached to any particular adult; nor do they have any formal education, but learn informally from the variety of adults they meet, all of whom have a responsibility as carers, playfellows and educators of the next generation. As Jan Relf argues, female separatist utopias can be escapist, representing a nostalgic return to the mother-child bond which is fetishised in the alternative world, reinforcing the archetype of woman as mother; alternatively, they can create 'a qualitatively different society from the one we historically inhabit' (Relf, 135, 142). Disinterested in maternity, Clyde achieves the latter, here based on a community of independent individuals, loose intergenerational bonds and an escape from biological femininity.

Nonetheless, although a heterosexual partnership has no meaning in Armeria as an economic or parental unit, or as an arena for joint perfection through complementarity, marriage is valued, rather remarkably, as a sanctioned lifelong commitment between two women. In this community of non-sexed persons, collective fellowship is not enough (unlike in *New Amazonia*) but recognises a need for special intimacy, and features relationship pairings that involve falling in love, shy revelations of feeling, fear of rejection, public declaration and a ritual commitment that is celebrated by the community. Women who choose to become each other's 'conjux' share a home and enjoy an affectionate, exclusive dynamic that includes many of the sensations associated with the heterosexual romance, finding unusual pleasure in each other's presence. Their shared physical affection shades into the erotic – the narrator gradually falls in love with her friend Ilex, whose touch 'made me feel a wild longing to prove her to be no [barbarian]' as her nationality is interpreted by some (Clyde, 174), and they analyse their feelings after the first declaration of love (Clyde, 329). The relationship appears non-sexual in the literal sense, and the novel may well be born of the ascetic distaste towards sexuality that was voiced by other feminists for whom it was inevitably associated with demeaning animality, brutal notions of men's 'conjugal rights' and obligatory childbearing. But it is worth noting that matters of homosexual and lesbian love were being discussed in tolerant tones in the *Adult* journal as early as 1897–1899 (Cunningham, 15–16) so the novel's silence about sex may be due to coyness rather than prurience. Whether lesbian or not, the relationships in the novel are certainly 'queer' in the sense of envisioning non-normative expressions of desire that trouble conventional boundaries between the homosocial and the homosexual. The use of invented words such as 'conjux', and 'kerôta' (being in love) create new categories of experience that evade the particular meanings established by a culture in which heterosexual pairing is the norm, born it seems out of a sense that men serve no constructive purpose in any of women's enjoyments or duties. As Relf suggests, it is by 'creating a new language of women's meanings' that separatist utopias can show women 'creating a new Symbolic order … a different order of reality' than the patriarchal norm that the reader inhabits (Relf, 142). Female marriage in *Beatrice* may or may not be sexless, but the novel implies that only by removing men from the equation altogether does a romantic partnership suit the needs of the emancipated woman.

Conclusion

The feminist utopias written during the era of the women's movement in Britain vary in their particulars, but collectively they envision the relationship as partnership based on affectionate friendship and intellectual companionship, one that respects the individuality of both partners rather than subscribing to stereotyped binary gender roles. Women's political enfranchisement is taken for granted as a condition necessary to dismantle patriarchal gender relations, but as far as marriage is concerned removing women's economic dependence on men is the primary liberation required. These are middle-class visions of wifehood – companionship is framed in term of intellectual pursuits, and housework is a nuisance that others can be paid to do, although some cross-class feminist solidarity is shown in the writers demanding better pay and recognition for domestic labour. Overwhelmingly the writers struggle to reconcile motherhood with the life of the emancipated woman, keen to reduce its role in women's lives and often liberate them from it altogether. The life of instincts – men's sexual, and women's maternal – is generally portrayed as entrapment in lower nature, a hindrance to evolution towards a life based more on mind and spirit and whose primary unit is humanity rather than the nuclear family. And while marriage is considered redeemable, it becomes less central in women's lives, recontextualised in a network of other modes of fellowship, romance and community. Patricia Stubbs shows that 'New Woman' fiction's portraits of marital disaster exhibit a rather conservative focus on women's 'private emotional experience' in isolation from 'any other kind of relation to people or material life', ignoring for example the new possibilities of employment available for self-supporting women (Stubbs xv). The utopia texts show a quite different picture – the possibilities of matrimony for women in a new context of relationships and material conditions, in which men have been reconstructed to be sexually self-controlled partners rather than masters, and women are liberated as breadwinners, intellectual companions and citizens.

Notes

1 Quoted in Charles J. Rooney Jr, *Dreams and Visions: A Study of American Utopias, 1867–1917* (Westport, CT: Greenwood Press, 1985), 15.
2 See for example Elaine Showalter, *A Literature of Their Own: from Charlotte Bronte to Doris Lessing*, 2nd edition (London: Virago Press, 1999), 184–87.
3 See Cynthia Eller, *Gentlemen and Amazons: The Myth of Matriarchal Prehistory, 1861–1900* (Berkeley: University of California Press, 2011), chapter 5. Mona Caird alludes to this in her feminist polemic *The Morality of Marriage*, 70–71.

4 Margaret Oliphant, quoted in Gail Cunningham, *The New Woman and the Victorian Novel* (London: Macmillan, 1978), 49.
5 Cunningham, *The New Woman and the Victorian Novel*, 48; and J.S. Mill quoted in Lloyd Fernando, *'New Women' in the Late Victorian Novel* (London: Pennsylvania State University Press, 1977), 13.
6 See for example Cunningham, *The New Woman and the Victorian Novel*.
7 See also Albinski, *Women's Utopias in British and American Fiction* (London: Routledge, 1988), 4–5, 8–9, and Lewes, *Dream Revisionaries*, chapter 4. For discussions of marital and domestic matters in US feminist utopias of the era, see Carol Farley Kessler, "The Grand Marital Revolution: Two Feminist Utopias (1874, 1919)", in *Feminism, Utopia and Narrative*, ed. Jones and Goodwin, and Kenneth M. Roemer, "Sex Roles, Utopia and Change: The Family in Late Nineteenth-Century Utopian Literature", *American Studies* 13:2 (1972). For a full discussion of *Gloriana*, see Ann Ardis, "'The Journey from Fantasy to Politics': The Representation of Socialism and Feminism in *Gloriana* and *The Image-Breakers*", in *Rediscovering Forgotten Radicals*, ed. Ingram and Patai.
8 For a discussion of the varied fin-de-siècle feminist views on male and female sexuality, see Lucy Bland, *Banishing the Beast: English Feminism and Sexual Morality, 1885–1914* (London: Penguin, 1995).
9 See Bland, "The Married Woman", 148–51.
10 Lewes, *Dream Revisionaries*, 6.
11 Angelique Richardson, *Love and Eugenics in the Late Nineteenth Century: Rational Reproduction and the New Woman* (Oxford: Oxford University Press, 2003), 8–9.
12 Alexis Lothian, "Introduction" to Corbett, *New Amazonia*, 2, 12–13.

Works Cited

Albinski, Nina. *Women's Utopias in British and American Fiction*. London: Routledge, 1988.
Albinski, Nina. 'The Laws of Justice, of Nature, and of Right': Victorian Feminist Utopias', in Falk Jones, Libby and Webster Goodwin, Sarah eds. *Feminism, Utopia and Narrative*. Knoxville: University of Tennessee Press, 1990.
Ardis, Ann. 'The Journey from Fantasy to Politics': The Representation of Socialism and Feminism in *Gloriana* and *The Image-Breakers*' in Angela Ingram and Daphne Patai eds. *Rediscovering Forgotten Radicals: British Women Writers 1889–1939*. Chapel Hill: University of North Carolina Press, 1993.
Beaumont, Matthew. 'The New Woman in Nowhere: Feminism and Utopianism at the Fin-de-Siecle', in Angelique Richardson and Chris Willis eds. *The New Woman in Fiction and in Fact: Fin-de-Siecle Feminisms*. Basingstoke: Palgrave, 2001.
Beaumont, Matthew. *Utopia Ltd: Ideologies of Social Dreaming in England 1870–1900*. Chicago, IL: Haymarket Books, 2009.
Bland, Lucy. 'The Married Woman, the 'New Woman' and the Feminist: Sexual Politics of the 1890s', in Rendall, Jane ed. *Equal or Different: Women's Politics 1800-1914*. Oxford: Basil Blackwell, 1987.
Bland, Lucy. *Banishing the Beast: English Feminism and Sexual Morality, 1885–1914*. London: Penguin, 1995.
Caird, Mona. *The Morality of Marriage, and Other Essays on the Status and Destiny of Woman*. London: George Redway, 1897.
Clapperton, Jane Hume. *Margaret Dunmore: or, A Socialist Home*, 2nd edition. London: Swann Sonnenschein & Co., 1894.

Clyde, Irene. *Beatrice the Sixteenth*. London: George Bell & Sons, 1909.

Cunningham, Gail. *The New Woman and the Victorian Novel*. London: Macmillan, 1978.

Corbett, Elizabeth Burgoyne. *New Amazonia: A Foretaste of the Future*. Seattle, Washington DC: Aqueduct Press, 2014.

Eller, Cynthia. *Gentlemen and Amazons: The Myth of Matriarchal Prehistory, 1861–1900*. Berkeley: University of California Press, 2011.

Fernando, Lloyd. *'New Women' in the Late Victorian Novel*. London: Pennsylvania State University Press, 1977.

Foster, Shirley. *Victorian Women's Fiction: Marriage, Freedom and the Individual*. London: Croom Helm, 1985.

Ingram, Angela and Daphne Patai. 'Introduction: 'An Intelligent Discontent with … Conditions', in Angela Ingram and Daphne Patai eds. *Rediscovering Forgotten Radicals: British Women Writers 1889-1939*. Chapel Hill: University of North Carolina Press, 1993.

Kessler, Carol Farley. 'The Grand Marital Revolution: Two Feminist Utopias (1874, 1919)', in Libby Falk Jones and Sarah Webster Goodwin eds. *Feminism, Utopia and Narrative*. Knoxville: University of Tennessee Press, 1990.

Ledger, Sally. 'The New Woman and the Crisis of Victorianism', in Sally Ledger and Scott McCracken eds. *Cultural Politics at the Fin de Siecle*. Cambridge: Cambridge University Press, 1995.

Lewes, Darby. *Dream Revisionaries: Gender and Genre in Women's Utopian Fiction 1870–1920*. Tuscaloosa: University of Alabama Press, 1995.

Garland Mears, A. [Amelia] A. *Mercia, the Astronomer Royal: A Romance*. London: Simpkin, Marshall, Hamilton, Kent & Co. Ltd, 1895.

Mellor, Anne K. 'On Feminist Utopias'. *Women's Studies*, Vol 9 (1982), pp 242–43.

Patai, Daphne. 'When Women Rule: Defamiliarization in the Sex-Role Reversal'. *Extrapolation*, Vol 23, No 1 (1982), pp 66–67.

Quissell, Barbara C. 'The New World that Eve Made: Feminist Utopias Written by Nineteenth-Century Women', in Kenneth M. Roemer ed. *America as Utopia: Collected Essays*. New York: B. Franklin, 1981.

Relf, Jan. 'Women in Retreat: the Politics of Separatism in Women's Literary Utopias'. *Utopian Studies*, Vol 2, No 1/2 (1991), pp 135, 142.

Richardson, Angelique. *Love and Eugenics in the Late Nineteenth Century: Rational Reproduction and the New Woman*. Oxford: Oxford University Press, 2003.

Roemer, Kenneth M. 'Sex Roles, Utopia and Change: The Family in Late Nineteenth-Century Utopian Literature'. *American Studies*, Vol 13, No 2 (1972), pp 33–47.

Rooney, Charles J. Jr. *Dreams and Visions: A Study of American Utopias, 1867–1917*. Westport, CT: Greenwood Press, 1985.

Showalter, Elaine. *A Literature of Their Own: from Charlotte Bronte to Doris Lessing*, 2nd edition. London: Virago Press, 1999.

Stubbs, Patricia. *Women and Fiction: Feminism and the Novel 1880–1920*. Brighton: Harvester Press, 1979.

Young, F.E. *The War of the Sexes*. London: John Young, 1905.

13 Marriage in Women's Short Fiction

Victoria Margree

Mrs Mallard's grief on learning of her husband's death is immediate and abandoned. And yet afterwards, facing the open window through which approach the sights and sounds of a world 'aquiver with the new spring life', she perceives that she feels something else too. For Louise – as the text now names her – knows that there will no longer be any 'powerful will bending hers', and that she is "Free! Body and soul free!".

Kate Chopin's 'The Story of an Hour' (1894) exemplifies how far the short story had developed over the course of the nineteenth century, in terms both of narrative innovation and of its explicit questioning of marriage. At just two pages in length, it exploits the form's character-istic economy to tell a story about matrimony that must have shocked readers, even in the scandalous 1890s. Eschewing complexity of plot, the narrative focuses on the movement of Mrs Mallard's thoughts in her awakening to her new freedom. We learn that hers was not a bad marriage particularly: she will weep genuine tears over the 'kind, tender hands folded in death' of the husband who had loved her, and whom she sometimes also loved. Chopin's story suggests instead that it is marriage itself that is the problem: that the institution entails conventions that regulate the behaviours and attitudes of the particular persons within it. But it is convention that wins out in the story's cruel twist, when the very much still-living Mr Mallard arrives home, unaware of his pur-ported demise, and Louise dies of what the doctors call heart disease compounded by 'joy that kills' – her anticipated years of self-belonging now but the dream of an hour.[1]

This chapter proposes that short fiction gave women writers of the nineteenth century particular freedom to explore the marriage ques-tion. Throughout the period female authors turned to the short story and there are few woman novelists who were not also practitioners of short fiction. Their reasons varied from the practical (short story writing could, for example, be more easily combined with the demands of man-aging a family) to the financial (especially in later decades, there was a burgeoning market for short fiction which offered swift remuneration) and the artistic. And yet the short story was typically considered a less serious form than the novel: something that novelists used to supplement their income, or that provided magazine editors with 'filler material' for padding out the pages around novel serializations, editorials and advertisements (Liggins et al., 3–4).

In what follows I argue in line with current scholarship that far from being an inferior form to the novel the short story is simply a different one, which brings distinctive possibilities and constraints. Where the Three Decker in particular comprised a vast canvass, short fiction works on an inevitably smaller scale, typically substituting for the intricate plotting of multiple story lines a single plot, and one from which, as Edgar Allen Poe had noted, '*no part can be displaced without ruin to the whole*' (qtd. in Liggins et al., 3). And in place of the realist novel's careful excavation of chains of causation, short fiction typically entails narrative elisions, whose gaps it falls to the reader to fill, or not. For these and other reasons the short story is often taken today to be characterised by a peculiar brevity, intensity and impressionistic quality, and therefore to be suited to the production of particular kinds of effect. But the distinctive possibilities of the short story are also a question of its status during this period. Emerging as a commercially important form through the periodicals market that flourished particularly with the expansion in literacy towards the century's end, the short story both benefited from a vogue for shortness and suffered from the elite denigration that this drew down upon itself. George Gissing, for example, famously parodied George Newness's *Tit Bits* publication in *New Grub Street* (1891) with his 'Chit Chat' magazine, created to provide what Gissing called a 'quarter-educated' readership with easily digested pieces of writing (Gissing, 460). William Makepeace Thackeray had earlier in the century urged Anthony Trollope to produce short stories for *Cornhill Magazine* (of which Thackeray was then editor), noting that the 'public love the tarts,' though he himself 'prefer[ed] bread and cheese' – thus contrasting the immediate gratification of the short story with the supposedly more substantial nourishment offered by the novel (qtd. in Liggins et al., 26). But if short stories tended to be seen as 'throwaway or "of the moment"' (Liggins et al., 32) – as an inferior form to the properly literary novel – more recently critics have argued that this gave it particular freedoms. Clare Stewart has noted, for example, that precisely because of its marginal status, short fiction was less subject to the censoring scrutiny of male editors, publishers and critics than was the novel.

I therefore concur with scholars for whom short fiction offered writers distinctive possibilities to engage in critical ways with their societies. As Clare Hanson has suggested: 'The formal properties of the short story – disjunction, inconclusiveness, obliquity – connect with its ideological marginality and with the fact the form may be used to express something suppressed/repressed in mainstream literature [...] the short story gives us the other side of the "official story" or narrative' (qtd. in Liggins et al., 16). In what follows I argue that women writers were able to exploit both the aesthetic possibilities and the minor status of the form to offer visions of married life that differed radically from official stories; whether sentimentalized representations of married idylls, or legalistic narratives of marital breakdown. Kelly Hager has noted that with the Divorce and Matrimonial Causes Act of 1857, a new codification was produced that meant that 'private life became increasingly more policed and standardized; [that] all legal stories of marriage and divorce would now be told using the same language and the same narrative cues' (Hager, 39). If the value of fictional treatments of marriage is that they broke with such standardization to find alternative ways of telling these stories, we will see that the short story as compared to the novel made possible still different narrative cues. These are put to use by women writers to produce stories of marriage that mainstream culture might have found less tasty morsels than bitter pills to swallow.

Early Stories

Although scholars have tended to regard the short story as emerging as a distinct form only in the middle or late nineteenth century, there are many examples of short fiction published in periodicals and collected in volumes before this, and which are – as Tim Killick has recently convincingly argued – worthy of critical attention. Two examples that provide interesting treatments of marriage are Maria Edgeworth's 'The Limerick Gloves' (1804) and Laetitia E. Landon's 'Sefton Church' (1834).

Edgeworth's story is a humorous narrative concerning the romance between tanner's daughter, Phoebe Hill, and Irish glove maker, Brian O'Neil, who has courted Phoebe by making her a present of some fine Limerick gloves. The couple's union is obstructed, however, by the objections Phoebe's parents raise to her marrying an Irishman. After comments by his wife arouse Mr Hill's suspicions, he sets out to prove that the innocent O'Neill has stolen his dog and is plotting to blow up the cathedral. After visiting a soothsayer gypsy king who confirms his beliefs, Mr Hill is finally put right only by the intervention of a kindly and wise local magistrate. Mr Hill learns that the gypsy king himself rather than O'Neill is guilty of the theft of his dog, and that the suspicious hole in the cathedral foundations is only the entrance for a rat that has been befriended by the children of a local widow whom O'Neill has been disinterestedly helping. The story ends happily, with O'Neill forgiving a contrite Mr Hill, and with the young couple set to marry.

A courtship tale and a comedy of misunderstandings, 'The Limerick Gloves' is exemplary of what Killick identifies as the pedagogic aim of Edgeworth's tales, which 'are notable for their insistence on good sense and sound character as reliable compasses for life's obstacles' (Killick, 81). In no sense anti-marriage, it tells instead of how what promises to be a successful marital union is nearly derailed through a father's lack of good sense. But in emphasising the power of paternal authority, no matter how distanced from sound judgement, the tale also points to the ways in which in the question of marriage the wishes of young women themselves are rendered peripheral. Upon learning that Phoebe's new gloves are from O'Neill, and that they signify his romantic interest in her, Mr Hill peremptorily commands 'Off with the gloves, Phoebe! When I order a thing, it must be done' (Edgeworth, 129). Phoebe's mother changes her view of O'Neill as a suitor only after he puts on a ball and sends Limerick gloves to twenty ladies by way of invitation; seeing that other families regard him as desirable match, Mrs Hill becomes anxious to 'secure the prize' (Edgeworth, 135). The marrying of daughters, 'The Limerick Gloves' suggests, is too often negotiated with the economic and social standing of families in mind, and with all too inadequate a consultation of the preferences of daughters themselves.

A very different sort of humour is employed in 'Sefton Church', with the omniscient, teasingly moralizing narrative voice of 'The Limerick Gloves' replaced by a first-person narrator who is world-weary and refined, and whose satire finds its target not in the misunderstandings that hinder lovers from marrying, but in the very idea of marriage at all. Our narrator begins by identifying marrying as the most absurd among life's biggest mistakes, since it is the only one that we can help – the others being 'to be born', 'to live' and 'to die'. The folly of marrying for love is the theme developed over the story's first few pages: the wedding day is correctly called '"the happiest day of one's life"' only because the couple 'are never particularly happy afterwards'; quarrels 'are only the refreshing necessities' of marital ennui; and the single happily married couple that our narrator can recall lived apart, in Amsterdam and Demerara, but sent 'each other such affectionate letters!' (Landon, 88). The only narrative event in this sketch is the wedding of a Miss Merton, to which the reluctant narrator is dragged, only to discover that the bridegroom has perhaps similar feelings about marriage and has earlier fled the scene. Catastrophe is forestalled, however, when another young man – a handsome naval lieutenant – steps forward to offer his hand instead, saying that he has just realised he has always loved Miss Merton. The lady gladly accepts, and the story ends with a wedding, if not the expected one.

The skill of Landon is to make her tale appealing to different kinds of readers, and for different reasons. One might consider its ending a happy and romantic one, and dismiss the cynical narrator as a curmudgeon. But by eschewing omniscient narration, Landon is able to avoid nailing her colours to the mast: readers are free to identify with or against a narratorial point of view that articulates a strong critique of the hegemony of marriage and of the condition of ignorance in which both sexes embark upon it. While our narrator is nowhere explicitly identified in terms of age or gender, their erudition, jadedness and apparent easy independence suggest someone older, unmarried and possibly male. As Harriet Devine Jump notes, this persona allows the young, at the time unmarried Landon 'to voice a scepticism that would be unthinkable in the conventional world of annual fictions' (Jump, 6) (where the story was published) – and, one might add, directly in the voice of a young woman. The very brevity of Landon's sketch allows her the freedom of suspending implied authorial judgement, in a way that might be difficult to maintain in a longer piece of fiction.

To the extent that they end with a marriage (actual or projected), both 'The Limerick Gloves' and 'Sefton Church' provide the conventional closure expected of the period's fiction. But en route to the altar, each deploys humour subtly to question the conditions under which young men and women enter into that blessed state.

Supernatural, Gothic and Uncanny Tales

While the stories by Edgeworth and Landon treat everyday subjects in domestic settings, as the century progressed authors increasingly turned to more phantasmagoric framings for their explorations of marriage, reflecting both the growing popularity of ghost stories and the continuing use of eighteenth-century female gothic tropes to explore women's vulnerability in patriarchal societies. While not a marriage story exactly, Rosa Mulholland's 'Not to Be Taken at Bed-Time' (1865) provides a dark take on the courtship narrative, relating the tale of Coll Dhu, a gloomy stranger who appears in the mountains of Connemara, Ireland, and employs witchcraft to make the beautiful Evleen Blake fall in love with him despite her strong antipathy. Coll's machinations succeed only in sending Evleen mad and the pair to their deaths. Despite its fantastic trappings the story signals the vulnerability of young women to men who, coveting their beauty and their family wealth, would override their will in order to make them their own. Themes of female vulnerability appear as well in the ghost stories of Charlotte Riddell, whose collection of predominantly haunted house narratives, *Weird Stories* (1882), was published in the same year as the second Married Women's Property Act, and was therefore written in a period of intense debate about the economic rights and responsibilities of married women. In several stories Riddell highlights the disastrous consequences of married women's economic powerlessness. In 'Old Mrs Jones' a woman is married for her fortune by a debauched doctor and then physically abused and murdered by him, echoing Frances Power Cobbe's warning that 'wife abuse' was an inevitable consequence of a legal principle that established a husband in a position of effective ownership over his wife. As Vanessa Dickerson has observed in her seminal study, *Victorian Ghosts in the Noontide: Women Writers and the Supernatural* (1996), the principle of coverture that prevailed prior to the Married Women's Property Acts of 1870 and

1882 was identified by many feminists at the time as a 'neo-Gothic condition' that rendered women legally dead, or at least ghostly (Dickerson, 137). Many writers of Victorian ghost fiction have exploited the genre's 'acceptability [as] a traditional form of entertainment' to explore this condition (Stewart, 112).

By the 1890s, the conventions of the ghost story and the gothic tale were being utilized by some women writers to produce devastating critiques of marriage. Charlotte Perkins Gilman's 'The Yellow Wallpaper' (1892) famously installs a tale of mental breakdown within what initially appears to be a haunted house narrative. While Gilman herself described the story as an attempt to persuade Silas Weir Mitchell of the disastrousness of his 'rest cure' for female nervous illness, it is also a damning critique of women's infantilization within traditional marriage.[2] In that respect, the story bears comparison with Edith Nesbit's much-anthologized 'Man-Size in Marble' (1893), in which a young husband ignores his wife's forebodings and leaves their home unsecured against vengeful reanimated marble-statue knights that are out roaming on All Hallow's Eve. As Nick Freeman has argued in his compelling analysis of the story as 'New Woman Gothic', although the husband's first-person narration presents us with an apparently determinedly modern couple living a bohemian idyll, the idea of this being a '"free union"' rather than a marriage is quickly revealed to be 'no more than a pose' as the reader realizes that the young husband systematically patronizes his wife and belittles her literary work, even as he depends on it for their income (Freeman, 458). In both Gilman's and Nesbit's stories, the husbands' disdain for their wives (interestingly both actual or aspiring writers) is simultaneously expressed and disguised in epithets that construct them as animals or children: 'little goose' and 'little girl' in Gilman's story; and 'pussy' in Nesbit's (Nesbit, 19, 23–24). Nesbit's narrator's refusal to credit his wife's intuition of danger leads directly to disaster as, arriving home far too late, he discovers her body fallen back against a table with one of the knight's 'grey marble finger[s]' clutched in her hand, and that not even by calling 'her by all her pet names' can he rouse her (Nesbit, 28). Nesbit and Gilman both exploit the licence accorded ghost fiction to end in brutal or shocking ways, leaving their readers with a closing image of a woman's broken body and broken sanity, respectively, in order to show how marriage frequently acts as a conduit for, rather than a protection against, the destructiveness to women that is endemic in patriarchal society.

While Gilman's and Nesbit's tales appear in the 1890s when the New Woman phenomenon had made criticism of marriage part of public discussion, it is possible to find uncanny fiction being used for this purpose much earlier. Rhoda Broughton's strikingly modern-seeming 'The Man with the Nose' (1872) is, like the Margaret Oliphant story discussed in the next section of this chapter, a tale of a honeymoon – that period when the expectations of both brides and bridegrooms are confronted by reality. Like Nesbit's tale, it is a story of the loss of a wife, told in the first person by a husband whose narration the reader may come to distrust. Indeed, both Nesbit's and Broughton's tales make themselves available to a double interpretation: they may be read at face value as stories of happy marriages destroyed by intrusions from without; or alternatively as tales of only superficially successful unions that unravel at least as much under the pressure of their own internal flaws. They might therefore be understood as what Hager calls 'failed marriage plots'; but ones partially hidden behind the formulaic conventions of genre fiction – still discernible, however, to the attentive reader (Hager, 7).

In 'The Man with the Nose' the wife within a honeymooning couple becomes troubled by repeated visions of a man with a peculiar nose, who seems to be commanding her to follow him, and who reminds her of a mesmeriser she once encountered as a child. When the couple stop at Lucerne, Switzerland, our narrator receives a letter recalling him to the sickbed of a great-uncle from whom he hopes to inherit, and insists on departing for England despite his wife Elizabeth's pleas not to leave her. Returning twelve days later he learns that she has gone from the hotel: despite desperately trying to find her, he discovers only that 'a dark gentleman with [a] peculiar physiognomy' has been seen leaving the district in a carriage, accompanied by 'a lady, lying apparently in a state of utter insensibility' (Broughton, 30–31). The final lines tell us that all this happened twenty years since; that the narrator has 'searched sea and land, but never have I seen my little Elizabeth again' (Broughton, 31).

Like Nesbit, Broughton manipulates her masculine narrative point of view to hint at a culpability in catastrophe that exceeds what the husband himself admits to. Both tales thereby problematize what might otherwise seem to be a dichotomy between the versions of masculinity represented by the monstrous figures who menace the young wives (the marble knights, the man with the nose) and by the 'good' husbands. Each tale actually insinuates that there is something deeply problematic too about the 'normal' masculinity of these men. Broughton's husband similarly infantilizes his wife, referring to her by a succession of diminutives, often combined with the possessive form: 'her little brown head', 'my little beloved', 'my little bride elect', 'my little one', 'poor little soul' (Broughton, 14–16, 20, 28). She is characterized or addressed as a child multiple times (Broughton, 24, 26–27, 29), and he refers to the 'dear little babyish notes she used to send me during our engagement!' (Broughton, 28). Again like Nesbit, Broughton shows the consequence of this infantilization in the husband's complacent response to his wife's perception of danger. When the man first appears to Elizabeth her husband considers it a dream and responds to her fear with mocking laughter (Broughton, 19–20). However, he is also capable of being moved to anger when Elizabeth refuses the role of 'timid' child-bride (Broughton, 15). When she reacts with 'strong irritation' to his suggestion that she has fancied seeing the man at their hotel, and asserts that he has seen him too – indeed, he *has* caught a brief glimpse of a tall figure in the shadows, but obfuscates – he is 'alarmed, and yet half angry' (Broughton, 24). This anger appears again when Elizabeth requests that he not leave her alone to return to England. The narrator has earlier presented himself as having been made happily slavish through his adoration of his fiancée (Broughton, 14), but this is now given the lie as, 'determined to have my own way', he demands 'dictatorially' to know '"any good reason why I *should* stay?"' (Broughton, 27). On returning after twelve days – longer than he promised her – he is indignant to find that she is not awaiting his arrival, and then discovering that she has left with a man, leaps to the conclusion that she has voluntarily deserted him (Broughton, 29). This husband may frame his story with himself as the chivalric, besotted and ultimately tragic, lover, but Broughton has him reveal through his own words a quickness to bullying and suspicion that his fondness for romantic conventionalities cannot hide.

But as Emma Liggins notes in her introduction to the re-issue of Broughton's *Twilight Stories* in which this story appears, there is also something else going on, an 'excess which finds its way into this alarming story' and which has to do with the sensuality and sexuality that Broughton as a 'sensation' writer is adept at evoking (Liggins, vi). The story's chief enigma is quite what it is about the man and his nose that is capable of producing such intense dread in Elizabeth. One explanation is that he really is the mesmeriser from her childhood, and that he is exerting upon her the hypnotist's conventional fascination. But as Liggins proposes, the 'prominent,' 'sharply chiselled' nose (Broughton, 20) is also 'a clear phallic reference', suggesting that at another level the story concerns sexuality.[3] As Liggins notes, it thereby enables Broughton not only 'to voice her heroine's anxieties about the conjugal act' but also to 'rais[e] the spectre of female sexual desire', since while Elizabeth fears and loathes the man who appears at her bed, she also feels irresistibly pulled towards him (Liggins, vi). Indeed, with its description of Elizabeth's childhood trauma in the aftermath of being mesmerized – '"I was very ill, very – I lay in bed for five whole weeks, and – and was off my head, and said odd and wicked things that you would not have expected me to say"' (Broughton, 16) – the story reads uncannily like a Freudian case study two decades before these appeared.

Just as interesting, however, are the aspects of the text that suggest that the narrator himself is involved in a suppression of sexuality. The early part of his narration is punctuated by expressions of anxiety about their being identifiable as a honeymooning couple, and thus, one might infer, as two people newly embarked upon a sexual relationship. He fears 'having the finger of derision pointed at us by waiters and land-lords'; to which Elizabeth responds by promising that they shall dress so that 'nobody will guess that we are bride and bridegroom' (Broughton, 14). But the narrator declares that 'we shall still have the *mark of the beast* upon us', and that they should therefore be sure to go to some-where with other honeymooners in order to become 'lost in the multi-tude of our *fellow-sinners*' (Broughton, 14–15; my italics). He evinces disgust for physical processes in the female body, and particularly for anything expressive of *appetite*: while on their boat on the Rhine he comments that 'There are few actions more disgusting than eating can be made' and observes a 'handsome girl … thrusting her knife halfway down her throat'; which leads a 'disgusted and frightened' Elizabeth to suggest that they leave the dining area (Broughton, 22).[4] In this context, his infantilization of Elizabeth takes on another layer of meaning. Early in their honeymoon tour, Elizabeth makes the narrator buy her a bonnet with feathers '"in order to look married"'; but he reports that 'the result is … a delicious picture of a child playing at being grown up, having practised a theft on its mother's wardrobe' (Broughton, 18). Elizabeth's anxiety to assume the role of married woman is met by the narrator's insistence on maintaining her – in his imagination at least – in a doll-like childishness that also implies sexlessness, suggesting that his 'fail[ure] to acknowledge his wife's sexuality' (Liggins, vi) might facilitate her fasci-nation with the terrible though magnetic man with the nose.

Neither clearly a supernatural story nor a realist one, 'The Man with the Nose' is perhaps better described as an *uncanny* tale. While it seems to call for a psychological reading, it cannot simply be read in psycho-logical terms: the man with the nose is witnessed by other characters and is therefore apparently no hallucination. But quite what is the nature of his powers (natural or occult); whether he is really the mesmerizer from Elizabeth's childhood; what he wants from her now and how he has found her – all remain unclear. Deploying ellipses, the story functions like a dream, substituting for cause-and-effect relationships a succession of haunting impressions that defy rational explanation but offer a prolif-eration of interpretative possibilities, installing a troubling strangeness at the heart of the familiar marriage plot.

The Fin-de-Siècle and the New Woman

The theme of sexual relationships in marriage could receive much less coded treatment by the 1890s, and the writers who were most bold in its depiction tended to be those associated with the New Woman phenome-non, although they were often obliged to use non-mainstream publishers and magazines. George Egerton is a key figure in the development of the short story towards what Clare Hanson has called 'plotless' short fictions that prioritize psychological states above external events (Hanson, 7).

Her well-known 'A Cross Line' (1893) utilizes a narrative technique of close focalisation to describe an extended fantasy whose images and syntax unmistakably signal sexual orgasm (Liggins et al., 74), as her heroine imagines herself dancing on an ancient stage, 'sway[ing] voluptuously' and 'giv[ing] each man what he craves' (Egerton, 266). Her protagonist is tempted to desert her marriage for a life with her lover – not because he understands her, but because he knows that he does not understand her. Ultimately she chooses to remain with her husband when she discovers that she is pregnant; though whether maternity is a new adventure, or a form of entrapment that compels adaptation to frustration and drudgery, is left to the reader to determine.

The theme of adultery is also treated in Netta Syrett's 'A Correspondence', published in the notorious *Yellow Book* in 1895. Young Cecily Armstrong asks her 'clever and accomplished' cousin Gretchen Verrol to impersonate her in letters to her fiancé, sculptor Noel Margrave, for fear that she herself is insufficiently cultured and intellectual for his tastes, and in so doing unwittingly kindles a romance between them. At the story's close, set a couple of years into their marriage, Cecily and Margrave are witnessed together with Gretchen at the theatre by an acquaintance, Mrs Yeo, who observes that Margrave has eyes and speech only for Gretchen, and Mrs Yeo has 'tears in her eyes' afterwards as she remembers the expression on the face of Mrs Margrave, the 'Poor girl! Poor child!' (Syrett, 328). Whether Margrave's infidelity is sexual as well as emotional is unclear, but it is perhaps not so much Margrave himself that the text deems culpable as the social conventions that regulate engagement and marriage. Syrett emphasises that the beautiful but unsophisticated Cecily and the older and experienced Margrave are, contrary to their social circle's opinion, fundamentally mismatched. While Cecily is guilty of perpetrating a fraud upon her lover through the letters, she attempts to undo the harm by confessing to the deception and calling off her engagement. But her mother is anxious to secure her daughter's marriage to the 'well connected and rich' Margrave and has 'worked it' so that the wedding takes place after all (Syrett, 316, 328). While this shows how men too can be treated as commodities on the marriage market, the man-of-the-world Margrave has presumably freely consented to the re-engagement; while Mrs Yeo comments indignantly to her husband that 'I don't believe the poor child [Cecily] was even consulted' (Syrett, 328). The theme of parental interference in marriage matches, treated with gentle irony in Maria Edgeworth's story, is taken up here with explicit presentation of the damage it can wreak, suggesting that despite the near century that separates the two tales, the preferences of young women themselves are still being marginalized. Syrett's story seems particularly to indict a failure in female solidarity: Cecily's mother has not protected but rather exposed her daughter to a disastrous marriage;

while the cousin who might have been her friend has betrayed her. But while all three protagonists are in a sense trapped, societal double standards afford the husband some license to obtain pleasure through an illicit relationship, while for his wife their marriage can mean nothing but misery and his lover is made vulnerable to the calamity (for a woman) of sexual disgrace.

One of the most interesting treatments of marriage in the short fiction of this decade comes not from a New Woman writer, however, but from an author usually considered a conservative voice on the Woman Question. Margaret Oliphant had defended the principle of coverture in the 1850s, objected to John Stuart Mill's depiction of marriage in *The Subjection of Women* (1869), and would attack Thomas Hardy and Grant Allen as members of an 'Anti-Marriage League' in her 1896 review of *Jude the Obscure*. While scholars agree that she came increasingly to support many feminist causes over the course of her long career (see, e.g. Williams), it is also thought by some that she retained a 'conservatism with regard to sexuality and divorce' (Heilmann, 214), disliking the stridency and attention to sexual matters of much fin-de-siècle feminism, and holding firm to her belief in a married woman's duty towards husband and family as one that superseded her desire for personal happiness (Heilman, 217, 222–23).[5]

It is this belief in wifely duty that makes 'A Story of a Wedding Tour' so fascinating. First published in 1894, the story appears in the midst of fin-de-siècle decadence and has a plot that would not seem out of place in a New Woman fiction. Janey becomes engaged to the much older Mr Rosendale, who proposes to her on the somewhat slight basis of their acquaintance from a train trip and a lunch. She does not love him, but being herself an unloved orphan, consents to marriage 'for the magic' of the words '"in love"' that are mistakenly used by others to describe his feelings for her (Oliphant, 426). But Rosendale is in fact an egotistical man who covets Janey only for her beauty and is utterly 'indifferent to herself' (Oliphant, 427). On honeymoon in France, an error in an announcement leads to him being stranded at a railway station while Janey's train propels her into the night. She need only wait for him a day at their next stop, but realising, like Chopin's Louise, what it is to be free, she instead takes flight, finding refuge at a village further along the railway route. Ten years pass, and Janey has made a happy life for herself and the son she had not known she was carrying, winning over her neighbours in St Honorat despite their suspicion that she is really unmarried and therefore a fallen woman. One day she recognises Rosendale's face in a passing train. He has also seen her, and furious, changes train at the next stop, in order to return and confront his wife. But on his arrival he has suffered some kind of collapse, and dies.

Like Syrett's tale, the story presents an indictment of women's status as commodities on the marriage market. Janey's value for her husband derives from her status as prize, as a beautiful young thing on the arm of a graceless middle-aged man. But she is also of value to him as sexual possession. Indeed, Oliphant points – albeit decorously – to the topic of sexual coercion in marriage. Her husband's brutishness takes the form not only of an 'unrestrained' temper that she perceives will one day manifest as physical violence, but also his expectation of whenever he chooses 'claiming her services as if she were his valet – a thing which had, more or less, happened already, and against which Janey's pride and her sense of what was fit had risen in arms' (Oliphant, 427–28). Upon realising that she is alone on the departing train, Janey's feelings commingle 'fright' at the prospect of his fury and a profound sense of safety: 'Was it possible that for the first time since that terrible moment of her marriage she was more safely by herself than any locked door or even watchful guardian could keep her, quite unapproachable in the isolation of the train? Alone!' (Oliphant, 427–28). The story's third-person narrator has at this point entirely assumed Janey's perspective, enjoining the reader into a sympathetic identification with her hopes and fears. As the train comes to a momentary halt, her thoughts assume a gothic character, her husband appearing in the guise of an almost supernatural monster as she imagines he might have 'climbed up somewhere, at the end or upon the engine, and was now to be restored to his legitimate place, to fall upon her either in fondness or in rage, delighted to get back to her, or angry with her for leaving him behind: she did not know which would be the worst' (Oliphant, 428). Here and elsewhere, the text makes caresses and blows equivalent. Each are violations imposed by virtue of a husband's legal if not moral right, and Oliphant points to the singular horror of having one's body belong to another person.

Janey's transformation into wife has been a profoundly alienating one, but once she grasps the chance of freedom that accident has delivered, she glimpses an authentic self that she had never previously known of: 'as she looked at herself in the glass [she] encountered the vision of a little face which was new to her. It was not that of Janey, the little governess-pupil; it was not young Mrs Rosendale. It was full of life, and meaning, and energy, and strength. Who was it? Janey? Janey herself, the real woman, whom nobody had ever seen before' (Oliphant, 431).

It is this apparent authorial endorsement of Janey's escape that makes the tale's ending so unexpected. While Rosendale's death in one sense secures Janey's freedom, at the same time it imprisons her in a guilt that will last her lifetime. It is not that Rosendale has become any more sympathetic a figure over the passing years: on the contrary, in the time that has elapsed his moral dissipation has become written upon his body as a physical degeneration that, combined with the shock of discovering his wife, kills him. To Janey, however, she is 'herself no less than the murderer of her husband' (Oliphant, 439). Having 'not blamed herself before' for her actions, she does so now, and the final line of the story tells us that she will never 'forgive herself, nor get out of her eyes the face she had seen, nor out of her ears the dreadful sound of that labouring breath' (Oliphant, 439). Janey's epiphany of guilt is the final striking impression of the text, and it jolts the reader out of our identification with her previous choices, posing the question of whether her abandonment of her husband was justified after all.

What is going on here? Should the reader feel dismay at Janey's self-condemnation and consider it tragically misplaced, or are we meant to understand that she really *is* guilty? Is this ending, so apparently discordant with the story's prevailing mood, added as Liggins et al. suggest 'to tone down the subversive implications of the narrative' (Liggins et al., 78)? Is it a sop to the conservative sensibilities of editors and readers of the *St James Gazette* and Blackwoods, with whom the story was published? I suspect not, or not simply. Rather, it seems likely that its equivocal ending proceeds from doubts that Oliphant really did feel about the moral probity of her protagonist's liberation. There are hints deployed earlier in the text that suggest that the narrator does not after all approve of Janey's flight from her marriage: she is described as having been 'elated and intoxicated with her freedom'; and in a conversation with the village priest, who urges Janey to recognise a husband's rights, we are told 'But Janey would hear no reason: had she heard reason either from herself or another, she would not have been at St Honorat now' (Oliphant, 439). Such narratorial observations suggest that Janey's actions have been motivated by an ultimately insupportable passion. When Janey recognises the invalid being lifted from the carriage as Rosendale, she exclaims '"He is my husband," … with awe in her heart' (Oliphant, 438–39). Rosendale seems an unlikely candidate to inspire 'awe', so the word perhaps instead refers to what the presence of the priest reminds us is the religious significance of marriage. Janey seems now to have arrived at an appreciation of marriage as an institution whose importance transcends the mere feelings of the particular persons within it, and that is the proper object of reverence. Furthermore, the final lines emphasise the separation of son from father that Janey's act has brought about. She is 'struck with a great horror' upon seeing that 'there could be no doubt that the boy was his father's heir' (Oliphant, 438–39). Her flight has denied a father his son, and her son his father, as well as denying that son the inheritance of family name and property. The narrative ends by reopening the question of what had been Janey's duty. She had chosen personal happiness and fulfilment, as many were urging women to do at the fin-de-siècle. Oliphant seems caught between championship of her protagonist's right to liberate herself from oppression, and a fear that this might after all amount only to an act of self-indulgence that, in disregarding the sanctity of marriage, does violence to the familial bonds required by a well-functioning society.

Conclusion

In Oliphant's honeymoon story from 1894, a new bride can voluntarily flee; in Broughton's from 1872 she has to be abducted, her possible willing complicity only hinted at. And while the traditionalist Oliphant seems unwilling to allow her heroine an uncompromised escape, neither do Egerton or Chopin in the stories discussed here, and Janey's ten years of freedom are of course much longer than Louise's single hour. That this is so testifies to the difficulty experienced by women writers of envisioning an alternative to traditional marriage, even as they increasingly explicitly pointed to its failings. By deploying the short story's formal condensation, its license to forgo closure in favour of endings that are shocking or unresolved, and by encoding subversive narratives within the formulaic plots of gothic and ghost stories, women writers over the century discovered the narrative possibilities of short fiction at the same time that they employed it as a vehicle to tell alternative stories about marriage: about the ignorance and vulnerability of young brides and bridegrooms; wives' economic and emotional repression, and their exposure to abuse; problems of sexual life in marriage; and the damage wrought by loveless and irreversible unions. In so doing they showed the short story to be very far from the inferior partner of the novel.

Notes

1 Chopin's story was in fact first published under the title 'The Dream of an Hour', in *Vogue* magazine, 6 December 1894.
2 The prominent American physician Silas Weir Mitchell advanced a treatment for neurasthenia, or hysteria, that required an almost complete abstention from physical and mental exertion, obliging the patient to undergo long periods of bed rest unrelieved by activities such as reading or sewing. Gilman herself underwent this treatment, and 'The Yellow Wallpaper' shows how this 'cure', with its enforced isolation and infantilization of the patient, caused rather than relieved intense distress and alienation.
3 Nick Freeman also reads the story in sexual terms, citing as further evidence 'its use of the bedroom as a site of anxiety and terror' (Freeman, 197).
4 My thanks to students on the course 'Victorian Women's Short Fiction' at the University of Passau for this observation.
5 Merryn Williams argues against Oliphant's typecasting as an anti-feminist, showing how she was in fact a thoughtful commentator on women's issues whose attitudes evolved over the course of fifty years towards a position that Williams calls 'Old Feminist' – concerned with equality before the law (Williams, 179). Ann Heilmann tells us that 'Oliphant never identified herself fully with the younger generation of women writers, and indeed intensely disliked the sexual politics of the New Woman' (Heilmann, 214), and for her even the later Oliphant 'cannot properly be regarded as a feminist in the political sense' since she 'favoured non-political, individual solutions' to women's problems (Heilmann, 220, 233).

Works Cited

Broughton, Rhoda. *Twilight Stories*, Emma Liggins ed. Brighton: Victorian Secrets, 2009.

Chopin, Kate. 'The Story of an Hour.' Accessed 15 December 2016. http://archive.vcu.edu/english/engweb/webtexts/hour/.

Devine Jump, Harriet, eds. *Nineteenth-Century Short Stories by Women: A Routledge Anthology*. London and New York: Routledge, 1998.

Dickerson, Vanessa D. *Victorian Ghosts in the Noontide: Women Writers and the Supernatural*. Columbia and London: University of Missouri Press, 1996.

Edgeworth, Maria. *Popular Tales*. Poughkeepsie: 1813. Google Books. Accessed 15 December 2016.

Egerton, George. 'A Cross Line' in Harriet Devine Jump eds. *Nineteenth-Century Short Stories by Women: A Routledge Anthology*. London and New York: Routledge, 1998.

Freeman, Nick. 'E. Nesbit's New Woman Gothic.' *Women's Writing*, Vol 15, No 3 (2008), pp 454–69.

Freeman, Nick. 'Sensational Ghosts, Ghostly Sensations.' *Women's Writing*, Vol 20, No 2 (2013), pp186–201.

Gilman, Charlotte Perkins. 'The Yellow Wallpaper'. Project Gutenberg ebook. Accessed 19 December 2016. www.gutenberg.org/files/1952/1952-h/1952-h.htm

Gissing, George. *New Grub Street*, John Goode ed. Oxford: Oxford World's Classics, 2008.

Hager, Kelly. *Dickens and the Rise of Divorce: The Failed-Marriage Plot and the Novel Tradition*. Farnham: Ashgate, 2010.

Hanson, Clare. *Short Stories and Short Fictions, 1880–1980*. New York: St Martin's Press, 1985.

Heilmann, Ann, 'Mrs Grundy's Rebellion: Margaret Oliphant between Orthodoxy and the New Woman.' *Women's Writing*, Vol 6, No 2 (2006), pp 215–37.

Killick, Tim. *British Short Fiction in the Early Nineteenth Century*. Aldershot: Ashgate, 2008.

Landon, Laetitia E. 'Sefton Church' in Harriet Devine Jump eds. *Nineteenth-Century Short Stories by Women: A Routledge Anthology*. London and New York: Routledge, 1998.

Liggins, Emma. 'Introduction' to *Twilight Stories*, Emma Liggins ed. Brighton: Victorian Secrets, 2009.

Liggins, Emma, Andrew Maunder and Ruth Robbins eds. *The British Short Story*. Houndmills, Basingstoke and New York: Palgrave Macmillan, 2011.

Mulholland, Rose. 'Not to be Taken at Bed-Time' in Richard Dalby ed. *The Virago Book of Victorian Ghost Stories*. London: Virago, 1988.

Nesbit, Edith. *The Power of Darkness: Tales of Terror*, David Stuart Davies ed. Ware: Wordsworth, 2006.

Oliphant, Margaret. 'A Story of a Wedding Tour' in Harriet Devine Jump ed. *Nineteenth-Century Short Stories by Women: A Routledge Anthology*. London and New York: Routledge, 1998.

Power Cobbe, Frances. 'Wife-Torture in England'. *Contemporary Review*. April 1878. Accessed 16 December 2016. www2.warwick.ac.uk/fac/arts/history/students/modules/hi398/timetable/seminar5/

Riddell, Charlotte. *Weird Stories*, Emma Liggins ed. Brighton: Victorian Secrets, 2009.

Stewart, Clare. '"Weird Fascination": The Response to Victorian Women's Ghost Stories' in Emma Liggins and Daniel D Duffy eds. *Feminist Readings of Victorian Popular Texts*. Aldershot: Ashgate, 2001.

Syrett, Netta. 'A Correspondence' in Harriet Devine Jump eds. *Nineteenth-Century Short Stories by Women: A Routledge Anthology*. London and New York: Routledge, 1998.

Williams, Merryn. 'Feminist or Antifeminist? Oliphant and the Woman Question' in Dale J Trela ed. *Margaret Oliphant: Critical Essays on a Gentle Subversive*. London: Associated University Presses, 1995.

14 Marriage, the March of Time and *Middlemarch*

Marlene Tromp

It is a noose, you know [...] And a husband likes to be master.
—Mr. Brooke, *Middlemarch*

If I may open with a very personal comment – one that I hope to tie to my argument shortly – I was very honored to be asked to write this afterword. This type of remark is usually not made so directly in a scholarly manuscript, but it makes sense to me to say so given what I will argue below about the study of gender in the academy, the cycles of feminist analysis of marriage across time, and *Middlemarch* (1872). I felt honored by this invitation because it suggested to me that work of young feminists in the academy – as I once was myself – addressing themselves to issues of feminist concern can have weight and bearing, and moreover can, alongside the work of others, make an impact on our field. Indeed, the culture at large has changed with regard to gender; this has permitted change in the academy, but, to date, that change has not been as great as we might have wished.

We may have finally gained a room of our own in which to write, but often this room is a very lonely one. A gender gap persists in universities in Australia (Baker 37), the US (where men outpace women at the highest ranks by a nearly four to one ratio) (Curtis), in Canada (Acker 743), and in the United Kingdom, with the Higher Education Statistics Agency finding that some institutions have only one female professor for every ten and research intensive universities regularly showing lower percentages of women (Grove). Lonely, indeed. Globally, women only earn about 50% of what men do ('Ten Years'), and the American Associate of University Women reports that even in industrialized nations with a highly educated populace, like the US, the gender wage gap is still 80% (just nudging up from the intensely activist period focused on this issue in the 1970s), a figure that is even lower for women of color, women with disabilities and women who are gender queer (Hill).

These factors make scholarship that centers on the concerns of women and their well-being just as critical now as it was decades ago. In addition, I would suggest that we can often do some of our most powerful work when we write together with a common purpose, as the scholars here have done. Our most significant challenges to the intellectual paradigm often gain force when we bring our voices together to speak to our colleagues. When I co-edited the volume on Mary Elizabeth Braddon (2000), I had a very senior colleague respond with disgust. He then proceeded to review the novelists in my single-authored manuscript on marital violence and sensation fiction, asking, 'Don't you want to write on someone or something important?' I believe that volume, alongside the work of others, helped resist that thinking, helped make future serious scholarly work on Braddon possible, although it would have been very difficult indeed to have published a single-authored manuscript solely on Braddon at that time. The force of those voices joined together was too substantial to ignore, and I watched with delight as the field responded and it even became possible for people to write dissertations on Braddon's work.

In Pierre Bourdieu's *Language and Symbolic Power* (1991), he argues that legitimate speech – which defines a socio-cultural field –

> occurs through the unceasing struggles between the different authorities who compete within the field of specialized production for the monopolistic power to impose the legitimate mode of expression, can ensure the permanence of the legitimate language and of its value, that is, of the recognition accorded to it.
>
> (55)

Such acts as this volume, then, can identify this work as legitimate and, moreover, shift the 'field' into which it enters. These speech acts are legitimized through what he calls 'rites of institution' (55), like the publication of this book. In this way, the authors here will transform the conversation once again. An edited volume serves as a very fine place to make the case that we must look at marriage anew in this cultural moment and to focus on women writers to do so. In collections like these, we do not write alone. In them, we can make a case for new study. Moreover, this is a significant time culturally and for higher education to bring these conversations to the fore, to raise our voices about power structures that not only impact characters in literature, but people in the workplace (including the academy), and in our cultures at large.

I would argue that the three waves of the feminist movement have all inspired critical reconsideration of marriage and gender relations. Each has caused us to turn again to the familiar and view it in entirely new ways. The first wave, rolling across Britain in the eighteenth and nineteenth centuries, often focused on property, marriage and traditionally 'male' rights such as suffrage and employment. Not only did this movement help to generate the fiction under consideration here, it made it virtually impossible to write on marital relations and the social context in which they existed without taking up these issues, whether the author intended to make a statement or not. Fiction often engaged the concerns that feminist (and anti-feminist) prose and activism raised with its attention to marriage and the woman's place in culture and domestic fiction and sensation fiction often did so centrally. Thus, what Carolyn Lambert has eloquently called a 'privately conducted struggle' came to be publicly consumed and debated in the fiction – fiction that often explicitly articulated itself as a part of the cultural conversation about marriage in real women's lives.

In the twentieth century, having won the right to the vote, to own property and to work outside home, second-wave feminism came alive to issues like gender equality and violence in these landscapes, including pay equity, sexual assault and intimate partner violence. In Victorian studies, this drew new attention to the very presence of women writers (beyond George Eliot) as voices on these issues and significant contributors to our understanding of the period. This movement helped to foster the work of scholars like Elaine Showalter, Sandra Gilbert and Susan Gubar, Catherine Hall, and Lenore Davidoff, Jenni Calder, Joan Perkin and Mary Lyndon Shanley, who, in introducing gender into the scholarly conversation and pointing to the cultural structures that had created material inequities and violences, began to recraft our articulation of the nineteenth century. Their work opened new ways of understanding what was at stake in the period and in the literature, as well as refiguring the canon to include authors whose names most people had forgotten.

A third wave of feminism, increasingly intersectional and global in its thinking, keenly aware of not just the psychology and social politics of marriage, but the complex material and interpersonal landscapes of marriage, has emerged. It has asked us to imagine the potential of a more diverse and less singular architecture for feminist readings and has seen value in understanding the tensions that emerge in literature. Third-wave readings, conscious of their own complex oppressions and less certain that the past represents a complete absence of enlightenment, might find the ways women actually did access power and voice. Second-wave scholarship influenced and inspired early work in this movement like my own, Pamela Gilbert's and Lisa Surridge's, among others. More recently, voices like those of Sharon Marcus, Elsie Michie and Kelly Hagar have challenged us to rethink some of our assumptions about marital relationships and their situation in the cultural fabric.

In each of these periods, we have taken stock – reflected on the new body of work that has been generated and attempted to discern, more clearly, the overarching trends. This particular cultural moment, in which so many of the advances of the last centuries seem contested by retrogressive political movements across the globe, demands that we again review the place of marriage in Victorian literature. This timely volume helps us to do just that, giving us an opportunity to examine our own assumptions and our past assessments. Much of this scholarship, as Lambert notes in her introduction, follows Kelly Hagar's fine work by considering the depiction of vexing marriages and asking how fiction offered a negative model – in Tamara S. Wagner's words, a 'how not to do it' guide.

What strikes me as most significant about this volume is its genuine capacity to bring fresh eyes to the nineteenth century, the fiction and the issues it raises. It reassesses novelists who have been imagined as largely conservative voices in the period (and sometimes dismissed as a result). This important reconsideration may help reshape our canon on not just marriage literature, but of the period more broadly. Emily Morris's challenge to rethink Charlotte Yonge's perceived conservatism, suggests that Yonge articulated marriage as a 'trial' that required the efforts of a community of women, a move that opens up this author in new ways to feminist considerations. Joanne Shattock's examination of Margaret Oliphant's oeuvre, argues that her novels increasingly engage marriage reform, but also the ways in which social and familial demands limit the reach of those reforms. Catherine Pope reads Florence Marryat's protest against marital violence as much stronger than previous critics have acknowledged, and, indeed, much stronger than many of her contemporaries, ultimately arguing that 'marital violence was both a threat and a reality' and 'challeng[ing] the idea that women's experiences were unsuitable for public consumption'. Discovering how literature articulates the challenges and failures of marriage is just as important as discovering those novels resist the bonds of matrimony.

Similarly, there are generic re-evaluations here that open our understanding of the fictional modes in which women novelists operated and that they manipulated. Carolyn W. de la L. Oulton's reassessment of Rhoda Broughton's work, in order to explore the ways in which more realist fiction exploited the tension building tools of sensation without recourse to sensational outcomes, suggests that 'struggles of apparently conforming women may be dramatic in ways that the more obvious spectacle offered by sensation plots fail to attain' – in other words, that in marriage, the real can be equally distressing to the sensational narratives we have associated with marital challenges. Frances Twinn suggests that *East Lynne* (1861) might be read in new ways, opining that the subtextual allusions actually raise the specter of real domestic strife and thus forestall a condemnation of women, bringing to the foreground the dark realities of marriage and thus 'joins the discourse of change and reform'. Tamara S. Wagner, in looking to Ellen Wood's later novel *Court Netherleigh* (1881), points to the way it forgoes the sexual betrayal, forgery and marriage for money of sensation fiction as it traces changes in conceptions of ideal marriage in reality and fiction to suggest how marriages can be mismanaged.

Turning to the more complexly psychological, Meredith Miller reads a canonical work anew, suggesting that bringing the two plots of *Daniel Deronda* (1876) together offers a reading that critiques English national and cultural heritage and reveals marriage as 'degenerate and pathological'. Marion Shaw introduces us to Gaskell's *Sylvia's Lovers* (1860) as a complex psychological study of marriage and particularly sympathizes with women trapped in marriages to obsessive men. Laura Allen examines Eliza Haweis's *A Flame of Fire* (1897) to illuminate new commentary on marriage, divorce and the law against the backdrop of the author's own vexing marriage. This work opens the canon by reconsidering canonical texts and introducing others.

Some of the pieces demonstrate what can come of the challenges inherent in marriage, and this represents the most hopeful strain in the volume. This movement resists the cynical notion that we simply trace a linear progression from the dark ages of the past to the enlightenment of the prsent. Carolyn Lambert's essay on Fanny Trollope explores the depiction, early in the century, of power struggles that can lead, over time, to a kind of mutual understanding. Eschewing the idealized depiction of the Victorian marriage, this series of novels demonstrates how a husband and wife might come to 'respect each other's skills and abilities'. This piece tares in interesting ways with Victoria Margree's study of short fiction, in which she argues that short fiction's 'formal condensation, its license to forgo closure [...] and encoding subversive narratives' offers new, liberatory possibilities in its depiction of marriage. By the century's end, as Rebecca Styler shows us, the much-understudied utopian fiction presents radically new models, in which relationships can be companionate and equal, similar to those between women. This fiction depicts women with full financial independence and freed or unconstrained by biological demands.

This volume scans the century, looking in new corners for insights and exploring familiar corners anew. It demonstrates that concerns early in the period (like those in Fanny Trollope's work) grew in more complex ways through the mid-century than we have previously imagined, being developed in mid-century work, both realist and sensational. It points to the ways in which women novelists deployed fictional conventions and generic modes to achieve their ends and to offer challenges without undermining the prospect of readership. It turns back to the pages of novels that we know well to offer readings of the literature nuanced by third-wave feminist concerns, and it brings to the fore novels and novelists that have been neglected. Finally, it helps us see the ways in which the suspensions, elisions, implicit and explicit analyses of marriage in fiction throughout the century, emerge in a paradigm shift that not only critiques the institution, but actually offers alternative and even utopian ways of understanding the very gendered relations, economics and identities in which marriage is grounded.

This volume provides a toolkit with which to rethink marriage in nineteenth-century fiction. We might consider, for example, *Middlemarch*, one of the century's greatest novels and one to which we often turn when discussing marriage. This novel has been described by Andrew Dowling as offering a 'wider eruption of speech about conjugal conflict' (336) and can be powerfully illuminated by the themes offered in this volume. Many critics have seen the ways in which nuanced assessments of economics are related to these concerns, from the barriers between Will and Dorothea in terms of her income and the codicil in Causabon's will to the financial pressures that create suffering in the Lydgates' marriage and the economic grime that humbles the Bulstrodes. Anna Kornbluh, in fact, has described the novel as an 'entangling of sympathy and economy' (941).

Indeed, this novel, like those Morris, Twin, Allen and Wagner discuss here, offers negative examples of failures that might be warnings to a wise reader. In their discussions, Dowling and Kornbluh focus, as most scholars have, on the marriages of the Lydgates, the Causabons and, finally, the Ladislaws. Ultimately, most critics read these marriages as unsatisfying and disempowering for women, particularly noting Dorothea's marriages and the quelling of her ambitions. Cara Weber reclaims what she calls the novel's 'melancholy' close with the argument that 'Eliot reveals marriage to be a situation apt to the posing of fundamental questions about human relatedness [...] register[ing] not only the suffering of women stifled, but also a general anxiety about human life together' and the ways such a depiction might inspire us to strive for more (494).

Arguments that despair over the limits placed on women by marriage in this novel, like so much other scholarship, overlook important threads that run against the grain of this element in the fabric of the novel and the cautions offered by this volume. While those limitations do exist in the narrative, there is more here to be uncovered. Catherine A. Civello has taken a step in this direction by arguing that widowhood achieves higher value than wifehood in Eliot's fiction, including *Middlemarch*, and she reads the novel's little recognized irony as call for reform (Civello). I would go even further to suggest that the host of metaphorically and literally murderous wives in the novel bespeak a kind power held by women in marriage that we have long neglected in our discussions of *Middlemarch*, particularly since we often focus primarily on Dorothea's limited frame of action, and, when we have looked at the behavior of Rosamond, it has often been with distaste.[1]

Several essays here highlight Victorian fiction's presentation of violence in marriage. Pope describes the way in which Marrayat 'challenged the highly influential misconception that the middle-class wife was always *protected* rather than threatened by her husband'. Miller notes that *Daniel Deronda* points out the 'bleak reality of marriage behind the veil of the public/private divide. These are embedded in a pointed critique of the relations between fiction and material life'. Miller specifically underscores Eliot's depiction of novel reading as a danger because it gave women a false picture of the experience they would have. I argue, in the spirit of these essays, that we can read *Middlemarch* more fully (as Miller has done *Daniel Deronda*), suggesting that it proposes not only this more realistic picture, but also a quality of durable power for women – as long as women maintained their 'feminine' qualities.

Dowling has already explained that *Middlemarch* 'publicized previously invisible types of cruelty in personal relationships and also allowed a new and more nuanced form of marital conflict to take shape' (336), particularly examining the emotional cruelty that is apparent, but the emotional abuses he describes are staged against the backdrop of literally murderous violence. Neglecting to read this emotional violence in the full and broad context of the novel, however, restricts the force of these more subtle images and their significance.[2] While Casaubon may be regarded as coldly cruel and Lydgate as blithely unaware, the physical violence to which Pope points is also present. The two marriages of Mrs Beevor, for example, explicitly define the kind of dangerous marriage against which the novel's emotional acts of violence lie. Lady Chettam, in a caveat regarding a woman ending her widowhood in re-marriage remarks that – like Dorothea, presumably – Mrs. Beevor's 'first husband was objectionable, which made [her remarriage] the greater wonder. And severely she was punished for it. They said Captain Beevor dragged her about by the hair, and held up loaded pistols at her' (516). This explicit reference to marital violence, from one of the most socially proprietous figures in the novel, makes clear what women can face.

From this brutal context, then, we are offered a model of navigation – imperfect, sometimes painful, but powerful. We have attended with less critical interest to women's response – an awareness for which this volume calls. *Middlemarch* does not leave women powerless and voiceless in response to these situations. Shortly after Mrs Beevor is mentioned, Lydgate references a wife who brooks no opposition from her husband, lodging the reference explicitly in the heart of his own marital conflict. During an unpleasant conversation about economizing with Rosamond, Lydgate remembers the woman to whom he had first proposed marriage – a woman accused of mariticide, or husband murder – and applies that image to his wife. 'His mind glancing back to Laure while he looked at Rosamond, he said inwardly, "Would *she* [Rosamond] kill me because I wearied her?"' (556). He later compares Rosamond to basil, a 'plant that flourished wonderfully on a murdered man's brains' (782). While this may seem simply to be the moderate trouble of the resistant wife, the parallels between Rosamond and Madame Laure suggest more.

Madame Laure, a beautiful and graceful stage actress for whom Lydgate had developed a passion, performed in a play in which she was meant to 'stab' her 'lover' because she mistook him for another character.

Her scripted assault (on the character played by her husband), however, ended in his actual death, and she collapsed in apparent shock. Lydgate leapt to the stage to attend to her suffering as a physician. Though rumors suggested otherwise, he believed the killing to have been accidental, and Madame Laure escaped legal action. Unable to stop thinking of her, Lydgate traced her to another city, and she told him that, indeed, she had intended to kill her husband. Rising to what he perceives as her defense, he offered reasons for which she might have been justified in freeing herself so violently from her marriage – reasons for which there might be a moral, if not legal, vindication:

> 'There was a secret, then,' he said at last, even vehemently. 'He was brutal to you: you hated him.'
> 'No! he wearied me; he was too fond: he would live in Paris, and not in my country; that was not agreeable to me.'
> 'Great God!' said Lydgate, in a groan of horror. 'And you planned to murder him?'
> 'I did not plan: it came to me in the play—*I meant to do it.*'
> Lydgate stood mute, and unconsciously pressed his hat on while he looked at her. He saw this woman – the first to whom he had given his young adoration – amid the throng of stupid criminals.
> 'You are a good young man,' she said. 'But I do not like husbands. I will never have another'.
>
> (143–44)

Madam Laure's murderous agency, her entire rejection of marriage, and her willingness to violate basic principles of human community, simply because she found that her husband's choices and behaviors were not 'agreeable', form the explicit backdrop of not only his marriage to Rosamond, but to all of the marriages in the novel. Indeed, Rosamond's responses to actions she finds disagreeable in Lydgate, overcome his will entirely.

What these scenes suggest is the power of women to respond actively to and manage a husband. Indeed, Lydgate's metaphoric acts of violence are quelled by Rosamond. In this same chapter, he speaks to her with 'fierceness' in his eye and 'violence' in his tone – a 'tone [...] which was the equivalent to the clutch of his strong hand on Rosamond's delicate arm.' While this evokes many newspaper and legal descriptions of marital violence, the narrator tells us, 'But for all that, his will was not a whit stronger than hers' (612). Later, he 'he wanted to smash and grind some object on which he could at least produce an impression, or else to tell her brutally that he was master, and she must obey. But [her] quiet elusive obstinacy [...] would not allow any assertion of power to be final [...] As to saying that he was master, it was not the fact' (621).

Her mastery of him, which began when he proposed to her in spite of his express intentions to remain single, carried on in defiance of his will throughout the novel. We learn early on that Rosamond 'never give[s] up anything [she] choose[s] to do' (329). Significantly, 'her pretty good-tempered air of unconsciousness' concealed 'her inward opposition to him without compromise of propriety' (604) and she maintained the appearance of a beautiful, 'amiable, docile creature' to even the sharp-eyed Farebrother. Still, Lydgate, like Laure's husband, dies 'prematurely' (782), his basil-plant wife happily remarrying once she is widowed.

Similarly, while we have read Dorothea as a victim of her marriages, she (like Rosamond) seldom relents in what she 'chooses to do.' Rosamond, a 'pattern-card of the finishing-school,' and Dorothea, a regal feminine beauty, both are literally described as models of 'perfect' womanhood by their husbands-to-be. Like Rosamond, Dorothea, too, has an 'inward fire.' Dorothea is described as 'ardent' over twenty-five times in the novel, and her ardent wishes thwart each of her family's and her husband's desires in the narrative. This ardency certainly does not suggest passivity, and, indeed, in the narrator's words, Dorothea embodies an 'ardent woman's need to *rule* beneficently' (emphasis added 339). Moreover, she refuses to be schooled by the men around her. In the same chapter that mentions Dorothea's wish to rule, Dorothea repeats a gentle defiance of Mr. Casaubon's wishes, and he retorts,

> Dorothea, my love, this is not the first occasion, but it were well that it should be the last, on which you have assumed a judgment on subjects beyond your scope [....Y]ou are not here qualified to discriminate. What I now wish you to understand is, that I accept no revision, still less dictation within that range of affairs which I have deliberated upon as distinctly and properly mine. It is not for you to interfere [...] and still less [for you to engage in acts] which constitute a criticism on my procedure.
>
> (352)

She, herself, feels that she may have overstepped, but her ardent desires consistently fail to match his wishes.

Virtually every wish he has that does not tare with her judgement, she repels. She refuses to commit herself to work on his 'Key to All Mythologies' when he is living – an act that, like Rosamond's passive resistance, may have hastened her husband's death. Nor will she submit to this work when he is gone, in spite of his explicit wish for this action. She refuses to remain passive in the face of his commands; she actually writes back to her deceased husband, 'Do you not see now that I could not submit my soul to yours, by working hopelessly at what I have no belief in' (506–7). Moreover, against the wishes of both her family and Casaubon – wishes he attempted to enforce with his testamentary will, social, and emotional force – she marries Casaubon's cousin, Will Ladislaw.

The pattern to which I draw attention in this novel would not have been alien to the Victorians. Elsewhere, I have argued that the threat of women's violence in marriage – even murderous violence – was present in mid-century Britain in a way we have not previously understood ("Throwing" 39). Famous matricides across the century, but particularly in the 1840s–1870s, made the Victorians conscious of the possibility of women choosing, like Madame Laure, to live as they liked, even if it meant murder. Sarah Chesham's infamous murder of her sons and husband with poisoned rice pudding, were only uncovered when another woman she had inspired to use the same stratagem was convicted of murder herself. Catherine Foster's poisoning of her husband after only ten days of marriage ("The Acton Murder" 7) was discovered only when the chickens died after eating his vomit that had been deposited on the dustheap. These cases inspired legislation restricting access to poison, but, just as significantly, they led the papers to speculate on how many women must murder their husbands *undetected* and to acknowledge the anxiety that women might be ridding themselves of husbands of which they disapproved.

Caroline Cock's case presents a striking example. Charged with stabbing her husband, John, with a dessert knife in one hand and their baby in the other in 1849, she was found not guilty, in spite of the significant circumstantial evidence against her. Their former lodger, Harriet De Morentin reported that Caroline 'said her husband had ill-used her [...] I believe she was jealous. De Morentin advice was that she should "govern her passion and get the better of it"' (Old Bailey 42). Caroline apparently took this advice, and remained, like Rosamond and Dorothea, characteristically 'feminine' in her resistance.

When visiting him in the home where he worked, other servants noted that 'he seemed vexed at her coming and she seemed a little out of temper with him' (Old Bailey 42), and they left the couple alone. Charlotte Grant, who had promised to come see John's new baby, returned to the kitchen and was surprised to find John prostrate on the floor. Grant turned to Caroline and said, 'Perhaps he is only faint, there is no occasion to fetch a doctor,' to which Caroline responded, '"For God's sake fetch a doctor; see what I have done," pointing to the body at the same time [. T]hen I looked at the man and saw blood on the top of the left waistcoat-pocket – I had not seen that before' (Old Bailey 40).

Imagine the scene with Caroline, as *The Times* painted her at trial: 'a diminutive woman [...] with a fine child in her arms' ("Central Criminal Court" 8). Grant and Caplin discovered the same when they entered the room: petite Caroline, infant cradled in her arms, standing above the body of her dying husband. The epitome of maternity and femininity, she must have hardly appeared to be a murderer. Caplin fell to her knees by his side and began to bathe his face with vinegar. She called to him, 'John, John, here is your wife,' and he replied faintly, 'What does she want?' The court had a particular question about this scene: did Caroline weep? Yes, Caplin reported, 'she wept, but recovered herself' (Old Bailey 43), a perfectly respectable feminine response.

Caroline claimed he had committed suicide, an act that, she said, had elicited not her anger, but her care and sensitivity. She knelt down to serve him. With their child safely in her arms, she kissed his 'quivering lips.' She called for help. Still, the medical expert who testified at the trial argued that suicide was a virtual impossibility. The wound was on the left side of his body, under his arm; the knife had entered directly into his heart. Not only was it nearly a direct transverse wound, it was 'inflicted with considerable force' – virtually impossible when one is stabbing oneself. Moreover, the knife was too far from the body, he testified, to have been placed in the kitchen sink by the wounded victim – though Caroline admitted no knowledge of the knife, she was the only one in the room who could have put it there. The forensic evidence suggested that someone else had driven the knife in (Old Bailey 47) and that Caroline was the only candidate.

Strikingly, if Caroline stabbed her husband on this occasion, it wouldn't have been first time. Elizabeth Smith, a fellow servant who had inspired some jealousy on Caroline's part, said that John had once prevented Caroline from hitting her, and that the enraged wife had stabbed John in the arm. Caroline had spoken of purchasing pistols to vent her jealousy, and complained that John was spending his earnings on a mistress, rather than her and her son. She had written to him, calling him a 'd—d devil' and remarking that she 'would to God you might be dead by the time this comes where you are; I feel that I should be glad never to see you again' (Old Bailey 50). Moreover, their former housemate indicated that Caroline told her that, "she had on one or two occasions stabbed [John], and she would again, she would kill him" (Old Bailey 49).

In spite of the circumstantial and forensic evidence in the case, along with the murder threats that Caroline had made, the jury acquitted her. The act had seemed strangely and intimately feminine and, in many ways, underscored the norms of womanhood. A single (well-placed) thrust with the small dessert knife did not seem to evoke murderousness, and this petite woman with her small child held in her arms did not seem to be a murderer. Likewise, neither Rosamond nor Dorothea violates the social norms of femininity. Even while both are opposing their husbands' will and doing as they wish, even in direct opposition of their husbands, each remains the model of a 'perfect lady' (156).

This volume teaches us to read this text anew. It asks us to be open to understanding in the full context of the novel the words of the widowed Dorothea when she remarks to the unhappy Rosamond, 'marriage stays with us like a murder' (749). Marriage certainly may be the noose that Arthur Brooke suggests, but, there is there is not a husband in *Middlemarch* who achieves the mastery that he expects, and the models of

Rosamond and Dorothea – two very different women – help us understand how women can maintain propriety and defy their husbands nonetheless. Moreover, as we read Rosamond, Dorothea, and the historical record of the period differently, we begin to carve out new spaces for intersectional feminist voices and analysis. This effort is not just one that is a reflection on the period, but one that has the potential to continue to shape the world we, as scholars, inhabit as well.

Notes

1 Linda K. Hughes has a fascinating reading of Rosamond as a 'metonym for the literary marketplace', in which she speaks to *Eliot's* lack of sympathy for all characters except Rosamond.
2 Indeed, Mario Ortiz-Robles has argued that disruptive/interruptive metaphors in Middlemarch point up the 'inescapable materiality of language' and the 'performative violence' embodied in the novel (18). He argues finally that it is 'Interruption', disruption in the text, that becomes a condition of possibility for reading ethically, since the constant oscillation between the order of cognition and the order of performance assures that whatever certainties representation, on the one hand, and performative violence, on the other, seem to guarantee are at best ephemeral and unstable.

Works Cited

Acker, Sandra, Michelle Webber, and Elizabeth Smyth. "Tenure Troubles and Equity Matters in Canadian Academe." *British Journal of Sociology of Education* 33, no. 5 (September 2012): 743–61.
"The Action Murder." *Times* [London, England] 8 April 1847, p 7. *The Times Digital Archive*. Web. 26 June 2015.
Baker, Maureen. "Perpetuating the Academic Gender Gap." *Atlantis*, Vol 34, No 1 (2009), pp 37–47.
Bourdieu, Pierre. *Language and Symbolic Power*. Ed. John B. Thompson, Trans. Gino Raymond and Matthew Adamson. Oxford: Polity Press, 1991.
Calder, Jenni. *Women and Marriage in Victorian Fiction*. London: Thames and Hudson, 1976. "Central Criminal Court." *The Times* (September 21, 1849), p 8.
Civello, Catherine A. "The Ironies of Widowhood: Displacement of Marriage in the Fiction of George Eliot." *Nineteenth-Century Gender Studies*, Vol 3, No 3 (Winter 2007). www.ncgsjournal.com/issue33/civello.htm
Curtis, John W. "Persistent Inequity: Gender and Academic Employment." Prepared for "New Voices in Pay Equity" An Event for Equal Pay Day, April 11, 2011. American Association of University Professors (April 11, 2011). https://www.aaup.org/NR/rdonlyres/08E023AB-E6D8-4DBD-99A0-24E5EB73A760/0/persistent_inequity.pdf.
Davidoff, Lenore and Catherine Hall. *Family Fortunes: Men and Women of the English Middle Class, 1780–1850*. Chicago, IL: University of Chicago Press, 1991.
Dowling, Andrew. "'The Other Side of Silence': Matrimonial Conflict and the Divorce Court in George Eliot's Fiction." *Nineteenth-Century Literature*, Vol 50, No 3 (1995), pp 322–36. doi:10.2307/2933672.

Gilbert, Pamela. *Disease, Desire and the Body in Victorian Women's Popular Novels.* Cambridge: Cambridge University Press, 1997.

Gilbert, Sandra and Susan Gubar. *The Madwoman in the Attic: The Woman Writer and the Nineteenth-Century Literary Imagination.* New Haven, CT: Yale University Press, 1979.

Grove, Jack. "Gender survey of UK professoriate, 2013." *Times Higher Education* (June 13, 2013). www.timeshighereducation.com/news/gender-survey-of-uk professoriate2013/2004766.article.

Hager, Kelly. *Dickens and the Rise of Divorce: The Failed-Marriage Plot and the Novel Tradition.* Farnham: Ashgate, 2010.

Hill, Catherine, et al. *The Simple Truth about the Gender Pay Gap.* American Association for University Women (AAUW). www.aauw.org/aauw_check/pdf_download/show_pdf.php?file=The-Simple-Truth.

Hughes, Linda K. 'Constructing Fictions of Authorship in George Eliot's "Middlemarch", 1871, 1872.' *Victorian Periodicals Review*, Vol 38, No 2 (2005), pp 158–79. www.jstor.org.ezproxy1.lib.asu.edu/stable/20084060.

Kornbluh, Anna. "The Economic Problem of Sympathy: Parabasis, Interest, And Realist Form in *Middlemarch*" *ELH*, Vol 77, No 4 (2010), 941–67. www.jstor.org.ezproxy1.lib.asu.edu/stable/40963115.

Marcus, Sharon. *Between Women: Friendship, Desire and Marriage in Victorian England.* Princeton, NJ: Princeton University Press, 2007.

Michie, Elsie B. *The Vulgar Question of Money: Heiresses, Materialism and the Novel of Manners from Jane Austen to Henry James.* Baltimore: The John Hopkins University Press, 2011.

Old Bailey Proceedings Online (www.oldbaileyonline.org, version 7.2), September 1849, trial of Caroline Cock (t18490917-1762): 49. Web. Accessed 29 June 2015.

Ortiz-Robles, Mario. "Local Speech, Global Acts: Performative Violence and the Novelization of the World." *Comparative Literature*, Vol 59, No 1 (Winter 2007), 1–22.

Perkin, Joan. *Women and Marriage in Nineteenth-Century England.* London: Routledge, 1989.

Shanley, Mary Lyndon. *Feminism, Marriage, and the Law in Victorian England, 1850–1895.* Princeton, NJ: Princeton University Press, 1989.

Showalter, Elaine. *A Literature of Their Own: British Women Novelists from Bronte to Lessing.* London: Virago Press, 1978.

Surridge, Lisa. *Bleak Houses: Marital Violence in Victorian Fiction.* Athens: Ohio University Press, 2005.

"Ten Years of the Global Gender Gap." World Economic Forum. www3.weforum.org/docs/WEF_Annual_Report_2015-2016.pdf.

Tromp, Marlene. *The Private Rod: Marital Violence, Sensation, and the Law in Victorian Britain.* Albany: SUNY Press, 2000.

Tromp, Marlene. 'Throwing the Wedding Shoe: Foundational Violence, Unhappy Couples, and Murderous Women.' *Victorian Review.* Special Issue on "Extending Families." Vol 39, No 2 (2013), 39–43.

Weber, Cara. "'The Continuity of Married Companionship': Marriage, Sympathy, and the Self in *Middlemarch*." *Nineteenth-Century Literature*, Vol 66, No 4 (2012), pp 494–530. doi:10.1525/ncl.2012.66.4.494.

Appendix A
Marriage 1800–1900: Timeline of Key Dates and Texts

1801	Jane Addison granted a divorce by private Act of Parliament
1804	Maria Edgeworth, 'The Limerick Gloves'
1834	Laetitia E Landon, 'Sefton Church'
1836	Act for Marriages in England
1837	Queen Victoria inherits the throne
1837	Caroline Norton, *Observations on the Natural Claim of a Mother to the Custody of her Child as affected by the Common Law Right of the Father*
1838	Caroline Norton, *The Separation of Mother and Child by the Law of Custody of Infants.*
1839	Caroline Norton, *A Plain Letter to the Lord Chancellor on the Infant Custody Bill*
1839	The Custody of Infants Act
1839	Frances (Fanny) Trollope, *The Widow Barnaby*
1840	Frances (Fanny) Trollope, *The Widow Married: A Sequel to The Widow Barnaby*
1840	Marriage of Queen Victoria and Prince Albert
1843	Frances (Fanny) Trollope, *The Widow Wedded; or the Adventures of the Barnabys in America* (1843)
1847	Charlotte Brontë, *Jane Eyre*
1849	Charlotte Brontë, *Shirley*
1850s	Langham Place circle established
1853	Aggravated Assaults Act
1853	Charlotte Yonge, *The Heir of Radcliffe*
1853	Elizabeth Gaskell, *Cranford*
1854	Barbara Leigh Smith, *A Brief Summary in Plain Language of the Most Important Laws of England concerning Women*
1854	Charlotte Yonge, *Heartsease; or The Brother's Wife*
1855	Caroline Norton, *Letter to the Queen on Lord Chancellor Cranworth's Marriage and Divorce Bill*
1855	Summary Jurisdiction (Married Women) Act
1855	Caroline Clive, *Paul Ferroll*
1857	Divorce and Matrimonial Causes Act
1857	Elizabeth Gaskell, *The Life of Charlotte Brontë*
1860	Elizabeth Gaskell, *Sylvia's Lovers*

1861	Eliza Lynn Linton, *East Lynne*
1861	Death of Prince Albert
1863	Margaret Oliphant, *Salem Chapel*
1864	Margaret Oliphant, *The Perpetual Curate*
	M E Braddon, *The Doctor's Wife*
1865	J S Mill elected to Parliament
1865	Charlotte Yonge, *The Clever Woman of the Family*
1865	Rosa Mulholland, 'Not to Be Taken at Bedtime'
1865	Florence Marryat, *Love's Conflict*
1866	Margaret Oliphant, *Miss Marjoribanks*
1867	Rhoda Broughton, *Cometh up as a Flower*
1870	Married Women's Property Act
1872	Rhoda Broughton, 'The Man with the Nose'
1873	Infant Custody Act
1876	George Eliot, *Daniel Deronda*
1877	Charlotte Yonge, *Womankind*
1877	Florence Marryat, *A Harvest of Wild Oats*
1878	Matrimonial Causes Act
1878	Francis Power Cobbe, 'Wife Torture in England'
1878	Florence Marryat, *Her World against a Lie*
1878	Florence Marryat, *Written in Fire*
1879	Florence Marryat, *The Root of all Evil*
1881	Mrs Henry Wood, *Court Netherleigh*
1882	Married Women's Property Act
1882	Charlotte Riddell, *Weird Stories*
1883	Margaret Oliphant, *The Ladies Lindores*
	Margaret Oliphant, *Hester*
1884	Margaret Oliphant, *The Wizard's Son*
1886	Infant Custody Act
1888	Jane Hume Clapperton, *Margaret Dunmore: or, A Socialist Home*
1889	Elizabeth Burgoyne Corbett, *New Amazonia: A Foretaste of the Future*
1890	Margaret Oliphant, *Kirsteen*
1890	Florence Dixie Douglas, *Gloriana: or the Revolution of 1900*
1891	Florence Marryat, *A Fatal Silence*
1892	Florence Marryat, *The Nobler Sex*
1892	Charlotte Perkins Gilman, 'The Yellow Wallpaper'
1893	Edith Nesbit, 'Man-Size in Marble'
1893	George Egerton, 'A Cross Line'
1894	Margaret Oliphant, 'A Story of a Wedding Tour'
1894	Kate Chopin, 'The Story of an Hour'
1895	Summary Jurisdiction (Married Women) Act
1895	Amelia Mears, *Mercia, The Astronomer Royal: A Romance*
1895	Netta Syrett, 'A Correspondence'
1897	Mona Caird, The Morality of Marriage
1897	Eliza Haweis, *A Flame of Fire*
1901	Death of Queen Victoria
1905	Florence Ethel Mills Young, *The War of the Sexes*
1909	Irene Clyde, *Beatrice the Sixteenth*

List of Contributors

Laura Allen is a doctoral student at Canterbury Christ Church University, United Kingdom, where she is undertaking research into the work of Mary Eliza Haweis focusing on her fictional and non-fictional discussions of marriage. She was given the VELFAC Award for Victorian Literature by Canterbury Christ Church University in 2015.

Carolyn Lambert is a visiting lecturer at the University of Brighton, United Kingdom, where she teaches nineteenth-century literature. She is the author of *The Meanings of Home in Elizabeth Gaskell's Fiction* (2013) based on her doctoral thesis. She has a chapter entitled 'Female Voices in Elizabeth Gaskell's *Mary Barton*' in a forthcoming publication from Bloomsbury edited by Adrienne E Gavin and Carolyn W. de la L. Oulton – *Women Writers of the 1840s and 1850s*. A further article entitled 'Cross-dressing in Nineteenth-Century Fiction and its Impact on the Family' will appear in a special issue of *Open Cultural Studies* to be published in 2017.

Victoria Margree is Senior Lecturer on the Humanities Programme at the University of Brighton, United Kingdom, and degree leader for the BA (Hons.) History, Literature and Culture. She specializes in the literary culture of the Victorian fin de siècle, with particular reference to popular and genre fiction. She has recently published articles on the feminist orientation of Edith Nesbit's short Gothic fiction (*Women's Writing* 21 April 2014) and on the relations of money, property and gender in the ghost stories of Charlotte Riddell (*Gothic Studies* 16 February 2014). Her current research relates to popular fiction writer Richard Marsh, and includes preparation of a co-edited essay collection as well as articles on Marsh's fictional depictions of professional authorship and his World War I serial short fiction.

Meredith Miller is Senior Lecturer in English at Falmouth University, United Kingdom. Her most recent monograph is *Feminine Subjects in Masculine Fiction: Modernity, Will and Desire, 1870–1910* (Palgrave, 2013). She is also the author of numerous scholarly articles on gender, sexuality and the popular novel as well as *The Historical Dictionary* *of Lesbian Literature* (Rowman and Littlefield, 2006). Alongside her academic work she is developing a growing list of published fiction.

Emily Morris teaches introductory and Victorian literature classes in the Department of English at St. Thomas More College and the University of Saskatchewan in Saskatoon, Saskatchewan, Canada. She has published articles on Elizabeth Gaskell in *The Gaskell Society Journal* (2009) and *Brontë Studies* (2013), as well as a chapter in *Evil and Its Variations in the Works of Gaskell*, edited by Mitsuhara Matsuoka (2015). She is a co-editor of *Place and Progress in the Works of Elizabeth Gaskell* (Ashgate 2015). Aside from Gaskell, her research interests include Charlotte Yonge, Elizabeth Barrett Browning, feminism and femininity, and relationships between health, material conditions and creative literary output.

Carolyn W. de la L. Oulton is Professor of Victorian Literature, and Co-Founder and Director of the International Centre for Victorian Women Writers at Canterbury Christ Church University, United Kingdom. She is the author of *Literature and Religion in Mid-Victorian England: from Dickens to Eliot* (Palgrave 2003), *Romantic Friendship in Victorian Literature* (Ashgate 2007), *Let the Flowers Go: A Life of Mary Cholmondeley* (Pickering and Chatto 2009), *Below the Fairy City: A Life of Jerome K. Jerome* (Victorian Secrets 2012) and *Dickens and the Myth of the Reader* (Routledge 2017). She is the series editor of *New Woman Fiction 1881–1899* (Pickering & Chatto 2010–2011) and co-editor (with SueAnn Schatz) of *Mary Cholmondeley Reconsidered* (Pickering & Chatto 2009) and (with Adrienne Gavin) *Writing Women of the Fin de Siècle: Authors of Change* (Palgrave 2011).

Catherine Pope gained her PhD from the University of Sussex in 2014 on feminism in the novels of Florence Marryat. She contributed an entry on Rhoda Broughton to OUP's *Oxford Bibliographies in Victorian Literature*, and is co-editor with Troy J. Bassett of Helen C. Black's Notable Women Authors of the Day (Victorian Secrets, 2011). Catherine is the founder of Victorian Secrets, a small press dedicated to publishing books from and about the nineteenth century.

Joanne Shattock is Emeritus Professor of Victorian Literature at the University of Leicester. She is general editor, with Elisabeth Jay, of a twenty-five-volume edition of *Selected Works of Margaret Oliphant* (Pickering & Chatto, 2011–2016), in which she has edited three volumes of Oliphant's journalism and fiction, and co-edited a fourth. She is working on a volume of essays on *Journalism and the Periodical Press in Nineteenth Century Britain* for Cambridge University Press.

Marion Shaw is Emeritus Professor of English at Loughborough University. Her research interests are in nineteenth-century literature and women's writing, particularly that of the interwar period. She has written/edited three books on Tennyson and for some years was editor of the *Tennyson Research Bulletin*. She is currently chair of the Tennyson Society Executive Committee. Some of her work has been textual editing, for example, a variorum edition of Elizabeth Gaskell's *Sylvia's Lovers*. She has also written a biography, *The Clear Stream*, about the Yorkshire novelist and social reformer, Winifred Holtby.

Rebecca Styler is a Senior Lecturer in English at the University of Lincoln, United Kingdom. Her specialist research interest lies in nineteenth-century women's religious writing. She is author of *Literary Theology by Women Writers of the Nineteenth Century* (2010), and a number of articles on Victorian women's spiritual biography and autobiography, as well as on Elizabeth Gaskell's fiction. Her current project is on ideas of God as a divine (earth) mother in British and US literature 1850–1920.

Marlene Tromp is Professor of English and Women and Gender Studies, Dean at Arizona State University's New College of Interdisciplinary Arts and Sciences, and Vice Provost of ASU's West Campus. She is the author of *Altered States: Sex, Nation, Drugs, and Self-Transformation in Victorian Spiritualism* (SUNY 2006), *The Private Rod: Sexual Violence, Marriage, and the Law in Victorian England* (UP Virginia 2000), and over twenty essays and chapters on nineteenth-century culture. She has edited or co-edited and contributed to *Abstracting Economics: Culture, Money, and the Economic in the Nineteenth Century* (Ohio University Press 2016); *Fear and Loathing: Victorian Xenophobia* (Ohio State UP 2013); *Victorian Freaks: The Social Context of Freakery in the Nineteenth Century* (Ohio State UP 2007); and *Mary Elizabeth Braddon: Beyond Sensation* (SUNY 2000). She has two new books under review, *Force of Habit: Life and Death on the Titanic*, which examines race, class, gender and big business in a global context, and *Intimate Murder: Sex and Death in Nineteenth Century Britain*, which explores deadly violence in sexual relationships. Tromp is an award-winning teacher and mentor. She is immediate past-president of the North American Victorian Studies Association and serves on the board of directors of the Nineteenth-Century Studies Association.

Frances Twinn is an independent scholar who holds a PhD the subject of which is 'The Landscapes of Elizabeth Gaskell's writing'. She is the author of a number of articles on aspects of Gaskell's writing. Frances edited *The Gaskell Journal* for four years from 2007 to 2010.

Tamara S. Wagner obtained her PhD from Cambridge University and is Associate Professor at Nanyang Technological University, Singapore. Her books include *Victorian Narratives of Failed Emigration: Settlers,*

Returnees, and Nineteenth-Century Literature in English (2016), *Financial Speculation in Victorian Fiction: Plotting Money and the Novel Genre, 1815–1901* (2010), and *Longing: Narratives of Nostalgia in the British Novel, 1740–1890* (2004). She has also edited collections on *Domestic Fiction in Colonial Australia and New Zealand* (2014), *Victorian Settler Narratives: Emigrants, Cosmopolitans and Returnees in Nineteenth-Century Literature* (2011), and *Antifeminism and the Victorian Novel: Rereading Nineteenth-Century Women Writers* (2009). Wagner currently works on a study of Victorian babyhood, with the working title *The Victorian Baby in Print: Infancy and Nineteenth-Century Popular Culture.*

Index

This index covers the introduction and following main chapters and chapter notes; the front matter, appendices and lists of works cited have not been indexed. **Bold** entries indicate a chapter on a particular author and/or work. Authors of chapters have been indexed and their chapters are indicated by ***bold italic*** entries. Cited authors have been indexed where there is discussion of their work in the text; citation references have not been indexed. Index entries that refer to chapter notes are indicated by the suffix n.